Counseling Theories

Essential Concepts and Applications

Samuel T. Gladding

Wake Forest University

PEARSON

Merrill
Prentice Hall

Upper Saddle River, New Jersey
Columbus, Ohio

Library of Congress Cataloging-in-Publication Data

Gladding, Samuel T.
    Counseling theories: essential concepts and applications/Samuel T. Gladding.
        p. cm.
    Includes bibliographical references and index.
    ISBN 0-13-113845-6
    1. Counseling—Textbooks. I. Title.
BF637.C6G5333 2005
158'.3—dc22

2004044710

Vice President and Executive Publisher: Jeffery W. Johnston
Publisher: Kevin M. Davis
Editorial Assistant: Amanda King
Production Editor: Mary Harlan
Copy Editor: Mary Benis
Design Coordinator: Diane C. Lorenzo
Photo Coordinator: Cynthia Cassidy
Text Design and Illustrations: Integra
Cover Design: Jason Moore
Cover Image: SuperStock. Paul Klee, "Marked Man" (detail), 1935, 146 (R 6), 32 × 29 cm, oil and watercolor
    on oil ground on gaze ib cardboard nailed on a frame, Kunstsammlung Nordhein Westfalen.
Production Manager: Laura Messerly
Director of Marketing: Ann Castel Davis
Marketing Manager: Autumn Purdy
Marketing Coordinator: Tyra Poole

This book was set in Berkeley by Integra. It was printed and bound by R. R. Donnelley & Sons Company.
The cover was printed by The Lehigh Press, Inc.

Photo Credits: David Buffington/Getty Images, Inc. – Photodisc, p. 76; ExxonMobil Corporation, p. 32; Getty Images, Inc. – Photodisc, p. 138; Steve Gorton/Dorling Kindersley Media Library, p. 2; Gary Kramer/USDA Natural Resources Conservation Service, p. 48; Michael Littlejohn/PH College, pp. 62, 90; Anthony Magnacca/Merrill, pp. 104, 224; Pennsylvania Dutch Convention and Visitors Bureau, p. 124; PH College, pp. 196, 210; Barbara Schwartz/Merrill, p. 168; Silver Burdett Ginn, p. 180; Paul A. Souders/Corbis, p. 152; and Peter Turnley/Corbis, p. 14.

Pearson Education Ltd.
Pearson Education Singapore Pte. Ltd.
Pearson Education Canada, Ltd.
Pearson Education–Japan

Pearson Education Australia Pty. Limited
Pearson Education North Asia Ltd.
Pearson Educatión de Mexico, S. A. de C. V.
Pearson Education Malaysia Pte. Ltd.

10 9 8 7 6 5 4 3 2 1
ISBN: 0-13-113845-6

To Pal,
   aka Inez Barnes Templeman,
      my maternal grandmother,
         a positive and dynamic influence,
            who accepted me unconditionally
            and taught me by example
               kindness, civility, generosity,
             and a love for others
                who are "different"

Samuel T. Gladding is the chair of and a professor in the Department of Counseling at Wake Forest University in Winston-Salem, North Carolina. He has been a practicing counselor in both public and private agencies since 1971. His leadership in the field of counseling includes service as president of the American Counseling Association, the Association for Counselor Education and Supervision, the Association for Specialists in Group Work, and Chi Sigma Iota (an international counseling honor society).

Gladding is the former editor of the *Journal for Specialists in Group Work* and the author of more than 100 professional publications. In 1999 he was cited as being in the top 1% of contributors to the *Journal of Counseling and Development* for the 15-year period 1978–1993. Some of Gladding's most recent books are *Counseling: A Comprehensive Profession* (5th ed., 2004); *The Creative Arts in Counseling* (3rd ed., 2005); *Community and Agency Counseling* (with Debbie Newsome) (2nd ed., 2004); *Group Work: A Counseling Specialty* (4th ed., 2003); *Family Therapy: History, Theory, & Process* (3rd ed., 2002); *Becoming a Counselor: The Light, the Bright, and the Serious* (2002); and *The Counseling Dictionary* (2001).

Gladding's previous academic appointments have been at the University of Alabama at Birmingham and Fairfield University (Connecticut). He also worked as director of children's services in a mental health center and in a private practice counseling group for a number of years. Gladding received his degrees from Wake Forest (B. A., M. A., Ed.), Yale (M. A., Religion.), and the University of North Carolina–Greensboro (Ph.D.). He is a National Certified Counselor, a Certified Clinical Mental Health Counselor, and a Licensed Professional Counselor (North Carolina). Gladding is a former member of both the Alabama Board of Examiners in Counseling and the Research and Assessment Corporation for Counseling. He is also a Fellow in the Association for Specialists in Group Work.

Dr. Gladding is married to the former Claire Tillson and is the father of three children—Ben, Nate, and Tim. In addition to counseling, he enjoys tennis, swimming, and humor.

Theories are like guiding lights. They give us some direction when we are with clients who have come to us in pain with problems or concerns they do not know how to address. Like light, theories can and do change. Some become brighter with time; others shift their focus. Some fade because they either lack a solid foundation or lose their relevance for the populations we serve. Wondrously new theories, like emerging lights, are generated as insightful clinicians and academics craft them out of the context in which people live.

Because this book is about counseling theories that are most prevalent at the beginning of the 21st century, it should be read in the light of its time. Some of the material covered will shine even brighter in the future whereas other ideas will falter or fade. In addition, some theories explained here may change their emphases. New ways of working with client populations will be created as practitioners discover other ways of helping individuals in mental distress. Thus, the knowledge gained from this text will be finite. To keep growing as a professional, you will have to study and read continuously about the latest developments in counseling and therapy circles.

So why should you study these theories at this time? They are the best and most complete that we know. Furthermore, they provide ways of conceptualizing the words and actions of clients and working constructively with them. In other words, these theories, if employed judiciously, will shed light on your work and give you direction. Without such a basis for making plans and decisions, you would have to rely on trial and error or intuition, neither of which is apt to be as efficient or effective.

This book is laid out developmentally so that you can see how various theories of counseling and therapy have emerged: psychoanalysis and psychoanalytic theories, Adlerian therapy, existential therapy, person-centered therapy, Gestalt therapy, reality therapy, behavioral therapy, cognitive and cognitive-behavioral therapy, rational emotive behavior therapy, transactional analysis, feminist therapy, Bowen family systems therapy, strategic family therapy, and solution-focused therapy. Each theory chapter presents important essentials without irrelevant details and follows a uniform outline: Major Theorist(s), View of Human Nature/Personality, Role of the Counselor/Therapist, Goals, Process and Techniques, Multicultural and Gender-Sensitive Issues, Evaluation of the Theory, Treating Linda with the Therapy, Summary and Conclusion, Summary Table, Learning More, Classroom Activities, and References.

The final chapter of the book discusses ethical and legal concerns related to counseling.

Throughout the book I have used the words *counselor* and *therapist* interchangeably, just as professionals in the helping fields commonly use them. Some individuals prefer other terms: *psychotherapist, psychologist, social worker, psychiatrist, psychiatric nurse, pastoral counselor,* or *mental health counselor.* However, I believe that using just *counselor* and *therapist* makes the text clearer, easier to read, and less distracting.

I would like to thank my colleagues both past and present for the many contributions they have made to my understanding of theories and the therapeutic process. My work and interactions with fellow clinicians in mental health, private practice, and

v

academic settings have allowed me to gain firsthand experience as a practicing coun-selor using major theories. For their constructive suggestions during the preparation of the manuscript, I thank reviewers Kenneth F. Hughey, Kansas State University; Julia K. Mirras, Middlesex Community College University; John Reese, Waubonsee Community College; and Eric A. Sleith, Jefferson Community College. I would also like to thank my editor at Prentice Hall, Kevin Davis, for continuously urging me to put my thoughts about theories on paper. Finally, I wish to express my gratitude for the support and love that my family, especially my wife, Claire, have shown me through this writing project. Our children—Ben, Nate, and Tim—are all teenagers now, and without a lot of understanding and some rare quiet moments, I could not have completed this project in a timely way.

I hope you will benefit from reading this book. In the writing process I have grown to appreciate even more the light that theories provide. Such may be the case with you as you reflect on the thoughts of the individuals who have provided the foundation for all that we do in counseling and therapy.

THE PRENTICE HALL COMPANION WEBSITE: A VIRTUAL LEARNING ENVIRONMENT

Technology is a constantly growing and changing aspect of our field that is creating a need for content and resources. To address this emerging need, Prentice Hall has developed an online learning environment for students and professors alike—Companion Websites—to support our textbooks.

In creating a Companion Website, our goal is build on and enhance what the textbook already offers. For this reason, the content for each user-friendly website is organized by topic and provides the professor and student with a variety of meaningful resources. Common features of a Companion Website include:

FOR THE PROFESSOR—

Every Companion Website integrates **Syllabus Manager™**, an online syllabus creation and management utility.

- **Syllabus Manager™** provides you, the instructor, with an easy, step-by-step process to create and revise syllabi, with direct links into Companion Website and other online content without having to learn HTML.
- Students may logon to your syllabus during any study session. All they need to know is the web address for the Companion Website and the password you've assigned to your syllabus.
- After you have created a syllabus using **Syllabus Manager™**, students may enter the syllabus for their course section from any point in the Companion Website.
- Clicking on a date, the student is shown the list of activities for the assignment. The activities for each assignment are linked directly to actual content, saving time for students.
- Adding assignments consists of clicking on the desired due date, then filling in the details of the assignment—name of the assignment, instructions, and whether it is a one-time or repeating assignment.
- In addition, links to other activities can be created easily. If the activity is online, a URL can be entered in the space provided, and it will be linked automatically in the final syllabus.
- Your completed syllabus is hosted on our servers, allowing convenient updates from any computer on the Internet. Changes you make to your syllabus are immediately available to your students at their next logon.

FOR THE STUDENT—

- **Chapter Objectives**—Outline key concepts from the text.
- **Interactive Self-quizzes**—Complete with hints and automatic grading that provide immediate feedback for students. After students submit their

answers for the interactive self-quizzes, the Companion Website **Results Reporter** computes a percentage grade, provides a graphic representation of how many questions were answered correctly and incorrectly, and gives a question-by-question analysis of the quiz. Students are given the option to send their quiz to up to four email addresses (professor, teaching assistant, study partner, etc.).

- **Web Destinations**—Links to www sites that relate to chapter content.
- **Message Board**—Virtual bulletin board to post or respond to questions or comments from a national audience.

To take advantage of these and other resources, please visit the *Counseling Theories: Essential Concepts and Applications* Companion Website at

www.prenhall.com/gladding

www.ResearchNavigator.com

Merrill Education is pleased to introduce Research Navigator—a one-stop research solution for students that simplifies and streamlines the entire research process. At www.researchnavigator.com, students will find extensive resources to enhance their understanding of the research process so they can effectively complete research assignments. In addition, Research Navigator has three exclusive databases of credible and reliable source content to help students focus their research efforts and begin the research process.

HOW WILL RESEARCH NAVIGATOR ENHANCE YOUR COURSE?

- Extensive content helps students understand the research process, including writing, Internet research, and citing sources.
- Step-by-step tutorial guides students through the entire research process from selecting a topic to revising a rough draft.
- Research Writing in the Disciplines section details the differences in research across disciplines.
- Three exclusive databases—EBSCO's ContentSelect Academic Journal Database, *The New York Times* Search by Subject Archive, and "Best of the Web" Link Library—allow students to easily find journal articles and sources.

WHAT'S THE COST?

A subscription to Research Navigator is $7.50 but is **free** when used in conjunction with this textbook. To obtain free passcodes for your students, simply contact your local Merrill/Prentice Hall sales representative, and your representative will send you the Evaluating Online Resource Guide, which contains the code to access Research Navigator as well as tips on how to use Research Navigator and how to evaluate research. To preview the value of this website to your students, please go to www.educatorlearningcenter.com and use the Login Name "Research" and the password "Demo."

BRIEF CONTENTS

CONTENTS

Note: Every effort has been made to provide accurate and current Internet information in this book. However, the Internet and information posted on it are constantly changing, so it is inevitable that some of the Internet addresses listed in this textbook will change.

Counseling Theories

Essential Concepts and Applications

CHAPTER 1

Theories and Therapies

He follows her words
*   to the end of her thoughts*
*   and hears the pain in her voice*
With empathy he tries to respond
*   structuring what he says*
*   through a theory that slowly unfolds*
*   like the pages of a book*
*   in the back of his mind—*
The session has begun!

Note: "The Session," by S. T. Gladding. Copyright 2003 by Samuel T. Gladding.

heories are essential to all helping professions. Credible theories are based on ideas, observations, and research. They are well crafted and are tested to verify whether they are effective and, if so, under what circumstances and with which populations. A sound theory is "essential to the meaningful practice of professional counseling" (Wilks, 2003, p. 278); from theories clinicians glean ideas of how to conceptualize and treat clients.

However, because some theories are better than others, it is important to examine the prominent theories of counseling and therapy and the ways in which they work. Theoretical knowledge frees counselors to operate in ethical, legal, and productive ways with those who seek their services.

This chapter explores what a theory is, what qualities characterize sound theories, why theories are important, how theoretical points of view have developed, and how counselors and therapists use theories singularly and eclectically in their practices.

WHAT IS A THEORY?

A *theory* is "a group of related laws or relationships that are used to provide explanations within a discipline" such as counseling (Sharf, 2004, p. 658). A theory is a model. Most counseling theories have been developed by exceptional practitioners and academicians, who have formulated their ideas on the basis of personal experiences, research, and observations.

In counseling, therapists employ theories as a guide to hypothesize about the formation of and possible solutions to problems or concerns. Based on their educational background, philosophy, and interests, as well as the needs of clients, effective counselors decide which theory or theories to apply to a situation. Not all approaches are appropriate for all counselors or all clients. Indeed, one theory may not be adequate for the same client over an extended period. Therefore, mental health professionals must not only choose their theoretical positions carefully but also regularly reassess them.

CHARACTERISTICS OF SOUND THEORIES

Some theoretical models are more thorough and versatile than others. According to Hansen, Stevic, and Warner (1986), a good theory is

1. *Clear, easily understood, and communicable.* It should make sense and be explainable.
2. *Comprehensive.* A good theory encompasses explanations for a wide variety of phenomena in human development.
3. *Explicit and heuristic.* A good theory of counseling is didactic in laying out its major tenets. It also generates research because of its design, inviting therapists to explore its uses.
4. *Specific in relating means to desired outcomes.* A well-crafted theory includes a way of achieving a desired end product. It contains guidelines that others can follow to obtain similar results.
5. *Useful to its intended practitioners.* A good theory is practical and provides strategies its followers may use under certain conditions or with specific populations.

In addition to these five qualities, a sound theory matches a counselor's personal philosophy of helping. Shertzer and Stone (1974) suggest that a counseling theory must fit like a suit of clothes. Some theories, like some suits, need tailoring; therefore, effective counselors realize the importance of alterations. Counselors who wish to be versatile and effective should learn a wide variety of counseling theories and know how to apply each without violating the theory's internal consistencies (Auvenshine & Noffsinger, 1984). Counselors should not be limited to just a pet theory or two, as the cartoon in Figure 1.1 humorously illustrates.

THE PRAGMATIC VALUE OF THEORIES

The practical value of a solidly formulated theory cannot be overstressed (Brammer, Abrego, & Shostrom, 1993). Theory helps explain what happens in a counseling relationship and assists the counselor in predicting, evaluating, and improving results. Furthermore, theory provides a framework for making scientific observations about counseling. Theorizing encourages a coherence of ideas and the production of new ideas (Gladding, 1990). It helps make sense out of a counselor's observations. As Prochaska and Norcross (2003) put it, "Without a guiding theory . . . clinicians would be vulnerable, directionless creatures bombarded with literally hundreds of impressions and pieces of information in a single session" (p. 5).

Boy and Pine (1983) elaborate even further on the practical value of theory by suggesting that theory is the *why* behind the *how* of counseling, providing a framework

FIGURE 1.1 "I'm working on my pet theory."

Note: Copyright Benita Epstein. Reproduced by permission of Benita Epstein.

within which counselors can operate. Counselors guided by theory can meet the demands of their roles because they have reasons for what they do. Boy and Pine point out six practical functions of theory:

1. Theory helps counselors find unity and relatedness within the diversity of experience.
2. Theory compels counselors to examine relationships they would otherwise overlook.
3. Theory gives counselors operational guidelines by which to work and helps them evaluate their development as professionals.
4. Theory helps counselors focus on relevant data.
5. Theory enables counselors to assist clients in effective behavior modification.
6. Theory assists counselors in evaluating old and constructing new approaches to the process of counseling.

   "The ultimate criterion for all counseling theories is how well they provide explanations of what occurs in counseling" (Kelly, 1988, pp. 212–213). The value of theories as ways of organizing information "hinges on the degree to which they are grounded in the reality of people's lives" (Young, 1988, p. 336).

THE EVOLUTION OF THEORIES

Theories, especially those related to counseling and therapy, have evolved over time with a sometimes checkered history.

ANTIQUATED THEORIES

Even before recorded time there are indications that people had theories about human functioning and mental disorders. Archeological records show that a practice known as *trephining*, essentially the drilling of holes in the skull, occurred in some early societies. Ancient people believed that individuals who were mentally disturbed were possessed by evil spirits. Thus, the holes were drilled to let the evil spirits out. In almost all cases, the treatment was worse than the disorder.

In medieval Europe that same theory continued, resulting in the practice of exorcism, which was meant to drive out evil spirits and restore mentally deranged individuals to health. Exorcism was initially performed by clergy, mainly in monasteries, and used techniques such as the laying on of hands and insulting the possessing demon(s) with obscene epithets.

As theological beliefs about evil spirit possession became more fully accepted by those in the secular world, more unpleasant means were used to drive out demons, such as flogging, starving, using chains, and immersing in hot water. The idea behind the treatment was that the possessing spirit(s) would leave a body that was an inhospitable host. Unfortunately, these remedies resulted in the demise of many persons who were mentally disturbed (Butcher, Mineka, & Hooley, 2003).

In Western societies subsequent treatment of people with mental conditions was slightly better because the theory of demon possession was mostly discredited. Thus, instead of being tortured to death, these individuals were locked up in institutions and "cared for." Sometimes they were given humane treatment whereas at other times they were chained up. There was almost no treatment besides physical restraint because there was no theoretical construct as to what should be done. Patients were sometimes placed on display for public amusement, and chaos reigned inside their facilities. The now-common term *bedlam* was the name of a particularly notorious institute in London, which housed many who were mentally disturbed and was renowned for its disarray and turmoil.

It was not until the 18th century that a new theory of treatment was formulated for working with individuals having emotional problems. That development occurred almost simultaneously in Europe and the American colonies; it was instigated by Benjamin Rust in North America, Phillip Pinel in France, and William Tuke in England. The humane theory proposed that mental patients be unchained and receive better treatment, such as time outdoors each day, a more nutritious diet, and communication with others. The idea was that people would get better when they received sunlight, good food, and kind attention.

This reform had varied success and gave rise to talk therapies, even before Sigmund Freud. Two early examples were initiated by Paul Dubois (1848–1918), a Swiss physician, and Pierre Janet (1859–1947), a French physician. Both of these professionals spoke to and with their mentally disturbed patients in a reasonable and logical manner (Corsini, 2000).

MODERN THEORIES

In more modern times theories of psychotherapy and counseling have emerged in relationship to definitions of free will and determinism (Wilks, 2003). For instance, theories such as psychoanalysis and behaviorism, both of which are covered in this text, grew out of biologic/psychic determinism and environmental determinism, respectively. More humanistic theories—such as existential, Adlerian, person-centered, and reality therapy, which are also covered in this book—are grounded in the idea that people have a degree of free will.

Regardless of their base, theories of counseling and psychotherapy have developed almost exponentially since the 1950s. In 1959 R. A. Harper identified only 36 systems of psychotherapy. By 1976 M. Parloff had discovered more than 130 therapeutic approaches, some of which were quite questionable. Only 3 years later, in 1979, *Time* reported that more than 200 therapies had been formulated (Prochaska & Norcross, 2003). Early in the 21st century more than 400 systems of psychotherapy and counseling have been generated worldwide, ranging from psychoanalysis to soap opera therapy (Corsini, 2000). Clearly, counselors today have a wide variety of theories from which to choose.

Although theory development has not stopped, Okun (1990) states that the present emphasis in counseling is on connecting theories instead of creating them. This focus rests on the fundamental assumption that "no one theoretical viewpoint can provide all of the answers for the clients we see today" (Okun, 1990, p. xvi).

Another current trend is that helping professionals adapt techniques and interventions from different theoretical approaches into their work without actually accepting the premises of some theoretical points of view. This flexibility can be seen in the widespread use of microskills in therapy circles. This approach focuses on atheoretical methods, such as active listening and empathy, that promote relationship formation and exploration of a problem or concern. The microskills approach, which is useful in many cases, does not develop a comprehensive way of addressing personal difficulties but assumes that some therapeutic skills transcend theory. Nonetheless, as counselors consider intrapersonal, interpersonal, and external factors when working with clients, it is theories that blend all these dimensions together in unique and effective ways.

THEORIES AND ECLECTICISM

Most modern professional counselors and psychotherapists identify themselves as eclectic, that is, "combining theories or techniques from a wide variety of therapeutic approaches" (Sharf, 2004, p. 641). These counselors use various theories and techniques to match their clients' needs, with "an average of 4.4 theories making up their therapeutic work with clients" (Cheston, 2000, p. 254). As needs change, counselors depart from one theory and adopt another—a phenomenon called *style-shift counseling*.

Counselors make changes related to their clients' developmental levels (Ivey & Goncalves, 1988). To be effective, counselors must consider how far their clients have progressed in their development, as described by theorists like Jean Piaget. For example, clients who are not developmentally aware of their environments may need a therapeutic approach that focuses on "emotions, the body, and experience in the here and now," whereas clients at a more advanced level of development may respond best to a "consulting-formal operations" approach, in which the emphasis is on thinking about actions (Ivey & Goncalves, 1988, p. 410). Counselors must start with where their clients are and help them develop in a holistic manner.

Even though eclecticism is able to draw on various theories, techniques, and practices to meet client needs, this approach does have its drawbacks. For instance, an eclectic approach can be hazardous if counselors are not thoroughly familiar with all aspects of the theories involved. In such situations counselors may become technicians who do not understand why certain approaches work best with specific clients at certain times and in certain ways (Cheston, 2000). Such as approach is sometimes referred to as "electric" because undereducated counselors try all methods that "turn them on." An electric orientation often does more harm than good.

To combat this problem, McBride and Martin (1990) advocate a hierarchy of eclectic practices and discuss the importance of having a sound theoretical base as a guide. They describe the first, or lowest, level of eclecticism as *syncretism*—a sloppy, unsystematic process of putting unrelated clinical concepts together. It is encouraged when graduate students are urged to formulate their own theories of counseling without first having experienced how tested models work. The second level of eclecticism is *traditional*. It incorporates "an orderly combination of compatible features from diverse sources [into a] harmonious whole" (English & English, 1956, p. 168). Theories are examined in greater depth and breadth than in syncretism, but no mastery is expected.

On a third level, eclecticism is described as professional or theoretical or as *theoretical integrationism* (Lazarus & Beutler, 1993; Simon, 1989). This type of eclecticism requires that counselors master at least two theories before attempting any combinations. This approach assumes a degree of equality between theories, which may not be accurate, and the existence of criteria "to determine what portions or pieces of each theory to preserve or expunge" (Lazarus & Beutler, 1993, p. 382).

A fourth level of eclecticism is called *technical eclecticism* and is exemplified in the work of Arnold Lazarus (1967, 2000). In this approach procedures from different theories are selected and used in treatment "without necessarily subscribing to the theories that spawned them" (Lazarus & Beutler, 1993, p. 384). The idea is that techniques, not theories, are used in treating clients. Therefore, after properly assessing clients, counselors can use behavioral methods (such as assertiveness training) with existential techniques (such as confronting persons about the meaning in their lives) if the situations warrant. This approach is in line with what Cavanagh (1990) proposes as a healthy way to conduct counseling. It requires counselors to have (a) a sound knowledge and understanding of the counseling theories used, (b) a basic integrative philosophy of human behavior that brings disparate parts of differing theories into a meaningful collage, and

(c) a flexible means of fitting the approach to the client. The critical variables in being a healthy eclectic counselor are a mastery of theory and an acute sensitivity to knowing which approach to use when, where, and how (Harman, 1977).

A final type of eclectic approach is the *transtheoretical model (TTM)* of change (Prochaska & DiClemente, 1992; Prochaska & Norcross, 2003). This model is developmentally based and has been empirically derived over time. It is "an alternative to technical eclectic approaches that tend to be inclusive to the point that various components are 'poorly' held together" (Petrocelli, 2002, p. 23). The model proposes five stages of change—precontemplation, contemplation, preparation, action, and maintenance—which are associated with varied behaviors:

- consciousness raising (e.g., observations, confrontations, and interpretations)
- dramatic relief (i.e., catharsis)
- environmental reevaluation (i.e., deeper consideration by clients of the effects of their behaviors on people they care about)
- self-reevaluation (i.e., an assessment of which values clients will enact and which they will let die)
- self-liberation (i.e., the belief that personal efforts play a crucial role in personal success in difficult situations)
- contingency management, counterconditioning, and stimulus control (i.e., behavioral processes to increase the probability of success when clients take action).

There are also five levels of change—symptom/situational problems, maladaptive cognitions, current interpersonal conflicts, family/systems conflicts, and intrapersonal conflicts. This model is depicted in Table 1.1.

"Counseling from a TTM perspective allows for a more *macroscopic approach* (involving a broad and comprehensive theoretical framework) and *personal adaptation* (involving an increase in critical, logical, accurate, and scientific-like thinking) rather than simple *personal adjustment*" (Petrocelli, 2002, p. 25). Its main drawbacks are its comprehensiveness and complexity and the fact that TTM has been tested only among limited groups, such as addictions populations.

THEORIES AND APPLICATION: THE CASE OF LINDA

The major theories discussed in subsequent chapters have significant differences in their approaches to counseling. To highlight those differences and show the ways in which therapists would operate from each of the theoretical perspectives, each theory is applied to a common case—that of a young woman named Linda. Comparing different theories at work with the same person should reveal those theories in action and permit an informed decision about their use, either singly or in combination.

Linda is a recently divorced, 32-year-old Caucasian woman who is seeking counseling because of relationship problems. Linda was married for 7 years but recently

TABLE 1.1

Levels × Stages × Processes of Change

Levels	Stages of change				
	Precontemplation	Contemplation	Preparation	Action	Maintenance
Symptom/situational	Consciousness raising Dramatic relief	Environmental reevaluation Self-reevaluation	Self-liberation	Contingency management Counterconditioning Stimulus control	
Maladaptive cognitions					
Interpersonal conflicts					
Family/systems conflicts					
Intrapersonal conflicts					

Note: From *Systems of Psychotherapy: A Transtheoretical Analysis*, 5th edition, by J. O. Prochaska and J. C. Norcross, © 2003. Reprinted with permission of Wadsworth, a division of Thompson Learning: www.thompsonrights.com. Fax 800 730-2215.

ended her relationship with her husband because she no longer found him exciting and thought he was being verbally abusive—for example, he often criticized her looks, weight, and dress. During her marriage Linda had had an abortion because her husband insisted and she did not feel she was ready to be a responsible parent yet. However, she states that her former husband's insistence on remaining childless was the primary reason for the abortion. That event took place about 2 years earlier, and Linda still has mixed emotions about it. When discussing it, her mood is both sad and angry.

Linda grew up in a lower-class neighborhood in a mid-size midwest city. Her father, Ralph, was a construction worker with a seventh-grade education. He drank heavily on weekends but otherwise seemed to have a good work ethic and a positive attitude toward his work. Ralph had definite opinions about politics, religion, and the place of women in society; and he never hesitated to voice his views, sometimes quite loudly. Linda kept her distance from him. Linda's mother, Marian, did not work outside the home. Instead, she took care of Linda and her siblings: Ted, 2 years older than Linda; Claudia, 13 months younger; and Patricia, 3 years younger. A high school graduate, Marian also took in sewing to earn extra income for the family. She was a rather quiet and introverted woman, and although Linda felt close to her in many ways, she never really identified with her mother. In fact, Linda reports that she is not emotionally close to her family at all.

As a teenager Linda was mildly rebellious. She occasionally skipped school and church services and also engaged in petty theft once at a local department store. She dated older boys, most of whom were friends of her brother. Linda was flirtatious but never really acted out sexually beyond some heavy petting. She states that her brother was her protector; she was grateful for his presence in her adolescent life. Otherwise, she thinks she would have probably gotten into trouble and may even have gotten married before finishing high school.

All of Linda's siblings graduated from high school but, like their parents, married young and got jobs either in a trade or in retail. Linda made good enough grades to be admitted to a regular 4-year college. However, she did not feel confident enough to apply because it would have gone against family norms. She states that her father discouraged her thoughts of further education. As a compromise, Linda enrolled in a local community college, where she completed a course in business administration. Since graduation she has drifted from job to job as an administrative assistant or a secretary, never challenged in any of her jobs. She admits to having a temper and says that she gets fed up with the treatment she receives from her bosses, who are sexist she thinks. She also gets tired of the routine work, especially the filing, which she has to do.

Linda likes to read romance novels, watch the home-and-garden television channel, and go to action movies. All of these activities make her feel better; they take her away from her mundane existence. Since her divorce, she has felt aimless, anxious, and depressed. She has not found a peer group of singles to associate with, and most of her former friends and acquaintances have either married or moved away. Both of her younger sisters are still in town, as are her parents, but Linda does not feel close to any of them. She finds them boring; they do not "stretch their minds." Thus, she sees them only once a week, for Sunday lunch, and leaves as soon as possible.

Linda reveals that she has had daydreams about ending her life by stepping out in front of a truck. However, she doubts that she would ever do such a thing. She has recently contemplated finding a new job and has given 2-weeks' notice to her current employer. She does not want life to pass her by, but she is beginning to think it is doing just that. Her voice sounds almost desperate as she asks for help.

SUMMARY AND CONCLUSION

The helping professions, especially counseling and psychotherapy, have evolved. Current ways of working with people who have concerns or problems are based on sound theories that have been researched and tested for effectiveness with client populations. Such was not always the case. The first theories for the treatment of people in mental pain were degrading, based on superstition, and potentially deadly. Clients were thought to be possessed by evil spirits that had to be driven out. This viewpoint eventually gave way to more humane approaches, and theories of treatment, initially slow to evolve, exploded in number during the last half of the 20th century.

Today, the creation and development of theories have slowed; movement is toward the combination of approaches and eclecticism. Most counselors and psychotherapists use multiple theories, and some focus more on techniques than theories. Nonetheless, the value of theories remains. They provide the foundation for the most effective counseling approaches.

REFERENCES

Auvenshine, D., & Noffsinger, A. L. (1984). *Counseling: An introduction for the health and human services.* Baltimore: University Park Press.

Boy, A. V., & Pine, G. J. (1983). Counseling: Fundamentals of theoretical renewal. *Counseling and Values, 27,* 248–255.

Bradley, R. W., & Cox, J. A. (2001). Counseling: Evolution of the profession. In D. C. Locke, J. E. Myers, & E. L. Herr (Eds.), *The handbook of counseling* (pp. 27–41). Thousand Oaks, CA: Sage.

Brammer, L. M., Abrego, P., & Shostrom, E. (1993). *Therapeutic counseling and psychotherapy* (6th ed.). Upper Saddle River, NJ: Prentice Hall.

Butcher, J., Mineka, S., & Hooley, J. (2003). *Abnormal psychology* (12th ed.). Boston: Allyn & Bacon.

Cavanagh, M. E. (1990). *The counseling experience.* Prospect Heights, IL: Waveland.

Cheston, S. E. (2000). A new paradigm for teaching counseling theory and practice. *Counselor Education and Supervision, 39,* 254–269.

Corsini, R. J. (2000). Introduction. In R. J. Corsini & D. Wedding (Eds.), *Current psychotherapies* (6th ed., pp. 1–15). Itasca, IL: Peacock.

English, H. B., & English, A. C. (1956). *A comprehensive dictionary of psychological and psychoanalytical terms.* New York: Longman Green.

Gladding, S. T. (1990). Let us not grow weary of theory. *Journal for Specialists in Group Work, 15,* 194.

Hansen, J. C., Stevic, R. R., & Warner, R. W. (1986). *Counseling: Theory and process* (4th ed.). Boston: Allyn & Bacon.

Harman, R. L. (1977). Beyond techniques. *Counselor Education and Supervision, 17,* 157–158.

Harper, R. A. (1959). *Psychoanalysis and psychotherapy: 36 systems*. Upper Saddle River, NJ: Prentice Hall.

Ivey, A. E., & Goncalves, O. F. (1988). Developmental therapy: Integrating developmental processes into the clinical practice. *Journal of Counseling and Development, 66*, 406–413.

Kelly, K. R. (1988). Defending eclecticism: The utility of informed choice. *Journal of Mental Health Counseling, 10*, 210–213.

Lazarus, A. A. (1967). In support of technical eclecticism. *Psychological Reports, 21*, 415–416.

Lazarus, A. A. (2000). Multimodal therapy. In R. J. Corsini & D. Wedding (Eds.), *Current psychotherapies* (5th ed., pp. 340–374). Itasca, IL: Peacock.

Lazarus, A. A., & Beutler, L. E. (1993). On technical eclecticism. *Journal of Counseling and Development, 71*, 381–385.

McBride, M. C., & Martin, G. E. (1990). A framework for eclecticism: The importance of theory to mental health counseling. *Journal of Mental Health Counseling, 12*, 495–505.

Okun, B. K. (1990). *Seeking connections in psychotherapy*. San Francisco: Jossey-Bass.

Parloff, M. (1976, February 21). Shopping for the right therapy. *Saturday Review*, pp. 14–16.

Patterson, C. H. (1985). *The therapeutic relationship*. Pacific Grove, CA: Brooks/Cole.

Petrocelli, J. V. (2002). Processes and stages of change: Counseling with the transtheoretical model of change. *Journal of Counseling and Development, 80*, 22–30.

Prochaska, J. O., & DiClemente, C. C. (1992). The transtheoretical approach. In J. C. Norcross & M. R. Goldfried (Eds.), *Handbook of psychotherapy integration* (pp. 300–334). New York: Basic Books.

Prochaska, J. O., & Norcross, J. C. (2003). *Systems of psychotherapy: A transtheoretical analysis* (5th ed.). Pacific Grove, CA: Brooks/Cole.

Sharf, R. S. (2004). *Theories of counseling and psychotherapy: Concepts and cases* (3rd ed.). Pacific Grove, CA: Brooks/Cole.

Shertzer, B., & Stone, S. C. (1974). *Fundamentals of counseling*. Boston: Houghton Mifflin.

Simon, G. M. (1989). An alternative defense of eclecticism: Responding to Kelly and Ginter. *Journal of Mental Health Counseling, 2*, 280–288.

Wilks, D. (2003). A historical review of counseling theory development in relation to definitions of free will and determinism. *Journal of Counseling and Development, 81*, 278–284.

Young, R. A. (1988). Ordinary explanations and career theories. *Journal of Counseling and Development, 66*, 336–339.

CHAPTER 2

Psychoanalysis and Psychoanalytic Theories

All our baggage is behind us
    as we rumble down the tracks
        past the people and the places
            that are changing
At each station we entrust
    that events now in our minds
        will come to have new meaning
            as we talk past fleeting scenery.

Note: "Baggage" by S. T. Gladding. Copyright 2003 by Samuel T. Gladding.

Even from a solely historical point of view, psychoanalysis is important. It was the first theory to gain public recognition and acceptance, especially in Europe and the Americas, for example, in Brazil and the United States. It was the genius of Sigmund Freud that created psychoanalysis, from his ideas all other psychoanalytic theories sprang—those of Anna Freud, Erik Erikson, Harry Stack Sullivan, Karen Horney, and Heinz Kohut. In addition, many prominent therapists in the history of counseling who did not become psychoanalysts were directly influenced by Freud's concepts, either through association with Freud himself or through instruction in his ideas—for example, Alfred Adler, Carl Jung, Albert Ellis, Rollo May, and Fritz Perls. Other theorists—including Carl Rogers, B. F. Skinner, and Otto Rank—developed theories in direct opposition to Freud's principles. Sigmund Freud and concepts of psychoanalysis permeate counseling literature. To be uninformed about psychoanalysis is to be an undereducated counselor.

MAJOR THEORIST: SIGMUND FREUD

The life of Sigmund Freud has been the focus of many books, such as Irving Stone's *Passions of the Mind*. His official biographer, Ernest Jones, wrote a definitive three-volume work (1953, 1955, 1957) on Freud's life and the development of his ideas.

Sigmund Freud was born in Freiburg, Austria, in 1856, the first son of Jacob Freud's second marriage (see Figure 2.1). Sigmund's mother, Amalia, gave him special privileges because she had higher hopes for her Sigmund than for the five daughters and two sons born later. In 1860 Freud's father moved the family to Vienna, and there Freud spent most of the remainder of his life.

An excellent student, Freud was limited in his occupational choices because of finances and the discrimination in Europe against Jews' entering certain occupations. Nevertheless, Freud enrolled at the University of Vienna in 1873 with the idea of pursuing medicine. He received his medical degree in 1881, having mastered research methods as well as the normal course work. He married Martha Bernays in 1886 and fathered six children, the youngest of whom, Anna, became famous in her own right as a child psychoanalyst.

FIGURE 2.1 Freud family genogram

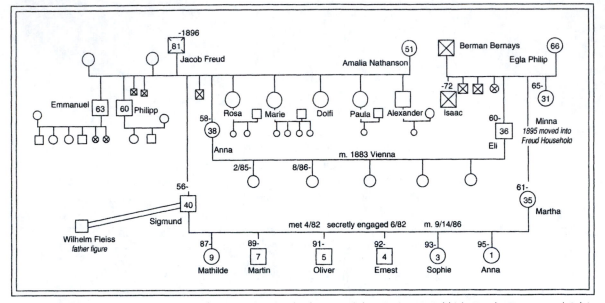

Note: From *Genograms: Assessment and Intervention* (2nd ed., p. 142) by Monica McGoldrick, Randy Gerson, and Sylvia Shellenberger. Copyright 1999 by Monica McGoldrick and Sylvia shellenberger. Copyright 1985 by Monica McGoldrick and Randy Gerson. Used by Permission of W. W. Norton & Company, Inc.

Freud supported his family through his private practice in psychiatry, working primarily with individuals with hysteria. Initially, he used hypnosis as his main form of treatment, a technique he had mastered in France under the tutelage of neurologist Jean Charcot. Though Freud was not a good hypnotist, he soon discovered that this deficit was beneficial. Indeed, much of his success depended on the relationship he developed during the treatment process rather than on the hypnosis. This revelation led Freud to explore how he might use his clinical relationship with a client in combination with the client's concentration to bring about change (Freud, 1925/1959).

During medical school Freud had been impressed with Joseph Breuer's cathartic method of treating people with hysteria. Breuer had his patients relive painful experiences and work through emotional events suppressed for years. Breuer's method also used hypnosis. Freud modified that approach by dropping the hypnosis and sitting behind his patients as they lay on couches. From this position he would press his hand on their foreheads whenever they began to block out memories, assuring them that they could remember long-forgotten important events and thoughts. Freud called this method *free association* and used it to explore the unconscious minds of his patients. The material uncovered in the process became the stuff of interpretation and analysis, and thus, psychoanalysis was born. Freud's work with others, as well as years of self-analysis, gave him new insight into the nature of persons, and he began to stress the importance of the unconscious in understanding personality (Monte, 1991).

Many of Freud's colleagues, and later the general public, were outraged by his emphasis on the importance of sexuality and aggression in the etiology of personality. Nevertheless, his ideas attracted a number of followers, and in 1902 he formally organized in his home the Wednesday Psychological Society, which met to discuss personality theory. This group, which at times included Carl Jung and Alfred Adler, became known in 1908 as the Viennese Psychoanalytic Society. It acquired international prominence when Freud and some of his followers accepted an invitation in 1908 to lecture at Clark University in the United States. Even though Freud suffered a number of personal and professional setbacks, his theory of psychoanalysis continued to grow and develop. Professional journals and international congresses devoted to the theory, as well as Freud's prolific and heuristic writings, assured the historical prominence of psychoanalysis. Freud died in London in 1939, a refugee from the Nazi occupation of Austria.

VIEW OF HUMAN NATURE/PERSONALITY

Freud's theory of psychoanalysis evolved throughout his lifetime. Many of its main tenets were set down in his books *The Interpretation of Dreams* (1900/1955), *New Introductory Lectures on Psychoanalysis* (1923/1933), and *The Ego and the Id* (1923/1947). The Freudian view of human nature is dynamic; that is, Freud believed in the transformation and exchange of energy within the personality (Hall, 1954). Much of what he described, however, is metaphorical because a majority of the hypotheses he proposed could not be proven scientifically at the time (Hergenhahn & Olson, 2003). Nevertheless, Freud hoped that his theory would eventually be empirically verified, and he developed techniques for working with his patients that were based on that hope. He focused particularly on levels of consciousness, the formation of personality, psychosexual development, and defense mechanisms.

LEVELS OF CONSCIOUSNESS

For Freud human nature can be explained in terms of a conscious mind, a preconscious mind, and an unconscious mind. The conscious mind is attuned to events in the present, to an awareness of the outside world. The preconscious mind is an area between the conscious and unconscious minds and contains aspects of both. Within the preconscious are hidden memories or forgotten experiences that can be remembered with the proper cues. For example, after a long separation a person may recall another person's name if enough reminders are generated. Finally, beneath the preconscious mind is the unconscious mind, the most powerful and least understood part of the personality. The instinctual, repressed, and powerful forces of the personality exist in the unconscious.

FORMATION OF PERSONALITY

Freud hypothesized that the personality is formed from the interaction of three developing parts—the id, the ego, and the superego—which are imbedded in the various conscious states. The id and the superego are confined to the unconscious, whereas the ego operates primarily in the conscious but also in the preconscious and the unconscious.

The id comprises the basic inherited givens of the personality and is present from birth. It is amoral, impulsive, and irrational and works according to the pleasure principle, that is, it pursues what it wants because it cannot tolerate tension. The id operates through drives, instincts, and images (such as dreaming, hallucinating, and fantasizing), a thought process known as *primary process*. Although primary process thinking may bring temporary relief, it is ultimately unsatisfying. Consequently, the id discharges energy to the ego, which is another way of obtaining what it wants.

If empowered and left on its own, the id would probably destroy a person or at least cause trouble by acting on its primitive, aggressive, and sexual drives. Those who let their ids guide their action lack insight into the consequences of what they are doing. The id contains basic life energy, collectively known as *eros*, and basic death instincts, known as *thanatos*. At first Freud associated eros with sexuality but later modified this idea, describing all life-preserving instincts as eros and the psychic energy that accompanies them as *libido*. The idea that each person has some sort of death wish was the result of Freud's observation of the destructiveness of World War I and his belief that humans, composed of inorganic matter, ultimately have a desire to return to this state of being. The premise of thanatos was never fully developed, but Freud saw it in acts of aggression, as well as in foolishly dangerous behaviors such as taking unnecessary risks.

To keep the person from being either too self-indulgent or too morally restrained, the ego moderates the wishes and desires of the id and the superego. The ego, the second system to develop, keeps the id from getting out of control and is, thus, often called "the executive of the mind." When the ego is fully developed, it functions to keep the desires of the id and the superego in check while realistically helping the person interact with the outside world. The ego works according to the reality principle, with reality being what exists (Hall, Lindzey, & Campbell, 1998). The ego devises ways to achieve appropriate goals, obtain energy for activities from the id, and keep the person in harmony with the environment. The ego's way of thinking is known as the *secondary process*, which is nothing more than rationally thinking through situations. A strong ego is essential to healthy functioning.

The superego, in contrast to the id, is the moral branch of the mind, operating according to what is ideal. The superego arises from the moral teachings of a child's parents and is said to function according to the moral principle. Through a mechanism known as the *ego ideal*, it strives for perfection and rewards actions that follow parental and societal dictates. For example, children who have been taught that neatness is a virtue feel good when they keep a neat room. On the other hand, those who act against what they have been taught are punished through the part of the superego called the *conscience*, which induces guilt. The superego locks a person into rather rigid moral patterns if given free reign. Because its goal is perfection, the superego sometimes forces people into restrained action or no action when they face a dilemma.

PSYCHOSEXUAL STAGES OF DEVELOPMENT

In addition to the levels of consciousness and his concept of personality, psychoanalysis is built on what Freud referred to as *psychosexual developmental stages*. Each of four main stages focuses on a zone of pleasure that is dominant at a particular time. In the first stage, the *oral stage*, the mouth is the chief pleasure zone. Children under the age of 1 are in this stage and obtain basic gratification from sucking and biting. In the second stage, the *anal stage*, children between the ages of 1 and 2 delight in either withholding or eliminating feces. This stage involves the first really significant conflict between a child's internal instincts and external demands, such as toilet training.

In the third stage, the *phallic stage*, children from 3 to 5 attempt to resolve their sexual identities. The chief zones of pleasure are the sex organs, and children of both genders must work through their sexual desires in a conflict of feelings known as the *Oedipus complex*. Freud thought that the conflict was clearer and more completely resolved in boys than in girls. Initially, both boys and girls are attracted to the mother because she is the source of great pleasure. Both genders see the father as a rival for the mother's love and attention. However, feelings about the mother change as boys and girls discover their own sexual identities.

For a boy there is a desire to possess his mother sexually. Yet there is a fear that if he makes his wishes known, his father, who is bigger and stronger, will become angry and castrate him. A boy assumes that his penis is the source of conflict between his father and himself and that girls, because they lack a penis, have been castrated. Although the boy may feel hostile toward his father, he represses his desire for his mother and eventually comes to identify with his father, thereby gaining vicarious satisfaction through father-mother interactions.

The Oedipus complex for a girl, sometimes called the *Electra complex*, is less clearly resolved. A young girl comes to notice that she does not have a penis and that boys do. Freud says she blames her mother for the lack of this valued organ and envies her father for possessing one (i.e., penis envy). Thus, she has both negative and positive feelings toward each parent and is sexually ambivalent at the end of this stage. She takes some consolation from learning that she has the ability to have babies because boys cannot. Therefore, she identifies with her mother and, according to Freud, hopes to receive later gratification by having children, especially boys.

The wishes of young boys and girls are not manifested directly during the phallic stage. Rather they are disguised in dreams, fantasy, and play. Nevertheless, the wishes are real and, if not resolved, will lead to future intra- and interpersonal difficulties. Freud thought that the basic ingredients of the adult personality had formed by the end of the phallic stage.

After the phallic stage, between the ages of 6 and 12, comes a period known as *latency*, at which time there is little manifest interest in sexuality. Instead, energy is focused on peer activities and personal mastery of cognitive learning and physical skills. Around puberty the last of the psychosexual phases occurs, the *genital stage*. If all has gone well previously, each gender takes more interest in the other, and normal heterosexual patterns of interaction appear. If there were unresolved difficulties in any of the first three stages, collectively known as the *pregenital stages*, the person may have difficulty adjusting to the adult responsibilities that begin in the genital stage. Freud believed that two difficulties could arise in the pregenital stages—excessive frustration or overindulgence—causing a person to become fixated, or arrested, at that level of development and overly dependent on the use of defense mechanisms.

Freud's psychosexual stages of development are the aspects of his theory that have been modified most by others who have stayed in the psychoanalytic tradition. Psychoanalyst Heinz Kohut (1971, 1984) proposed a much less sexually based view of childhood development. His psychodynamic approach is known as *object-relations theory*. An *object* is anything that satisfies a need, whether it is a person or a thing. It is used interchangeably with the term *other* to refer to an important person to whom the child and later the adult become attached. Others are perceived by an infant as not-me objects for gratifying basic and instinctive needs, rather than as individuals with separate identities.

Kohut's theory proposes that children introject what they perceive from others as good and both reject and project what they perceive as bad. In this way, children form an identity with others through interactions, both real and imagined. The challenge for children "is to learn to negotiate with this outside world without trading away satisfaction of such fundamental needs as love, security, and esteem for individual autonomy and a sense of self" (Bankart, 1997, p. 179). Mature individuals are both independent and attached to others, able to integrate all aspects of themselves and avoid *splitting*, a defense mechanism that keeps incompatible feelings separate from oneself.

Erik Erikson (1963, 1982) went even further than Kohut in modifying Freud's psychosexual theory of development. For Erikson development extends over the life span, and psychosocial factors are more important than psychosexual ones. Thus, Erikson's theory extends Freud's development emphasis from birth to death and focuses on the achievement of specific life-enhancing tasks. Like a number of other modifiers of Freud's theory, Erikson emphasizes the central role of the ego in life tasks rather than the interplay between the id, the ego, and the superego. Because of this emphasis, he and other theorists like him are sometimes known as *ego psychodynamic theorists*. Erikson's stages of development and the accompanying ages and tasks are presented in Table 2.1.

TABLE 2.1	Stage	Age	Tasks
Erikson's stages of development	Trust vs. mistrust	Birth to 1	Emphasis on satisfying basic physical and emotional needs
	Autonomy vs. shame/doubt	2 to 3	Emphasis on exploration and developing self-reliance
	Initiative vs. guilt	4 to 5	Emphasis on achieving a sense of competence and initiative
	Industry vs. inferiority	6 to 12	Emphasis on setting and attaining personal goals
	Identity vs. role confusion	12 to 18	Emphasis on testing limits, achieving a self-identity
	Intimacy vs. isolation	18 to 35	Emphasis on achieving intimate interpersonal relationships
	Generativity vs. stagnation	35 to 65	Emphasis on helping next generation, being productive
	Integrity vs. despair	65 +	Emphasis on integration of life activities, feeling worthwhile

Note: From *Counseling: A Comprehensive Profession* (4th ed., p. 190) by Samuel T. Gladding. Copyright 2000. Reprinted by permission of Pearson Education, Inc., Upper Saddle River, NJ.

DEFENSE MECHANISMS

Defense mechanisms are the last crucial part of Freud's theory as it relates to human nature and personality. Basically, *defense mechanisms* protect a person from being overwhelmed by anxiety, through adapting to situations or distorting or denying events. Such mechanisms are normal and operate on an unconscious level. Anna Freud (1936) and other ego psychodynamic theorists elaborated on Freud's original ideas. Among the main defense mechanisms are the following:

- **Repression.** Repression is the most basic defense mechanism, the one on which others are built. Using this mechanism, the ego involuntarily excludes from consciousness any unwanted or painful thoughts, feelings, memories, or impulses. The ego must use energy to keep excluded areas from consciousness, but sometimes the repressed thoughts slip out in dreams or verbal expressions. Repression is considered the cornerstone, or foundation-stone, of psychoanalysis (Nye, 2000).
- **Projection.** Persons using projection attribute an unwanted emotion or characteristic to someone else in an effort to deny that the emotion or characteristic is part of themselves. For example, a woman may say that her boss is angry at her instead of saying that she is angry at her boss.
- **Reaction formation.** With this mechanism anxiety-producing thoughts, feelings, or impulses are repressed and their opposites are expressed. For example, a host at a party may shower a disliked guest with attention. A reaction formation is often detected by the intensity with which the opposite emotion is expressed.
- **Displacement.** Displacement channels energy away from one object to an alternative, that is, to a safe target. For instance, a person who has had a hard day at the office may come home and yell at the dog. A positive form of displacement is known as *sublimation*, in which a drive that cannot be expressed directly is channeled into constructive activities. For example, those who are unable to express themselves sexually may take care of children. Freud thought sublimation was a major means of building civilization.
- **Regression.** In regression a person returns to an earlier stage of development. For example, after suffering a trauma during early adolescence, a child may begin to wet the bed. Virtually all people regress if placed under enough pressure or stress.
- **Rationalization.** Rationalization allows a person to find reasonable explanations for unreasonable or unacceptable behaviors, in order to make them sound logical and acceptable. An individual might say, "I did it because everyone else was doing it," or "I really didn't think it was going to be worth the time I'd have to spend, so I didn't do it."
- **Denial.** A person in denial does not consciously acknowledge an unpleasant or traumatic event or situation. Denial protects people from having to face painful experiences. For instance, a couple may deny that they are having marital problems even though both are aware that the relationship is deteriorating. Denial may initially help a person cope with certain situations, such as war, but if perpetuated, it ultimately becomes destructive.
- **Identification.** In identification a person incorporates the qualities of another, thereby removing any fear that person might have of the other and giving him or her new behavioral skills. For example, a child might identify with a feared

parent. Identification, like sublimation, differs from other defense mechanisms in that it can help a person realistically solve problems.

Freud's view of human nature stresses conflict between conscious and unconscious forces (Arlow, 2000; Monte, 1991). The theory is deterministic, holding that a person's adult personality is formed by resolving the gender-specific stages of childhood. If a person has a traumatic childhood and fails to resolve a psychosexual stage, that person will need to work through this unresolved stage later in life.

ROLE OF THE COUNSELOR/THERAPIST

Professionals who practice psychoanalysis play the role of experts. They encourage their clients to talk about whatever comes to mind, especially childhood experiences. To create an atmosphere in which clients feel free to express difficult thoughts, psychoanalysts, after a few face-to-face sessions, often have clients lie down on a couch while the analyst remains out of view, usually seated behind the client's head. The analyst's role is to let clients gain insight by reliving and working through unresolved past experiences that come into focus during therapy sessions. To help clients deal realistically with unconscious material, therapists encourage them to project onto the therapists emotions associated with others in the clients' lives. Unlike some other approaches, psychoanalysis encourages clinicians to interpret for their clients.

Overall, psychoanalytic therapists employ both active and passive techniques. Psychological assessment instruments are sometimes employed, especially projective tests such as the Rorschach Ink Blots. Practitioners of psychoanalysis almost always use diagnostic labels to classify clients and from those labels develop treatment plans. Psychoanalysts rely on the latest edition of the American Psychiatric Association's *Diagnostic and Statistical Manual (DSM)*, the standard reference for diagnoses.

GOALS

The goals of psychoanalysis vary according to the clients being treated. However, clinicians of this persuasion focus mainly on personal adjustment, usually inducing a reorganization of internal forces within the persons they see. In most cases a primary goal is to help clients become more aware of the unconscious aspects of their personalities, including repressed memories and wishes too painful or threatening to have been dealt with initially. Repression does not stop thoughts from having influence; it just makes identifying them more difficult. Psychoanalysis strives to help clients gain insight into themselves.

A second major goal, often tied to the first, is to help clients work through developmental stages not previously resolved. If accomplished, clients become unstuck and are able to live more productively. However, working through unresolved developmental stages may require a major reconstruction of the personality. As a consequence, psychoanalysis is often a long, intense, and expensive process (Nye, 2000).

A final goal of psychoanalysis is helping clients cope with the demands of the society in which they live. According to this theory, unhappy people are not in tune with themselves or society. Thus, psychoanalysis stresses environmental adjustment, especially in the areas of work and intimacy. The focus is on strengthening the ego so that perceptions and plans become more realistic.

PROCESS AND TECHNIQUES

Psychoanalysis is a time-consuming process. Clients are usually seen a minimum of three times a week for a number of months or even years. Psychoanalytic techniques are most often applied within a specific setting, such as a therapist's office or the interview room of a hospital. Among the most prominent techniques are free association, dream analysis, analysis of transference, analysis of resistance, and interpretation. Although each technique is examined separately here, in practice they are integrated into the process of therapy.

FREE ASSOCIATION

Repressed material in the unconscious is always seeking release. On a daily basis this material may be expressed in the form of sexual or aggressive jokes or through Freudian slips, errors of speech such as "I loathe you" instead of "I love you." In psychoanalysis, clients are encouraged to relax and freely recall early childhood memories or emotional experiences. During free association clients abandon the normal way of censoring thoughts by consciously repressing them and instead say whatever comes to mind, even if the thoughts seem silly, irrational, suggestive, or painful. In this way the id is requested to speak, and the ego remains silent (Freud, 1936). Unconscious material thus enters the conscious mind, and there clinicians interpret it.

At times clients resist free association by blocking their thoughts, denying their importance, or both. Often such resistance is concerned with significant earlier unresolved relationships. Nonetheless, therapists attempt to help clients work through their resistance, assuring them that even seemingly trivial thoughts or feelings are important. Many times such assurance is enough to overcome the resistance.

DREAM ANALYSIS

Clients report dreams to their therapists on a regular basis. Freud believed that dreams were "the royal road to the unconscious," an attempt to fulfill a childhood wish or express unacknowledged sexual desires. He insisted on getting at the nature of dreams by breaking them down into parts and treating them in as much detail as possible (Capuzzi & Black, 1986).

In dream analysis, clients are encouraged to dream and remember dreams, even though not everything in a dream is considered important. Clinicians are especially sensitive to two aspects—the *manifest content* (obvious meaning) and the *latent content* (hidden but true meaning) (Jones, 1979)—and help to interpret both. Some dream symbols are obvious, such as hostility expressed as death or an accident (Nye, 2000). Other symbols are vague and difficult to interpret. Freud's method of dream analysis is considered the first scientific approach to the study of dreams.

ANALYSIS OF TRANSFERENCE

Transference is the term that denotes a client's response to a clinician as if the clinician were some significant figure in the client's past, usually a parent figure. Analysts encourage transference and interpret the positive or negative feelings expressed. The release of feelings is therapeutic, providing an emotional catharsis, but the real value lies in clients' increased self-knowledge, which comes through therapists' analysis of the transference. Clients who experience transference and learn from it are then freed to move on to another developmental stage (Singer, 1970). It should be stressed that "working through" transference is a continual process that "consists of repetition, elaboration, and amplification" (Arlow, 2000, p. 37). Understanding and insight grow with each analysis of the transference experience.

ANALYSIS OF RESISTANCE

Sometimes clients make initial progress while undergoing psychoanalysis and then slow down or stop. Their resistance to the therapeutic process may take many forms, such as missing or being late for appointments, not paying fees, persisting in transference, blocking thoughts during free association, or refusing to recall dreams or early memories. When resistance occurs in any form, clinicians must deal with it immediately. Analysis of resistance can help clients gain insight into it as well as other behaviors. But if resistance is not dealt with, the therapeutic process will probably come to a halt.

INTERPRETATION

Interpretation is part of the other techniques already examined and complementary to them. Through interpretation therapists help clients understand the meaning of past and present personal events. The technique also encompasses explanations and analysis of clients' thoughts, feelings, and actions. However, counselors must carefully time the use of interpretation. If it comes too soon in a relationship, it can drive a client away. On the other hand, if it is not employed at all or is used infrequently, a client may fail to develop insight. Only when clients are ready can interpretation make a significant impact on their growth and development.

MULTICULTURAL AND GENDER-SENSITIVE ISSUES

Sigmund Freud and his theory of psychoanalysis were influenced by the times in which they emerged: the late Victorian Era and the beginning of the 20th century. Consequently, many of the concepts and ideas that developed in psychoanalysis are not considered relevant in the 21st century. Because Freud worked with upper-class Viennese women, almost all of whom suffered from hysteria, some clinicians today dismiss psychoanalysis as an irrelevant theory.

Nonetheless, a good deal of psychoanalysis has transcended cultural barriers. For instance, outside the United States, the greatest number of practitioners of psychoanalysis live in Brazil, a very diverse society. In addition, the work of Erik Erikson in studying the development of children and child-rearing practices in American Indian cultures and his emphasis on the ego have helped to make psychoanalysis more palatable for some cultural groups. Furthermore, concepts ranging from transference to defense mechanisms seem to have relevance for people in different parts of society.

Gender-sensitive issues are another story. Freud's concept of the Electra complex and penis envy is largely discredited now (Horney, 1967). Nevertheless, many women avoid psychoanalysis and its offshoots because of what they consider a bias in psychoanalytic theory, which sees women as inferior to men because they do not resolve the Electra complex as completely as men resolve the Oedipal complex.

EVALUATION OF THE THEORY

STRENGTHS AND CONTRIBUTIONS

As developed by Freud and modified by others, psychoanalysis has several unique emphases. First, psychoanalysis emphasizes the importance of sexuality and the unconscious in human behavior. Before this theory came into being, sexuality (especially childhood sexuality) was denied, and little attention was paid to unconscious forces. Now, many theories acknowledge both the importance of the person as a sexual being and the power of the unconscious mind.

Another positive aspect of this theory is that it lends itself to empirical studies; it is heuristic. Since the early 1900s Freud's proposals have generated a tremendous amount of research. Much of the research supporting the theory has been reported in the form of case histories and reactions in journals such as the *American Psychoanalytic Association Journal*, the *International Journal of Psychoanalysis*, and the *Psychoanalytic Review*. A good deal of the research attacking the theory has been reported as empirical studies in other reputable journals. The theory itself challenges researchers to develop sophisticated methods of inquiry so that studies can be comparable.

A third interesting aspect of psychoanalysis is that it provides a theoretical base of support for a number of diagnostic instruments. Some psychological tests, such as the

Thematic Apperception Test and the Rorschach Ink Blots, are rooted in psychoanalytic theory. Many other tests used by counselors and therapists are outgrowths of this theory or reactions to it.

Another strength of the psychoanalytic approach is that it reflects the complexity of human nature. Clinicians of any theoretical persuasion can gain a greater appreciation of human development and various associated problems by understanding psychoanalysis (Monte, 1991).

A fifth strength of psychoanalysis is that it has grown and developed through the years, as opposed to having stagnated. Nye (2000) reports that there are 10,000 practicing classical psychoanalysts in the United States, and many other professionals undoubtedly engage in a modified form of psychoanalysis, such as ego psychology or object-relations theory. Psychoanalysis continues to evolve and most recently has emphasized adaptive processes, social relations, and brief forms of treatment.

Another contribution of psychoanalysis is that it appears to be effective for those who suffer from a wide variety of disorders, including hysteria, narcissism, obsessive-compulsive reactions, character disorders, anxiety, phobias, and sexual difficulties (Arlow, 2000).

One final strength of psychoanalysis is that it stresses the importance of developmental growth stages. This emphasis has influenced a significant amount of investigation since Freud's time, especially the work of Erikson (1963) and Levinson et al. (1978). Such knowledge of human development is invaluable when proposing an individual treatment plan.

LIMITATIONS AND CRITICISMS

Despite the unique emphases of psychoanalysis, most professional counselors and therapists do not use this approach. First of all, psychoanalysis is time-consuming and expensive. A person undergoing psychoanalysis is usually seen three to five times a week for a period of years (Bankart, 1997; Nye, 2000). Although psychoanalytically oriented psychotherapy (as opposed to psychoanalysis) is an alternative to long-term treatment, the effectiveness of briefer versions of psychoanalysis is debatable.

Another drawback is that psychoanalysis does not seem to lend itself to working with older clients. Thus, many psychoanalysts will not see clients over the age of 50.

A third limitation of psychoanalysis is that it has been claimed almost exclusively by psychiatry, despite the wishes of Freud (Vandenbos, Cummings, & Deleon, 1992). Counselors and therapists without medical degrees have had a difficult time getting extensive training in psychoanalysis (Turkington, 1985). In a 1988 settlement the American Psychoanalytic Association, the most prestigious psychoanalytic society in the United States, "agreed that roughly 40 percent of its training slots [would] be filled by psychologists and other non-medically trained mental health professionals" (Bule, 1988, p. 15). Still, psychoanalysis tends to be a rather restricted profession. Most nonmedical mental health professionals are members of the American Academy of Psychoanalysis and the National Psychological Association for Psychoanalysis, organizations that are less prestigious than the American Psychoanalytic Association (Arlow, 2000).

A fourth limitation of psychoanalysis is that it is based on many concepts that are not easily communicated or understood. The id, the ego, and the superego, for instance, might be represented in more easily understood ways. Psychoanalytical terminology seems at times to be overly complicated.

Another criticism of the psychoanalytic approach, especially the theory created by Freud, is that it is deterministic. For example, Freud attributed certain limitations in women to their gender. This controversial aspect of his theory has subsided because of the influence of ego psychology and women scholars' interpretation of Freud (Winkler, 1986), yet the appropriateness of psychoanalysis for women continues to be questioned.

Still another limiting aspect of the psychoanalytic approach is the fact that psychoanalysis does not lend itself to the needs of most individuals who seek professional counseling. The psychoanalytic model has become associated with people who have major adjustment difficulties or who want or need to explore the unconscious. However, many individuals who seek counseling have less disruptive developmental or situational problems or disorders.

TREATING LINDA WITH PSYCHOANALYSIS AND PSYCHOANALYTIC THERAPIES

CONCEPTUALIZATION

From a psychoanalytic perspective you notice several problems in Linda's life. She states that she never felt close to her mother and is not close to her father either. You therefore hypothesize that she has never really resolved the phallic/Electra stage of childhood. If that is true, then it is little wonder that she has not been able to sustain a marriage and that she continues to have trouble with her bosses at work. Linda's psychosexual development is a major theme that you identify immediately.

You also note, not surprisingly, that Linda is dependent on a number of defense mechanisms, one of which is repression of her hostile thoughts about the way she has been and is being treated in her life. Instead of dealing with these thoughts and feelings constructively and in a straightforward manner, Linda uses escape literature, movies, and television to help her feel better. Overall, Linda has a stronger-than-average death wish and a weak ego. She has not found satisfaction in either love or work, and she is most likely diagnosable under one of the *DSM* categories dealing with depression or personality disorder.

TREATMENT PROCESS

As a psychoanalyst you are the expert who directs the course of therapy. You are particularly interested in Linda's past and in any early childhood memories. You hope that Linda can gain insight into her situation by reliving past experiences and thereby resolving them. In order to help Linda, you employ a number of procedures to bring out repressed and unconscious material. For example, you encourage Linda to engage in free association and dream analysis. Your ultimate goal is to enable her to adjust to society and to be intimate with others as she chooses.

You begin by seeing Linda four times a week for 1 hour at a time, stressing to her that treatment is likely to take years. In order to be unobtrusive and yet facilitate Linda's therapy, you have her lie down on a couch while you sit behind her head. In addition to free association and dream analysis, you try other standardized psychoanalytic techniques, including analysis of transference, analysis of resistance, and interpretation.

All of these procedures release unconscious material that Linda has repressed. Sometimes the process is a struggle, and Linda is surprised at what she says. For example, she blurts out that she *loathed* (instead of *loved*) her father. The interpretation of the latent content of her dreams astonishes her, too. And with you she works through her transference of feelings related to her father and her former husband.

Through the process of psychoanalysis, Linda gains insight into her defense mechanisms and comes to understand why she has been depressed and has become obsessed with escape materials. When she ends treatment after 3 years, at age 35, she has made considerable progress, manifest in a less passive and more productive role within her family, especially with her mother. She has also begun to date and is feeling optimistic that her next relationship will be healthy.

SUMMARY AND CONCLUSION

Psychoanalysis is considered by many practitioners to be the grandparent of most modern theories of counseling. Although Freud's ideas are controversial, his thoughts about human nature and the helping process are comprehensive. Since his death they have been elaborated on and refined by his daughter, Anna Freud, and by many of his followers, such as Heinz Kohut and Erik Erikson. Psychoanalysis, along with modifications to the approach, is still widely practiced, especially in psychiatry.

Overall, psychoanalysis is biologically based and stresses biological causality, psychosexual development, the dynamics of the mind, and defense mechanisms. This approach makes use of the *DSM* diagnoses. However, psychoanalysis is not used by many counselors and therapists beyond those with medical degrees because it is costly, time-consuming, and restricted in regard to training programs. This approach is also not applicable for the client populations that most counselors and therapists serve. It needs to provide the public and professionals in the helping fields with more empirical evidence of its effectiveness.

SUMMARY TABLE: PSYCHOANALYSIS AND PSYCHOANALYTIC THEORIES

Major Theorists

Sigmund Freud	Anna Freud
Heinz Kohut	Erik Erikson

View of Human Nature/Personality

Personality development during early childhood
Psychosexual stages of development
Emphasis on the unconscious
Ego defense mechanisms
Biological, deterministic aspects of behavior

Role of the Counselor/Therapist

Functions as expert
Encourages transference
Focuses on unconscious materials
Breaks through defense mechanisms
Uses interpretation

Goals

Make the unconscious conscious
Work through unresolved developmental stages
Help client learn to cope and adjust
Reconstruct client's personality

Process and Techniques

Several sessions per week
Free association
Analysis of transference
Exploration of dreams
Interpretation of conscious and unconscious material
Attention to resistance
Encouragement of client insight

Multicultural and Gender-Sensitive Issues

Practiced worldwide
Inappropriate for some cultures because of emphasis or techniques
Shunned by many women, because the theory sees them as inferior and less developed

Strengths and Contributions

Emphasizes sexuality and the unconscious
Supports diagnostic instruments and diagnoses
Is multidimensional
Continues to evolve
Focuses on developmental stages

Limitations and Criticisms

Time-consuming and expensive
Limited mainly to psychiatry
Focused on pathology
Deterministic
Inefficient for less disturbed individuals

LEARNING MORE

A number of periodicals are devoted to the theory, research, and practice of psycho-analysis. Among the best are the following:

American Journal of Psychoanalysis
Bulletin of the Menninger Clinic
Contemporary Psychoanalysis
International Journal of Psychoanalysis
Journal of Clinical Psychoanalysis
Journal of American Psychoanalytic Association
Modern Psychoanalysis .
Psychoanalysis and Psychotherapy
Psychoanalytic Inquiry
Psychoanalytic Psychology
Psychoanalytic Quarterly
Psychoanalytic Review

In addition to journals, there are several training institutes where clinicians can learn psychoanalysis processes and skills. Associations to contact about training include
American Psychoanalytic Association
309 East 49th Street
New York, NY 10017
212-752-0450
http://www.apsa.org/pubinfo/about.htm

National Psychological Association for Psychoanalysis
150 West 13th Street
New York, NY 10011-7891
212-924-7440
http://www.npap.org/

An interesting historical website, which is also a resource for training and education, is the Sigmund Freud Museum, Vienna home page.

CLASSROOM ACTIVITIES

1. Think of examples of defense mechanisms that you have seen employed or have used yourself. Share your examples with a classmate and then with the class as a whole.
2. What specific aspects of psychoanalysis do you think need further research? Why? Write down your responses and share them with the class.
3. In a group of three to five, discuss the appeal of psychoanalysis and determine why your group believes it is still an attractive theory for both many practitioners

and many clients. Also as a group critique the theory in regard to its appropriateness as a counseling approach for most clinicians today.

REFERENCES

Arlow, J. A. (2000). Psychoanalysis. In R. J. Corsini & D. Wedding (Eds.), *Current psychotherapies* (6th ed.) (pp. 16–53). Itasca, IL: Peacock.

Bankart, C. P. (1997). *Talking cures*. Pacific Grove, CA: Brooks/Cole.

Baruth, L. G., & Huber, C. H. (1984). *An introduction to marital theory and therapy*. Pacific Grove, CA: Brooks/Cole.

Bule, J. (1988, November). Psychoanalysis barriers tumble. *APA Monitor, 19*(1), 15.

Capuzzi, D., & Black, D. K. (1986). The history of dream analysis and the helping relationship: A synopsis for practitioners. *Journal of Humanistic Education and Development, 24*, 82–97.

Erikson, E. H. (1963). *Childhood and society* (2nd ed.). New York: Norton.

Erikson, E. H. (1982). *The life cycle completed*. New York: Norton.

Freud, A. (1936). *The ego and the mechanisms of defense* (J. Strachey, Trans.). New York: International Universities Press.

Freud, S. (1900/1955). *The interpretation of dreams* (J. Strachey, Trans.). London: Hogarth.

Freud, S. (1923/1933). *New introductory lectures on psychoanalysis* (W. J. H. Sprott, Trans.). New York: Norton.

Freud, S. (1923/1947). *The ego and the id* (J. Strachey, Trans.). London: Hogarth.

Freud, S. (1925/1959). An autobiographical study. In J. Strachey (Ed. & Trans.), *The standard edition of the complete psychological works of Sigmund Freud* (Vol. 20, pp. 7–74). London: Hogarth.

Hall, C. S. (1954). *A primer of Freudian psychology*. New York: New American Library.

Hall, C. S., Lindzey, L., & Campbell, J. B. (1998). *Theories of personality* (4th ed.). New York: John B. Wiley.

Hergenhahn, B. R., & Olson, M. H. (2003). *An introduction to theories of personality* (6th ed.). Upper Saddle River, NJ: Prentice Hall.

Horney, K. (1967). On the genesis of the castration complex in women. In K. Horney, *Feminine psychology* (pp. 37–53). New York: Norton.

James, R. K., & Gilliland, B. E. (2003). *Theories and strategies in counseling and psychotherapy* (5th ed.). Boston: Allyn & Bacon.

Jones, E. (1953). *The life and work of Sigmund Freud* (Vol. 1). New York: Basic Books.

Jones, E. (1955). *The life and work of Sigmund Freud* (Vol. 2). New York: Basic Books.

Jones, E. (1957). *The life and work of Sigmund Freud* (Vol. 3). New York: Basic Books.

Jones, R. M. (1979). Freudian and post-Freudian theories of dreams. In B. B. Wolman (Ed.), *Handbook of dreams: Research, theories, and applications*. New York: Litton.

Kohut, H. (1971). *The analysis of the self*. New York: International Universities Press.

Kohut, H. (1984). *How does psychoanalysis cure?* Chicago: University of Chicago Press.

Levinson, D. (1978). *The seasons of a man's life*. New York: Knopf.

Levinson, D. J., Darrow, C. N., Klein, E. B., Levinson, M. H., & McKee, B. (1978) *The seasons of a man's life*. New York: Knopf.

Monte, C. F. (1991). *Beneath the mask: An introduction to theories of personality* (4th ed.). Fort Worth, TX: Holt, Rinehart, & Winston.

Nye, R. D. (2000). *Three psychologies: Perspectives from Freud, Skinner, and Rogers* (6th ed.). Pacific Grove, CA: Brooks/Cole.

Singer, E. (1970). *Key concepts in psychotherapy* (2nd ed.). New York: Basic Books.

Slipp, S. (1988). *The technique and practice of object relations family therapy*. New York: Aronson.

Turkington, C. (1985). Analysts sued for barring non-MDs. *APA Monitor, 16*(5), 2.

Vandenbos, G. R., Cummings, N., & Deleon, P. H. (1992). A century of psychotherapy: Economic and environmental influences. In D. K. Freedheim (Ed.), *History of psychotherapy: A century of change* (pp. 65–102). Washington, DC: American Psychological Association.

Wallace, W. A. (1986). *Theories of counseling and psychotherapy*. Boston: Allyn & Bacon.

Winkler, K. J. (1986). Scholars prescribe Freud's "talking cure" for problems. *Chronicle of Higher Education, 33*(8), 4–6.

Adlerian Therapy

When we were young
    we played jacks in the sun
        near the old concrete stoop
            by the porch,
Unaware that in the game
    were early previews
        of enactments
            on who we would become.

Note: "Jacks" by S. T. Gladding. Copyright 2003 by Samuel T. Gladding.

dlerian counseling is an internationally popular form of psychotherapy. It is based on the common sense thinking of Alfred Adler, who was a contemporary of Sigmund Freud and proposed his ideas in the early days of psychotherapy. Adler had a keen interest in people and their motivations for behavior. He noted the inherent social interest of individuals and based his ideas for therapy around this concept. From the Adlerian point of view the essence of normality is having a feeling of concern for others (Corsini, 1988). Such an emphasis is manifested in activities that center around social development, cooperation, and education.

In addition to his emphasis on social interests, Adler focused his theory on the influence of early memories on a person's life. The impact of one's family was another focus of Adler's, especially the ordinal position that children have in their family of origin, for example, first, second, last, only. Adler based his therapeutic approach on including such concepts as lifestyle, beliefs (or fictions), psychological environment, and the importance of striving for completeness and wholeness.

MAJOR THEORIST: ALFRED ADLER

Alfred Adler was born in 1870 in Penzig, Austria, a suburb of Vienna. He was the second of six children in a middle-class Jewish family (see Figure 3.1). Adler shared a close relationship with his mother until his younger brother was born. Then, feeling abandoned, he sought the support of his father. Adler was also close to his older brother, Sigmund.

Adler was a sickly child and was injured often. He was run over in the street, suffered from rickets, and almost died of pneumonia at age 5. At age 3 he had witnessed the death of a younger brother. It is little wonder that he was later attracted to the profession of medicine.

To make up for his physical limitations, Adler spent a great deal of his childhood outside playing with other children and went out of his way to cultivate their friendship. Initially, he was not a good student; he did so poorly in mathematics at the secondary level that his teacher suggested his father take him out of school and apprentice him to a shoemaker. Adler reportedly overheard the conversation and studied to overcome this deficiency. Eventually, he became skilled in math.

FIGURE 3.1 Adler family genogram

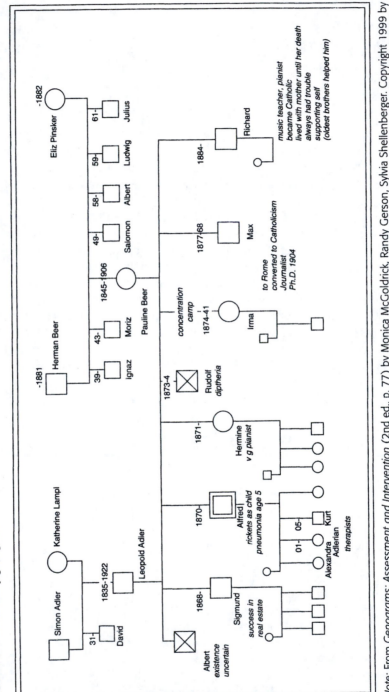

Note: From *Genograms: Assessment and Intervention* (2nd ed., p. 77) by Monica McGoldrick, Randy Gerson, Sylvia Shellenberger. Copyright 1999 by Monica McGoldrick and Sylvia Shellenberger. Copyright 1985 by Monica McGoldrick and Randy Gerson. Used by permission of W. W. Norton & Company, Inc.

In 1895 Adler received a degree in medicine from the University of Vienna. In his first practice he worked as an ophthalmologist, but his interests turned to neurology and finally to psychiatry. As a practicing psychiatrist, Adler was invited in 1902 to join Freud's Vienna Psychoanalytic Society, where he quickly gained prominence. Adler always thought of himself as a colleague rather than a disciple of Freud and disagreed early on with much of Freud's theoretical approach, especially his emphasis on biology and sexuality. Adler developed a theoretical orientation that was less deterministic and more practical and hopeful. Unlike Freud, Adler stressed the importance of subjective feelings rather than biological drives as the primary motivating force of life (Datler & Gstach, 2001).

Because of his differences with Freud, Adler resigned as president of the Vienna Psychoanalytic Society in 1910 and also gave up his coeditorship of the *Journal of Psychoanalysis*, a periodical he had cofounded with Freud. Adler then established the rival Society of Individual Psychology.

During World War I Adler served as a physician in the Austrian army. After the war, in 1922, he was instrumental in setting up child guidance clinics in the Vienna schools and eventually in other parts of Europe. All the while Adler worked to refine his theory and spoke widely in Europe and the United States. Adler fled Hitler's rise to power and in 1932 was appointed to a position in medical psychology at the Long Island College of Medicine. He died of a heart attack in 1937 while on a lecture tour in Aberdeen, Scotland. He was survived by his wife, two daughters, and a son.

Although Adler was a popular speaker and the author of more than 300 published papers and books, he has not generally received credit for many of the concepts he formulated. Such terms as *inferiority complex, social interest, empathy*, and *lifestyle* originated with Adler and were quickly absorbed by other scholars and the public. His theory waned in popularity during the 1940s and 1950s, was revitalized during the 1960s and 1970s, and has been widely used since that time. An excellent introduction to Adlerian theory is *The Practice and Theory of Individual Psychology* (Adler, 1969).

VIEW OF HUMAN NATURE/PERSONALITY

Adler thought that people were primarily motivated by *social interest*, a "feeling of being part of the social whole" and having an interest in others as well as a "need and willingness to contribute to the general social good" (Corsini & Wedding, 2000, p. 469). Thus, social interest is "not only an interest in others but an interest in the interests of others" (Ansbacher, 1977, p. 57).

In addition, Adler's theory holds that conscious aspects of behavior, rather than the unconscious, are central to the development of personality. A major Adlerian tenet is that individuals strive to become successful, that is, the best they can be. Therefore, their behavior is goal-directed and purposeful. Underlying this paramount belief is Adler's conviction that each person strives for growth and has a need for wholeness. "Adler gave his theory the name Individual Psychology to emphasize the holistic perspective, with the term *Individual* deriving from the Latin *individuum*, meaning 'indivisible'" (Mosak & Maniacci, 1998, p. 19).

The tendency of people to try to fulfill their own unique potential is a process Adler called *striving for perfection* or *completeness* (Adler, 1964). Another tendency for each person to feel initially inferior to others, if not overcome, leads to an inferiority complex and can become the basis for defining one's personality. A person who overcompensates for feelings of inferiority develops a superiority complex (Ansbacher & Ansbacher, 1964), which Adler described as a neurotic fiction that is unproductive.

Adler believed that people are as influenced by future goals as by past causes. His theory places considerable emphasis on birth order: those who share ordinal birth positions (for example, firstborns) may have more in common with one another than with siblings from the same family (Dreikurs, 1950). Five ordinal positions are emphasized in Adlerian literature on the family constellation: firstborns, secondborns, middle children, youngest children, and only children (Dreikurs, 1967; Dreikurs & Soltz, 1964; Sweeney, 1998).

- **Firstborns.** Firstborns are initially the "reigning monarchs" of a family because they receive undivided attention from parents. They are socialized to conform, achieve, behave, and please. They take responsibility when parents are absent and often act as parent substitutes in large families. All firstborns experience the loss of their unique position in the family when a second child is born. The experience of being "dethroned" may cause them to become resentful or help them better understand the significance of power and authority.
- **Secondborns.** The position of secondborn is an enviable one, according to Adler, but does have drawbacks. Secondborns never have to worry about issues of power and authority because they are born into a family atmosphere in which they will never be dethroned. Usually, these individuals are more outgoing, carefree, and creative and less concerned with rules than firstborns. They frequently pursue roles not taken by firstborns and are likely to be just the opposite of their older siblings.
- **Middle children.** Children born in the middle positions of a family often feel squeezed in and treated unfairly. They do not develop the close, personal types of alliances that an oldest or a youngest child may form; but because of their position, middle children learn a great deal about family politics and the art of negotiation. These skills can prove useful in manipulating events to get what they want and choosing areas where they can be successful.
- **Youngest children.** Youngest children in the family have difficulties and opportunities that are different from those of their older siblings. Youngest children receive a great deal of attention from others, who are likely to cater to their needs. These children may become charmers but may also have difficulty breaking out of the role of baby or family pet. They face the danger of becoming spoiled but at the same time may make great strides in achievement because of role models provided by older siblings.
- **Only children.** Any child born 7 or more years apart from siblings is psychologically an only child. These children, as a group, are never dethroned and are at an advantage, like oldest children, in receiving a great deal of attention. They may

mature early and become high achievers. They may also develop rich imaginations because of the amount of time they spend alone. Major disadvantages are that only children may become pampered and selfish and may not be well socialized.

In addition to birth order, the family environment is important to a person's development, particularly in the first 5 years of life. Adlerian theory stresses that by age 5 each person creates a *lifestyle*, or style of life, which is one's characteristic way of living and pursuing long-term goals. This lifestyle is gained primarily through interacting with other family members. A negative family atmosphere might be authoritarian, rejecting, suppressive, materialistic, overprotective, or pitying (Dreikurs & Soltz, 1964), whereas a positive family atmosphere might be democratic, accepting, open, and social. Nevertheless, perception of the family atmosphere, rather than any events themselves, is crucial to the development of a lifestyle (Adler, 1964).

Individuals are also guided by their *fictions*, that is, their subjective evaluations of themselves and their environments. Five basic mistakes are caused by fictions (Mosak, 2000, p.73):

1. *Overgeneralizing*—viewing everything as the same, for example, believing that all African-Americans think similarly
2. *False or impossible goals of security*—trying to please everyone, for example, being aggressive or passive to please certain individuals
3. *Misperceptions of life and life's demands*—believing that one never gets any breaks
4. *Minimization or denial of one's worth*—thinking that one will never amount to anything
5. *Faulty values*—believing in the necessity of being first no matter what needs to be done to achieve that goal

In contrast, a healthy style of life focuses on three main areas—society, work, and sexuality. Adlerian theory places strong emphasis on contributing to society. It also holds that work is essential for human survival and that we must learn to be interdependent. Furthermore, individuals must define their sexuality, in regard to self and others, in a spirit of cooperation rather than competition. Adler mentions two other challenges of life, although he does not fully develop them—spirituality and coping with self (Dreikurs & Mosak, 1966). Adlerian theory emphasizes that every life task requires *courage*, a willingness to take risks without knowing what the consequences may be.

ROLE OF THE COUNSELOR/THERAPIST

Adlerian counselors function primarily as diagnosticians, teachers, and models in the egalitarian relationships they establish with their clients. Adlerian clinicians try to assess why clients are oriented to a certain way of thinking and behaving. Counselors make an assessment by gathering information on the family constellation and clients' earliest memories. They then share interpretations, impressions, opinions, and feelings with their clients and concentrate on promoting the therapeutic relationship. Clients, in turn, are encouraged to examine and change a faulty lifestyle by developing social interests (Adler, 1927, 1931). Adlerians frequently share hunches or guesses with clients and are often directive when assigning clients homework—for example, suggesting that they act as if they were the persons they want to be.

Adlerian counselors employ a variety of techniques, some of which are borrowed from other approaches. Adler was not specific in detailing how counselors should operate when using his theory. As a general rule, Adlerian therapists make little use of assessment tools, such as psychological tests, but usually employ life-history questionnaires to gather data. They generally avoid the types of diagnoses found in the *DSM* but use their own language (for example, "discouraged") to describe the dynamics they encounter within clients.

GOALS

The goals of Adlerian counseling revolve around helping persons develop healthy, holistic lifestyles. This focus may mean educating or reeducating clients about what such lifestyles are, as well as helping them overcome feelings of inferiority.

One of the major goals of Adlerian therapy is to encourage clients to cultivate social interest (Adler, 1931). According to Adler, *social interest* is an innate potentiality "that must be consciously developed or trained" (Watts, 1996, p. 169). A faulty style of life is self-centered and based on mistaken goals and incorrect assumptions associated with feelings of inferiority. These feelings might stem from being born with a physical or mental defect, being pampered by parents, or being neglected. In order to correct the feelings and stop inappropriate forms of behavior, counselors assume the roles of teachers and interpreters of events. In short, Adlerian counseling deals with the whole person, and clients must ultimately decide whether to pursue social or self-interests (Kern & Watts, 1993).

PROCESS AND TECHNIQUES

Adlerian techniques are practiced in conjunction with the four different phases of treatment that are part of the Adlerian therapeutic process (Nystul, 2000). These phases are identified as establishing a relationship, performing analysis and assessment, promoting insight, and reorienting (Dreikurs, 1967; Kottman & Warlick, 1990; Mosak, 2000).

ESTABLISHING A RELATIONSHIP

Establishing a counseling relationship is crucial if the goals of Adlerian counseling are to be achieved, and certain techniques enhance this process. Adlerian counselors try to develop a warm, supportive, empathic, friendly, and egalitarian relationship with clients.

They are encouraging and try to win the respect of their clients. Adlerian counseling is seen as a collaborative effort (Adler, 1956), with encouragement and hope a part of the process. Counselors actively listen and respond in much the same way that person-centered counselors do (James & Gilliland, 2003), trying to help their clients define specific goals and discover what prevents the achievement of these goals. Counselors may focus on clients' strengths but may confront at times, pointing out clients' inconsistencies. The primary counseling objectives are to maintain a flexible interaction process that stresses clients' responsibilities and abilities (Dinkmeyer & Sperry, 2000).

PERFORMING ANALYSIS AND ASSESSMENT

After a relationship has been established, Adlerian counselors concentrate on analyzing their clients' lifestyles, examining family constellations, early memories, dreams, priorities, and ways of responding. As previously noted, the family constellation and the atmosphere in which children grow greatly influence both self-perception and perceptions of others. Clients are encouraged to recall early memories, especially events before the age of 10. Adler (1931) contended that people remember childhood events that are consistent with their present view of self, others, and the world in general. Adlerian counselors look both for themes and for specific details within these early recollections (Slavik, 1991; Statton & Wilborn, 1991; Watkins, 1985). Figures from the past are treated as prototypes rather than specific individuals; they may represent clients' attitudes toward power, weakness, men, women, or almost anything else. Recent and past dreams are also a part of lifestyle analysis. Adlerian theory holds that dreams are a possible rehearsal for future courses of action, making recurrent dreams especially important.

A look at client priorities is also helpful in understanding style of life and ways of responding. Unless challenged, a client may persist in one predominant lifestyle that is filled with basic mistakes (Mosak, 2000). These faulty or irrational views of life, or fictions, are delineated in an earlier section. In this second phase of counseling, lifestyle priorities and ways of responding are challenged.

PROMOTING INSIGHT

Counselors next try to help clients develop insight, especially by asking open-ended questions and offering interpretations. *Open-ended questions*, that is, those that invite a thoughtful response of more than a few words, allow clients to explore patterns in their lives that may have gone unnoticed. *Interpretation*, from an Adlerian perspective, often takes the form of intuitive guesses, sometimes based on counselors' general knowledge of ordinal positions and family constellations. However, true to the eqalitarian spirit of the process, a client is never forced to accept a counselor's point of view. *Empathy*, the ability to feel what it is like to be the client, is especially important in this process.

REORIENTING

To accomplish behavioral change and put insight into action, counselors use specific techniques.

- **Confrontation.** In this process counselors challenge clients to consider their own private logic. When clients examine their logic, they often realize they can change both it and their behavior.
- **Asking the question.** In this procedure counselors ask, "What would be different if you were well?" Clients are often asked this question during the initial interview, but it is appropriate at any time.
- **Encouragement.** Encouragement implies faith in a person (Dinkmeyer & Losoncy, 1996; Dreikurs & Soltz, 1964). Counselors encourage their clients by stating their belief that behavior change is possible. Encouragement is the key to making productive lifestyle choices.
- **Acting "as if."** Clients are instructed to act as if they are the persons they want to be, for instance, the ideal persons they see in their dreams (Gold, 1979). Adler originally got this idea from Hans Vaihinger (1911), who wrote that people create the worlds they live in by making assumptions about the world.
- **Spitting in the client's soup.** In this technique counselors point out certain behaviors to clients, thereby ruining the payoff for the behaviors. For example, a mother who always shows up her daughter in order to feel superior may continue to do so after the behavior has been pointed out but will no longer reap the reward of feeling superior.
- **Catching oneself.** Clients learn to become aware of self-destructive behaviors or thoughts. At first, counselors may help in the process, but eventually clients take over this responsibility.
- **Task setting.** Clients initially set short-range, attainable goals and eventually work up to long-term, realistic objectives.
- **Push button.** Clients are encouraged to realize that they have choices about the stimuli to which they will pay attention. They are taught to create the feelings they want by concentrating on their thoughts. The technique is like pushing a button because clients can choose to remember negative or positive experiences (Mosak, 2000).

In the process of using these techniques, counselors must avoid the "*tar baby*," that is, "the perceptions on life that the client carries into counseling and attempts to fit into the counselor. Anger, discouragement, seductiveness, martyrdom, and a host of other traps are set for the unwary counselor as the client resists change" (James & Gilliland, 2003, p. 121).

MULTICULTURAL AND GENDER-SENSITIVE ISSUES

Because of its emphasis on social interest, Adlerian counseling is well suited for use in multicultural and gender-sensitive areas (Sharf, 2004). For example, many minority cultures in the United States—such as Native Americans, Asian-Americans, and Latinos—value social interaction and social groups. The Adlerian approach emphasizes that healthy individuals need to extend themselves beyond themselves and their families, regardless of the cultural groups to which they belong. Such a concept often requires learning about and understanding different cultural groups. In that process individuals learn much about themselves and may also realize that certain Adlerian concepts may need to be modified within a cultural context.

Likewise, the Adlerian approach is sensitive to equality issues between the genders (Ansbacher & Ansbacher, 1978). Adler believed that both men and women want to be superior, perfect (that is their best), and never inferior. He referred to this attitude in women as the *masculine protest*, since men in his era held superior roles to those of women. Because Adler's concern for women's rights and equality is still a part of Adlerian theory and practice, both women and men find Adlerian counseling appropriate.

EVALUATION OF THE THEORY

STRENGTHS AND CONTRIBUTIONS

Adlerian therapy has a number of unique emphases that make it an important theory. The Adlerian approach fosters an egalitarian atmosphere through positive counseling techniques. Rapport and commitment are enhanced, thereby increasing the chances for change. Adlerian counselors offer encouragement and support and approach their clients with an educational orientation and an optimistic outlook on life.

Adlerian therapy is also versatile over the life span. "Adlerian theorists have developed counseling models for working with children, adolescents, parents, entire families, teacher groups, and other segments of society" (Purkey & Schmidt, 1987, p. 115). Play therapy for children ages 4 to 9 seems to be especially effective, allowing children to communicate through the language of play and then verbally talk about their feelings (Kottman & Warlick, 1990). An approach that emphasizes verbal and behavioral consequences is recommended for adolescents, particularly those dealing with the faulty goals typical of this age group (Kelly & Sweeney, 1979; Sweeney, 1998). Parents may benefit from Adlerian theory through educational support groups that help them understand their children better and plan effective intervention strategies (Dinkmeyer, 1982a, 1982b; Dinkmeyer, McKay, & Dinkmeyer, Jr., 1997; Dinkmeyer, McKay, McKay, & Dinkmeyer, Jr., 1998). The Adlerian approach has been successfully applied to complex family interactions, too (Lowe, 1982; Walsh & McGraw, 1996).

In addition, the Adlerian approach is useful in the treatment of a variety of DSM disorders—conduct disorders, antisocial disorders, anxiety disorders of childhood and adolescence, some affective disorders, and personality disorders (Seligman, 1997).

Another valued aspect is the Adlerian contribution to other helping theories and to the public's knowledge and understanding of human interactions. Adlerian concepts such as freedom, phenomenology, interpretation of events, life scripts, growth, and personal responsibility are found in existential, Gestalt, rational emotive behavior, person-centered, and reality-based counseling and therapy. Adlerian terms such as *inferiority complex* have also become part of the public's vocabulary.

A final strength of Adlerian therapy is that it can be employed selectively in different cultural contexts (Brown, 1997). For instance, the concept of encouragement is appropriately emphasized in working with Hispanic and Asian American groups, which have traditionally emphasized collaboration, whereas the concept of sibling rivalry may be highlighted with traditional European North Americans, who stress competition.

LIMITATIONS AND CRITICISMS

The Adlerian approach, like any theory, has limitations and weaknesses. First of all, the therapy lacks a firm, supportive research base. Relatively few empirical studies clearly outline the effectiveness of Adlerian counseling (Wallace, 1986). More investigations are needed if the theory is to develop systematically. Journals devoted to the Adlerian viewpoint, such as the *Journal of Individual Psychology*, may rectify this situation.

In addition, the Adlerian approach is vague in regard to some of its terms and concepts. Corey (2001) notes that Adler emphasized practice and teaching rather than theoretical definitions and organization. Although a number of prominent educators—such as Dreikurs, Mosak, Dinkmeyer, and Sweeney—have attempted to clarify the Adlerian approach, some of its ideas remain unclear. Adler was especially nebulous about how to work with clients.

A third factor that may be considered a drawback is that this therapy may be too optimistic about human nature. Adler, who called his theory "individual psychology," stressed social cooperation and interest. Some critics consider his view neglectful of other life dimensions, such as the power and place of the unconscious (Prochaska, 1984).

Yet a fourth possible limitation of the Adlerian approach centers on some of its basic principles. For instance, a concept like democratic family structure may not fit well with clients whose cultural contexts stress a lineal social relationship, such as that of traditional Arab Americans (Brown, 1997). If all basic principles of Adlerian counseling cannot be followed, then the impact of the theory may be lessened.

Finally, the Adlerian approach relies heavily on verbal erudition, logic, and insight and may thus be limited in its applicability to clients who are not intellectually bright (James & Gilliland, 2003). This limitation applies to many theories and is not singularly targeted to Adlerian counseling.

TREATING LINDA WITH ADLERIAN THERAPY

CONCEPTUALIZATION

From an Adlerian viewpoint Linda is a person who is discouraged; she has tried to be successful but has failed. Yet she is goal directed and wants more in her life than escape mechanisms. Linda is also seeking to connect socially. Her family life and her former husband were both less than ideal. In addition, Linda has an inferiority complex that has kept her from reaching her potential vocationally and interpersonally. As the secondborn child in her family and the first girl, Linda is in an enviable position.

However, her negative perception of her family and its authoritarian, suppressing, and rejecting attitude have handicapped her.

Linda has bought into a couple of Adlerian fictions that hinder her, too. She has over-generalized, believing that she will never get a break. And she has minimized her worth as a person; hence, her thoughts about suicide. In essence, Linda's style of life—especially as it relates to work, society, and sexuality—has been unhealthy and needs to be rectified.

TREATMENT PROCESS

As an Adlerian therapist you recognize first that Linda is discouraged. To promote a positive relationship with Linda, you are warm, supportive, empathic, encouraging, and collaborative in working with her. You actively listen and give her feedback. In addition, you ask Linda about early childhood memories; they center around staying clean, being neat, being proper, and doing what she was told. These are not pleasant recollections, and you share your impressions of what it must have been like as you continue to develop your relationship with Linda. You note that Linda has developed a faulty lifestyle that has made her overly dependent on the opinions of others. Therefore, in the therapeutic session you take the role of being an interpreter and teacher.

As therapy progresses, you as well as Linda begin to concentrate on her strengths. You ask her what her dreams are and how she would like to respond to situations around her. To give Linda practice in being the person she wishes to be, you invite her to act as if she were that person. In addition, you ask Linda open-ended questions and allow her to explore her life more closely, especially in regard to how she wants it to be.

As therapy moves toward a conclusion, you help Linda become reoriented to a new life by confronting her and challenging her private logic, which tells her that she is not capable of being more than she is now. You also ask her the question about how her life would look if she were well. You encourage her to live a more productive lifestyle and to catch herself when she begins to have destructive or negative thoughts. You also urge Linda to set short-term goals, such as taking a course at a nearby college, hoping that the achievement of these short-term goals will lead to long-term goals. Overall, you help Linda strive toward her own perfection, or completeness, and resist getting trapped into her former unproductive lifestyle.

SUMMARY AND CONCLUSION

Alfred Adler, a contemporary of Sigmund Freud, developed a theory of individual psychology, based on the premise that people have a specific concern and need for social interest. The theory has been clarified and expanded since his death, especially by Rudolph Dreikurs and Don Dinkmeyer, making the approach more understandable and popular, particularly in North America. Adlerian theory is a socially based, interpersonal, and subjective (i.e., phenomenological) approach to counseling. It emphasizes the future, holism, collaboration, and choice and focuses on the importance of childhood (i.e., working through real or perceived unresolved situations) and behavioral goals. Ordinal family positions, lifestyle, and the importance of socialization and encouragement are a few concepts that have made strong contributions to the helping professions.

The Adlerian approach stresses definable stages and techniques and is widely practiced in school and institutional settings. Its popularity can be attributed to its hopefulness and its useful application in multiple settings, such as in groups and families. Even as more research needs to be conducted on its practice, this approach remains a popular way of working with people of all stages and backgrounds.

SUMMARY TABLE: ADLERIAN THERAPY

Major Theorists

Alfred Adler	Rudolph Dreikurs
Don Dinkmeyer	Thomas Sweeney

View of Human Nature/Personality

Emphasis on social interest
Focus on birth order
Personality expressed in lifestyle
Future goals influential

Role of the Counselor/Therapist

Establishes egalitarian relationship
Models, teaches, and assesses
Shares hunches, directs, encourages

Goals

Cultivate client's social interests
Correct faulty assumptions and goals
Develop client's insight
Change behavior through acting "as if"

Process and Techniques

Four-stage process: establishing a relationship, performing analysis and assessment, promoting insight, and reorienting
Multiple techniques: using empathy, support, and collaboration; stressing client strengths and awareness; examining memories and dreams; interpreting, challenging, confronting, task setting

Multicultural and Gender-Sensitive Issues

Emphasizes social interest
Is appropriate for most cultural groups, requires modification for some

Is sensitive to gender equality
Sees both men and women as wanting to be superior

Strengths and Contributions

Supportive egalitarian relationship
Versatile approach
Useful therapy for specific disorders
Contribution of ideas and vocabulary

Limitations and Criticisms

Weak research on effectiveness
Vagueness of concepts and terms
Narrow approach

LEARNING MORE

A number of periodicals feature articles on the theory, research, and practice of Adlerian therapy. A journal specifically devoted to Adlerian therapy is the *Journal of Individual Psychology*.

Adlerian theory is practiced worldwide; its emphasis on social living makes it a popular approach in counseling and therapy. For more information on Adlerian organizations and institutes, contact

North American Society of Adlerian Psychology
65 East Wacker Place, Suite 1710
Chicago, IL 60601-7298
312-629-8801
http://www.alfredadler.org/affiliates.html

CLASSROOM ACTIVITIES

1. With another classmate, discuss how Adlerian counseling might be used in the following settings: a mental hospital, a public secondary school, a rehabilitation center, and a community agency.
2. As a class, divide into five groups according to Adler's description of the five ordinal positions in a family: firstborns, secondborns, middle children, youngest children, and only children. Appoint a scribe in each group to take notes. Then discuss with other group members your perceptions of being a child in that position. Have each scribe report back to the class as a whole.
3. Divide into groups of three with each member taking the role of counselor, client, or observer. Try to implement some of the specific ways an Adlerian counselor would work with clients who have the following problems: depression, anxiety, poor self-identity, and phobias. After each role play, discuss what you observed and learned.

REFERENCES

Adler, A. (1927). *Understanding human nature.* Greenwich, CT: Fawcett.

Adler, A. (1931). *What life should mean to you.* Boston: Little, Brown.

Adler, A. (1956). *The individual psychology of Alfred Adler: A systematic presentation in selections from his writings* (H. L. Ansbacher & R. R. Ansbacher, Eds.). New York: Norton.

Adler, A. (1964). *Social interest: A challenge to mankind.* New York: Capricorn.

Adler, A. (1969). *The practice and theory of individual psychology.* Patterson, NJ: Littlefield, Adams.

Ansbacher, H. L. (1977). Individual psychology. In R. J. Corsini (Ed.), *Current personality theories.* Itasca, IL: Peacock.

Ansbacher, H. L., & Ansbacher, R. R. (Eds.). (1964). *Superiority and social interest.* Evanston, IL: Northwestern University Press.

Ansbacher, H. L., & Ansbacher, R. R. (Eds.). (1978). *Cooperation between the sexes.* New York: Anchor.

Brown, D. (1997). Implications of cultural values for cross-cultural consultation with families. *Journal of Counseling and Development, 76,* 29–35.

Corey, G. (2001). *Theory and practice of counseling and psychotherapy* (6th ed.). Pacific Grove, CA: Brooks/Cole.

Corsini, R. J. (1988). Adlerian groups. In S. Long (Ed.), *Six group therapies* (pp. 1–43). New York: Plenum.

Corsini, R. J., & Wedding, D. (Eds.). (2000). *Current psychotherapies* (6th ed.). Itasca, IL: Peacock.

Datler, W., & Gstach, J. (2001, June 26). Alfred Adler and his time. Presentation to the Wake Forest Vienna Theorists class. University of Vienna, Vienna, Austria.

Dinkmeyer, D. (1982a). *Developing understanding of self and others (DUSOD-1).* Circle Pine, MN: American Guidance Service.

Dinkmeyer, D. (1982b). *Developing understanding of self and others (DUSOD-2).* Circle Pine, MN: American Guidance Service.

Dinkmeyer, D., & Losoncy, L. E. (1996). *The skills of encouragement.* New York: Saint Lucie Press.

Dinkmeyer, D., McKay, G. D., & Dinkmeyer, D., Jr. (1980). *Systematic training for effective teaching (STET).* Circle Pine, MN: American Guidance Service.

Dinkmeyer, D., McKay, G. D., & Dinkmeyer, D., Jr. (1997). *The Parents Handbook: Systematic training for effective parenting (STEP).* Circle Pine, MN: American Guidance Service.

Dinkmeyer, D., McKay, G. D., McKay, J. L., & Dinkmeyer, D., Jr. (1998). *Parenting teenagers: Systematic training for effective parenting/Teen (STEP/Teen).* Circle Pine, MN: American Guidance Service.

Dinkmeyer, D., & Sperry, L. (2000). *Adlerian counseling and psychotherapy* (3rd ed.). Upper Saddle River, NJ: Prentice Hall.

Dreikurs, R. R. (1950). *Fundamentals of Adlerian psychology.* Chicago: Alfred Adler Institute.

Dreikurs, R. R. (1967). *Psychodynamics, psychotherapy, and counseling.* Chicago: Alfred Adler Institute.

Dreikurs, R. R., & Mosak, H. H. (1966). The tasks of life. I: Adler's three tests. *Individual Psychologist, 4,* 18–22.

Dreikurs, R. R., & Soltz, V. (1964). *Children: The challenge.* New York: Hawthorne.

Gold, L. (1979). Adler's theory of dreams: An holistic approach to interpretation. In B. B. Wolman (Ed.), *Handbook of dreams: Research, theories, and applications.* New York: Van Nostrand Reinhold.

James, R. K., & Gilliland, B. E. (2003). *Theories and strategies in counseling and psychotherapy* (5th ed.). Boston: Allyn & Bacon.

Kelly, E. W., Jr., & Sweeney, T. J. (1979). Typical faulty goals of adolescents: A base for counseling. *School Counselor, 26,* 236–246.

Kern, C. W., & Watts, R. E. (1993). Adlerian counseling. *Texas Counseling Association Journal, 21,* 85–95.

Kottman, T., & Warlick, J. (1990). Adlerian play therapy. *Journal of Humanistic Education and Development, 28,* 125–132.

Lowe, R. N. (1982). Adlerian/Dreikursian family counseling. In A. M. Horne & M. M. Ohlsen (Eds.), *Family counseling and therapy* (pp. 329–359). Itasca, IL: Peacock.

Mosak, H. (2000). Adlerian psychotherapy. In R. J. Corsini & D. Wedding (Eds.), *Current psychotherapies* (6th ed.) (pp. 54–98). Itasca, IL: Peacock.

Mosak, H. H., & Maniacci, M. P. (1998). *Tactics in counseling and psychotherapy.* Itasca, IL: Peacock.

Nystul, M. S. (2000). *Introduction to Counseling: An Art and Science Perspective.* Needham Heights, MA: Allyn & Bacon.

Prochaska, J. O. (1984). *Systems of psychotherapy: A transtheoretical analysis* (2nd ed.). Homewood, IL: Dorsey.

Purkey, W. W., & Schmidt, J. J. (1987). *The inviting relationship.* Upper Saddle River, NJ: Prentice Hall.

Seligman, L. (1997). *Diagnosis and treatment planning in counseling* (2nd ed.). New York: Plenum.

Sharf, R. S. (2004). *Theories of psychotherapy and counseling* (3rd ed.). Pacific Grove, CA: Brooks/Cole.

Slavik, S. (1991). Early memories as a guide to client movement through life. *Canadian Journal of Counselling, 25,* 331–337.

Statton, J. E., & Wilborn, B. (1991). Adlerian counseling and the early recollections of children. *Individual Psychology, 47,* 338–347.

Sweeney, T. J. (1998). *Adlerian counseling* (4th ed.). Muncie, IN: Accelerated Development.

Vaihinger, H. (1911). *The philosophy of "as if."* New York: Harcourt, Brace, & World.

Wallace, W. A. (1986). *Theories of counseling and psychotherapy.* Boston: Allyn & Bacon.

Walsh, W. M., & McGraw, J. A. (1996). *Essentials of family therapy.* Denver, CO: Love.

Watkins, C. E., Jr. (1985). Early recollections as a projective technique in counseling: An Adlerian view. *AMHCA Journal, 7,* 32–40.

Watts, R. E. (1996). Social interest and the core conditions: Could it be that Adler influenced Rogers? *Journal of Humanistic Education and Development, 34,* 165–170.

Existential Therapy

CHAPTER 4

He struggles with life
    as he rides the subways
        in the bowels of New York City
Afraid he may have lost a dream
    he nurtured in the open fields
        outside of Lincoln, Nebraska.

Note: "The Dream" by S. T. Gladding. Copyright 2003 by Samuel T. Gladding.

The basis for existentialism comes from the 19th century theologian and philosopher Soren Kierkegaard. He was the first to develop a philosophy focused on the pursuit of becoming an individual, "formulating truth as a guidepost, and emphasizing the necessity of commitment. His approach was named 'existentialism' by German and French theorists Martin Heidegger and Jean Paul Sartre. The approach was later formulated into a therapeutic process by Swiss psychiatrist Ludwig Binswanger" (Austin, 1999, p. 53).

The essence of existentialism as a therapeutic approach is represented in the writings of several prominent American theorists—including Sidney Jourard, Abraham Maslow, Irvin Yalom, Rollo May, Clemmont Vontress, and Clark Moustakas—even though its philosophical roots are European. Other notable contributors to existentialism include Fyodor Dostoyevski, Albert Camus, Edmund Husserl, Friedrich Nietzsche, Martin Buber, and Victor Frankl. In recent years the most prominent practitioners of existential psychotherapy in the United States and Europe have been Rollo May, Victor Frankl, Irvin Yalom, and Clemmont Vontress. Of these, May (1961) and Frankl (1962) are probably the best-known theorists.

As a group, existentialists differ widely in their emphases. For example, Dostoyevski stressed the importance of consciousness, Kierkegaard concentrated on human anxiety and dread, and Buber focused on the treatment of persons in "it" or "thou" relationships, that is, treating others as inanimate objects or as unique individuals. However, despite their diversity, existentialists hold some beliefs in common:

- the importance of anxiety, values, freedom, and responsibility in human life
- an emphasis on finding meaning in one's actions

MAJOR THEORISTS: ROLLO MAY AND VICTOR FRANKL

Rollo May was born in 1909 in Ada, Ohio. Like Alfred Adler, May was the second of six children; but unlike Adler, May was the oldest son in his family. The relationship between May's parents was discordant, leading May to describe his boyhood home life as unhappy. Consequently, he became a loner and a rebel during his adolescence (Rabinowitz, Good, & Cozad, 1989).

In 1930 May graduated with a degree in English from Oberlin College and accepted a position teaching English at Anatolia College in Greece. During two of his summer vacations there, he traveled to Vienna and enrolled in seminars conducted by Alfred Adler, which sparked his interest in psychoanalysis. However, during his years in Greece, he was also extremely lonely and began working incessantly, which resulted in a breakdown. As he reflected years later, "I had learned enough psychology at college to know that these symptoms meant that something was wrong with my whole way of life. I had to find some new goals and purposes for my living and to relinquish my moralistic, somewhat rigid way of existence" (May, 1985, p. 8).

In 1933 May returned to the United States to enter Union Theological Seminary, where he was strongly influenced by Paul Tillich, an existential theologian. After a brief career as a Congregationalist minister, May decided to pursue a degree in clinical psychology at Columbia University, but tuberculosis interrupted his studies. He struggled with the illness for almost 2 years, during which time he was strongly impressed with the writings of the Danish existentialist Soren Kierkegaard. After his recovery May completed his doctorate at Columbia in 1949 and joined the faculty of the William Allanson White Institute in New York City.

May's most influential book, *The Meaning of Anxiety*, was published a year later. May believed that anxiety could work for the good as well as the detriment of people. He lectured on this subject at some of the most distinguished universities in the United States, including Yale and Harvard, while continuing to practice psychotherapy and serve "as an adjunct faculty member at the New School of Social Research and New York University" (Rabinowitz et al., 1989, p. 437). May was a cofounder of the Association for Humanistic Psychology in the 1960s and later wrote two other well-known books, *Love and Will* (1969) and *The Courage to Create* (1975). In the 1980s he retired to the San Francisco area, where he concentrated on writing about the meaning of myths for modern society and continued to promote a humanistic approach to psychology. May died on October 22, 1994, at the age of 85.

Victor Frankl was born in 1905 in Vienna, Austria. He received a medical degree in 1930 and a Ph.D. in 1949 from the University of Vienna. Frankl established the Youth Advisement Centers in Vienna and directed them from 1928 to 1938. He also held several hospital appointments in the city between 1930 and 1942.

Although Frankl was a contemporary of Freud and Adler and had interactions with both, he became interested in existentialism in the 1930s while reading philosophers such as Heidegger, Scheler, and Legan. He began formulating his ideas about an existential approach to counseling, using the term *logotherapy* as early as 1938. The Greek word *logo* implies a search for meaning.

During World War II Frankl was imprisoned from 1942 to 1945 in Nazi concentration camps at Auschwitz and Dachau, where his parents, a brother, and his wife died. The impact of the concentration camps crystallized his thoughts about the meaning of life and suffering, and it was partly his determination to share those beliefs that kept him alive.

In 1947 Frankl joined the faculty of the University of Vienna and later became associated with the United States International University in San Diego, lecturing widely at many prestigious universities throughout the world. He wrote extensively also; his best-known books are *Man's Search for Meaning* (1962), which has been translated into 24 languages, and *The Will to Meaning* (1969b). "According to Frankl, the *will to meaning* is the central drive of human existence" (Dollarhide, 1997, p. 181), but meaning is attained as a by-product of discovery rather than through direct pursuit.

Frankl is sometimes referred to as the founder of the third school of Viennese psychotherapy (i.e., logotherapy), with Freud's psychoanalytic theory first and Adler's individual psychology second. On September 2, 1997, at the age of 92, Frankl died of heart failure in Vienna and is buried there.

VIEW OF HUMAN NATURE/PERSONALITY

As a group, existentialists believe that people form their lives by the choices they make. Even the worst situations, such as the Nazi death camps, provide an opportunity to make important life-and-death decisions, such as whether to struggle to stay alive (Frankl, 1969b). Existentialists focus on this freedom of choice and the action that goes with it, viewing people as the authors of their lives. Existentialists contend that people are responsible for any choices they make and that some choices are healthier and more meaningful than others. For example, individuals who prize creativity, service to others, friendship, and self-growth within a community or family environment may, as Abraham Maslow describes, have peak experiences, in which they feel truly integrated and connected with the universe in a very emotional way (Hoffman, 1990). Such persons are characterized as having "a holistic perspective of the world, [having] a natural tendency toward synergy [cooperative action], [being] intrapsychic, interpersonal, intercultural and international, [being] more consciously and deliberately metamotivated" (Chandler, Holden, & Kolander, 1992, p. 168).

On the other hand, individuals who are self-indulgent may feel a sense of normlessness and valuelessness. They may experience what Frankl (1959) calls an *existential vacuum*, a sense that life has lost all meaning. Carried to an extreme, these individuals would develop a disorder Frankl calls *noogenic neurosis*, characterized by a feeling that one has nothing to live for (Das, 1998).

According to Frankl (1962), the "meaning of life always changes but it never ceases to be" (p. 113). Meaning goes beyond self-actualization and exists at three levels: (a) ultimate meaning (e.g., an order to the universe); (b) meaning of the moment; and (c) common, day-to-day meaning (Das, 1998). Frankl believes we can discover life's meaning in three ways:

- by doing a deed—that is, by achieving or accomplishing something
- by experiencing a value, such as a work of nature, culture, or love
- by suffering—that is, by finding a proper attitude toward unalterable fate

Existentialists believe that psychopathology is a failure to make meaningful choices and maximize one's potential (McIllroy, 1979). Choices may be avoided and potentials unrealized because of the anxiety involved in action. Anxiety is often associated with paralysis, but May (1977) argues that normal anxiety can be healthy and motivational and can help people change. Clients may leave existential counseling more anxious than they began, but in such cases they are consciously aware of their anxiety and can therefore channel it toward constructive use (May, 1967). Thus, existentialism, unlike other theories, focuses on the meaning of anxiety in human life, emphasizing the inner person and the ways in which authentic individuals search for value in life. By being aware of feelings and the finite nature of human existence, people come to make healthy, life-enhancing choices.

ROLE OF THE COUNSELOR/THERAPIST

There are no uniform roles that existential counselors adopt; indeed, the existential approach to counseling is unique in its diversity. Nor is there agreement among existentialists about how to systematically formulate their ideas into a uniform way of helping others. Part of the reason for this variety among practitioners is that existentialists believe every client is distinctive, regardless of similar concerns, heritages, or backgrounds. Therefore, counselors are sensitive to the discrete aspects of their clients' characteristics, "such as voice, posture, facial expression, even dress and apparently accidental movements of the body" (May, 1939, p. 101). Basically, existential counselors concentrate on being authentic with their clients and entering into deep and personal relationships with them.

In the therapeutic process it is not unusual for counselors to share personal experiences with their clients to deepen the relationship and help clients realize a shared humanness and struggle. Buhler and Allen (1972) suggest that existential counselors focus on person-to-person relationships that emphasize mutuality, wholeness, and growth. Counselors who practice from a Frankl perspective are Socratic in engaging their clients in dialogue (Das, 1998). However, all existential counselors serve as a model of how to achieve individual potential and make decisions. They concentrate on helping clients experience subjective feelings, gain clearer self-understanding, and move toward a new way of being in the world. The focus is on living productively in the present, not recovering a personal past. They also "focus on ultimate human concerns (death, freedom, isolation, and meaninglessness)" (May & Yalom, 2000, p. 284).

Existential counselors do not use psychological tests, nor do they make diagnoses in accordance with the latest *DSM*. Both of these procedures would be antithetical to the thrust of the approach, which stresses the uniqueness of each client. It is interesting to note, however, that some psychological instruments, such as the Purpose of Life Test, are based on existential premises and that the *DSM* deals with anxiety on several levels.

GOALS

The goals of existential therapy include helping clients realize the importance of meaning, responsibility, awareness, freedom, and potential. Existential therapists hope that during the course of counseling, clients will take more responsibility for their lives: "The aim of therapy is that the patient experience his existence as real" (May, Angel, & Ellenberger, 1958, p. 85). If all works well, clients are freed from being observers of events and become shapers of meaningful personal activity.

Clients become more responsible through the relationships they build with counselors, in which the clients become aware of personal freedom. Thus, a major goal of existential counseling is for clients to shift from an outward to an inward frame of reference, no longer depending on the judgment of others but evaluating their own activities first. Further goals include

- making clients sensitive to their existence
- calling attention to clients' unique traits and characteristics
- helping clients improve their encounters with others
- assisting clients in establishing a will to meaning
- encouraging clients to make a decision about both present and future directions in life (Cunningham & Peters, 1973; Das, 1998; May, 1975; Reeves, 1977)

PROCESS AND TECHNIQUES

Because the existential approach is not a clearly defined process for most of its practitioners, specific techniques are rarely used repeatedly. In fact, the existential approach claims fewer techniques than almost any other model of counseling. "Approaching human beings merely in terms of techniques necessarily implies manipulating them," and manipulation is opposed to what existentialists espouse (Frankl, 1967, p. 139).

This apparent weakness is paradoxically a strength because it allows existential counselors to concentrate on building deep and meaningful relationships with their clients, thereby helping them become more aware of themselves and others. It also allows counselors to borrow ideas from other areas and to use a wide range of professional skills in a highly personal manner. Thus, they are free to use techniques as widely diverse as desensitization and free association or to disassociate themselves from these practices entirely (Corey, 2001).

Clients usually benefit from existential counselors who are able to address client needs in a multidimensional and highly customized way. For example, depressed persons tend to adopt emotion-focused strategies for dealing with their pain, whereas nondepressed individuals use multiple and vying strategies (Stevens, Pfost, &

Wessels, 1987). Existential counselors can offer a variety of approaches—some that may be cognitively or even behaviorally based, as well as some that may be emotionally oriented—to help depressed individuals and assist them in seeing options. Of uppermost importance is the existential view that counselors work with clients in an open and inquiring manner and thereby accept the truth unique to each individual (Kemp, 1976).

In addition, developing some vision of the true, the good, and the beautiful is essential from an existential counseling perspective. Such a vision gives meaning to individuals' personal lives and humanizes society as well (Partenheimer, 1990). However, sometimes the process of finding personal truth requires a willingness to work through ambiguity. In such cases existential counselors have a most effective and powerful tool to aid in exploration—their relationships with their clients. Ideally, counselors transcend their own needs and focus on their clients during this phase of therapy (Wallace, 1986), remaining open and self-revealing in an attempt to help their clients become more in touch with personal feelings and experiences. The emphasis is on authenticity, honesty, and spontaneity.

Existential counselors also make use of confrontation; clients are confronted with the idea that everyone is responsible for his or her life. For this purpose existential counselors borrow some techniques from other models, such as imagery exercises, awareness exercises, and goal-setting activities. For example, counselors may lead clients through a typical day in their lives 5 years in the future. Through this process clients are able to see more clearly the meaning in life by recognizing the choices they are making now that will shape their futures.

MULTICULTURAL AND GENDER-SENSITIVE ISSUES

Because existentialists concentrate on human conditions that are universal in all walks of life and all circumstances, this approach to counseling is probably as multicultural as any. A leading proponent of the existentialist approach in the United States, Clemmont Vontress, is African American and has proposed existential theory as a base for multicultural counseling (Vontress, 1979; Vontress, Johnson, & Epp, 1999). In addition, Victor Frankl's form of existential counseling, logotherapy, is particularly adaptable to multicultural counseling and therapy, having grown out of the cultural oppression of the Jews during the Holocaust (Ivey, D'Andrea, Ivey, & Simek-Morgan, 2002).

Gender issues are deemphasized in the existential approach. Both men and women have feelings of meaninglessness, isolation, and anxiety with which they must deal. Even though ways of addressing these feelings and other conditions in life may vary with the genders, a common emphasis remains within existentialism on working with men and women in unique ways that help them transcend common human difficulties.

EVALUATION OF THE THEORY

STRENGTHS AND CONTRIBUTIONS

One strength of existential counseling is its emphasis on the uniqueness of each individual. It is a very humanistic way of working with others (Yalom, 1980). It also stresses continued human growth and development, offering hope to clients through directed readings and therapeutic encounters with the counselor. The life of Victor Frankl is a good illustration of this strength. Furthermore, existential therapy recognizes that anxiety is not necessarily a negative condition. Anxiety is a part of human life and can motivate some individuals to make healthy and productive decisions.

Another contribution of existential counseling is its effectiveness in multicultural and gender counseling situations. Because of its global view of human existence, existential counseling allows clinicians to focus on the person of the client in an I-thou manner without regard to ethnic, social, or sexual background (Jackson, 1987; Epp, 1998).

In addition, an existential approach gives counselors access to a tremendous amount of philosophy and literature that is both informative and enlightening about human nature. This philosophical base has the potential to support a systematic counseling theory. Existential theory also helps connect individuals to universal problems faced by humankind, difficulties such as the search for peace and the absence of caring (Baldwin, 1989).

Finally, an existential approach is valuable to practitioners because it can be combined with other perspectives and methods, such as those based on learning principles and behaviorism, to treat extremely difficult problems, such as alcoholism. In such cases a major focus is on the existential value of facing "life problems and feelings through honest expression" (Wilbur, Roberts-Wilbur, & Morris, 1990, p. 157).

LIMITATIONS AND CRITICISMS

Despite its strengths and contributions the existential approach has not produced a fully developed model of counseling. Professionals who stress developmental stages of counseling are particularly vehement in this criticism. Existential therapy also lacks educational and training programs; the uniqueness of each practitioner prohibits the systematic teaching of theory. As a result, Wallace (1986) wonders whether the existential approach will last without Rollo May's continued presence. A related limitation is that existential counseling is difficult to implement beyond an individual level because of its subjective nature. Existentialism lacks the type of methodology and validation processes prevalent in most other therapeutic approaches and the uniformity and systematic outline that beginning counselors readily understand.

Another shortcoming of existential therapy, according to some critics, is that existentialists as a group do not diagnose or test their clients. Critics claim that the failure to evaluate and diagnose may be irresponsible; therapists may miss opportunities to assess their clients more thoroughly and subsequently gear their practices more specifically to clients' needs.

Finally, critics charge that existential counseling theory and therapy are closer to existential philosophy than to other counseling theories and therapies. This distinction and separation limit the usefulness of existential counseling.

TREATING LINDA WITH EXISTENTIAL THERAPY

CONCEPTUALIZATION

From an existential perspective Linda seems to be living a meaningless life, just drifting. She has contemplated suicide and is anxious about her ability to succeed at work and in relationships. Thus, her life is characterized by a feeling that she has nothing to live for. Although Linda has made a number of bad choices, you, as an existentialist, believe she is capable of making healthy choices and maximizing her potential.

TREATMENT PROCESS

As an existential therapist you focus on the uniqueness of Linda and her distinctiveness. In counseling you attempt to be authentic with her and to enter into a deep relationship. You self-disclose and share with Linda some of your own struggles as she reveals hers. You try to serve as a role model for her and help her focus on living a productive life in the present.

Your hope in working with Linda is that she will take more responsibility for her life. You want her to shift from an outer to an inner frame of reference, from which she can evaluate situations first. You want her to be more sensitive to herself. In order to help her in envision the good and the beautiful, you borrow several techniques from guided imagery and use them with her. You also confront Linda with the fact that she alone is responsible for her life. Because Linda likes to read, you assign her books on the lives of Victor Frankl and Rollo May and some of the popular fiction of Irvin Yalom. When she returns for her appointments, you discuss the books with her and talk about how each of these individuals has had to overcome obstacles to find meaning in life.

Linda leaves therapy with a new sense of herself and others. She begins to engage in social activities within the community and to explore opportunities for personal and professional growth. She maintains a relationship with you even after treatment has officially ended.

SUMMARY AND CONCLUSION

Existentialism is both a philosophy and a philosophical approach to counseling. It has European roots but has been adopted and adapted by a number of prominent American clinicians. The approach is centered on the premise that human beings have universal feelings and experience universal conditions, such as anxiety, loneliness, death, and the search for meaning in existence. Leading existentialists of the 20th century include Rollo May and Victor Frankl. Notable therapists today include Irvin Yalom and Clemmont Vontress.

There is no uniform existentialist approach to counseling, although one form of existentialism, Frankl's logotherapy, is more systematic than any other. Nonetheless, the focus in all forms of existentialism is on the relationship between counselor and client, and on that relationship a dialogue about issues relevant to the client is built. In the process of counseling, existentialists confront and share personal experiences. Most borrow techniques from other approaches and concentrate on working with clients in the moment, using whatever techniques further insight and movement within clients to address their concerns.

In recent years some have argued that existential psychotherapy is a positive psychology because it focuses on both possibilities and limitations and recognizes human potential without succumbing to an unrealistic optimism (Bretherton & Orner, 2003). Existential counseling remains an effective approach for working in multicultural and gender-sensitive venues.

SUMMARY TABLE: EXISTENTIAL THERAPY

Major Theorists

Rollo May   Irvin Yalom
Victor Frankl   Clemmont Vontress

View of Human Nature/Personality

Belief in human freedom and choice of lifestyle
Focus on meaning of anxiety, meaning of life, relevance of individual experience

Role of the Counselor/Therapist

Emphasize authenticity
Understand clients as unique individuals
Stress personal relationship, modeling, sharing experiences

Goals

Help clients realize responsibility, awareness, freedom, potential
Shift clients from outward to inward frame of reference

Process and Techniques

Use of counseling relationship that is open, inquiring, accepting
Variety of borrowed and diverse techniques

Multicultural and Gender-Sensitive Issues

Recognizes and respects culture and uniqueness
Transcends gender differences
Focuses on meaningfulness for all individuals

Strengths and Contributions

Emphasizes human interests and concerns
Recognizes uniqueness of individuals
Focuses on anxiety as a motivator
Uses a wide range of philosophy and literature
Stresses continuous growth
Is strongly multicultural and gender sensitive
Connects individuals to universal problems

Limitations and Criticisms

Is not a fully developed theory
Lacks training facilities
Is subjective
Lacks uniformity and teachable processes
Does not benefit from diagnosis and testing
Is closer to philosophy than to other therapies

LEARNING MORE

A number of periodicals on existential theory may be helpful in exploring this approach to counseling.

Journal of Humanistic Psychology
Journal for the Society of Existential Analysis
Journal of Phenomenological Psychology
Review of Existential Psychology and Psychiatry

In addition to journals, several training institutes and professional associations allow clinicians to learn more about existentialism in therapeutic settings.

Society for Existential Analysis
BM Existential
London, England WC1N 3XX
Telephone: 07000 473337
E-mail: exist@cwcom.net

Excellent website for exploring existential psychotherapy is

http://members.aol.com/timlebon/extherapy.htm#ExistentialLinks

CLASSROOM ACTIVITIES

1. Rollo May believed that the best counselors are those who have been wounded, that is, who have suffered and been healed. In small groups discuss what experiences counselors might use to help them best understand themselves and their

clients. What are the advantages of having experienced situations similar to those of your clients? What are the disadvantages?

2. Tell how you think an existential counselor might work with the following types of clients: an alcoholic, a school-phobic child, a spouse abuser, and an unemployed person. Do you think the techniques the counselor might use would be different or basically the same in each case? Why?

3. What experiences have been most meaningful in your life—for example, graduation, love relationships, birth of children? How do you think existential therapists might use such significant and momentous life experiences in their work with clients?

REFERENCES

Austin, L. (1999). *The counseling primer.* Philadelphia: Accelerated Development.

Baldwin, C. (1989). Peaceful alternatives: Inner peace. *Journal of Humanistic Education and Development, 28,* 86–92.

Bretherton, R., & Orner, R. (2003). Positive psychotherapy in disguise. *Psychologist, 16,* 136–137.

Buhler, C., & Allen, M. (1972). *Introduction to humanistic psychology.* Pacific Grove, CA: Brooks/Cole.

Chandler, C. K., Holden, J. M., & Kolander, C. A. (1992). Counseling for spiritual wellness: Theory and practice. *Journal of Counseling & Development, 71,* 168–176.

Corey, G. (2001). *Theory and practice of counseling and psychotherapy* (6th ed.). Pacific Grove, CA: Brooks/Cole.

Cunningham, L. M., & Peters, H. J. (1973). *Counseling theories.* Upper Saddle River, NJ: Prentice Hall.

Das, A. K. (1998). Frankl and the realm of meaning. *Journal of Humanistic Education and Development, 36,* 199–211.

Dollarhide, C. T. (1997). Counseling for meaning in work and life: An integrated approach. *Journal of Humanistic Education and Development, 35,* 178–187.

Epp, L. R. (1998). The courage to be an existential counselor: An interview with Clemmont E. Vontress. *Journal of Mental Health Counseling, 20,* 1–12.

Frankl, V. (1959). The spiritual dimension in existential analysis and logotherapy. *Journal of Individual Psychology, 15,* 157–165.

Frankl, V. (1962). *Man's search for meaning: An introduction to logotherapy.* New York: Washington Square Press.

Frankl, V. (1967). *Psychotherapy and existentialism: Selected papers on logotherapy.* New York: Washington Square Press.

Frankl, V. (1969a). *Psychotherapy and existentialism: Selected papers on logotherapy.* New York: Simon & Schuster.

Frankl, V. (1969b). *The will to meaning: Foundations and applications of logotherapy.* New York: New American Library.

Hoffman, E. (1990). Abraham Maslow's legacy for counseling. *Journal of Humanistic Education and Development, 29,* 2–9.

Ivey, A. E., D'Andrea, M., Ivey, M. B., & Simek-Morgan, L. (2002). *Theories of counseling and psychotherapy: A multicultural perspective* (5th ed.). Pacific Grove, CA: Brooks/Cole.

Jackson, M. L. (1987). Cross-cultural counseling at the crossroads: A dialogue with Clemmont E. Vontress. *Journal of Counseling and Development, 66,* 20–23.

Kemp, C. G. (1976). Existential counseling. In G. S. Belkin (Ed.), *Counseling directions in theory and practice.* Dubuque, IA: Kendall/Hunt.

May, R. (1939). *The art of counseling.* New York: Abingdon-Cokesbury.

May, R. (Ed.). (1961). *Existential psychology.* New York: Random House.

May, R. (1967). Part three: Psychotherapy. In *Psychology and the human dilemma* (pp. 87–160). Princeton, NJ: Van Nostrand.

May, R. (1969). *Love and will.* New York: Norton.

May, R. (1975). *The courage to create.* New York: Bantam.

May, R. (1977). *The meaning of anxiety* (Rev. ed.). New York: Norton.

May, R. (1985). *My quest for beauty.* New York: Norton.

May, R., Angel, E., & Ellenberger, H. (Eds.). (1958). *Existence.* New York: Simon & Schuster.

May, R., & Yalom, I. (2000). Existential psychotherapy. In R. J. Corsini & D. Wedding (Eds.), *Current psychotherapies* (6th ed., pp. 273–302). Itasca, IL: Peacock.

McIllroy, J. H. (1979). Career as life-style: An existential view. *Personnel and Guidance Journal, 57,* 351–354.

Partenheimer, D. (1990). Teaching literature toward a humanistic society. *Journal of Humanistic Education and Development, 29,* 40–44.

Rabinowitz, F. E., Good, G., & Cozad, L. (1989). Rollo May: A man of meaning and myth. *Journal of Counseling and Development, 67,* 436–441.

Reeves, C. (1977). *The psychology of Rollo May.* San Francisco: Jossey-Bass.

Stevens, M. J., Pfost, K. S., & Wessels, A. B. (1987). The relationship of purpose in life to coping strategies and time since the death of a significant other. *Journal of Counseling and Development, 65*, 424–426.

Vontress, C. (1979). Cross-cultural counseling: An existential approach. *Personnel and Guidance Journal, 58*, 117–122.

Vontress, C. E., Johnson, J. A., & Epp, L. R. (1999). *Cross-cultural counseling: A casebook*. Alexandria, VA: American Counseling Association.

Wallace, W. A. (1986). *Theories of counseling and psychotherapy*. Boston: Allyn & Bacon.

Wilbur, M. P., Roberts-Wilbur, J., & Morris, J. R. (1990). A humanistic alternative for counseling alcoholics. *Journal of Humanistic Education and Development, 28*, 146–165.

Yalom, I. D. (1980). *Existential psychotherapy*. New York: Basic Books.

5 CHAPTER

Person-Centered Therapy

I can still hear your voice
from a distance
beneath the California sun
Calmly reminding me
(and my anxiety)
That unless I am true to myself
and genuine with you
we do not have a relationship.

Note: "Remembrance from a Carl Rogers Encounter" by S. T. Gladding. Copyright 2003 by Samuel T. Gladding.

Person-centered counseling was created by Carl Rogers in the early 1940s. It was considered a radical approach when it began because it differed greatly from the primary theories in used. At that time the predominant theories of counseling were therapist centered (e.g., the work of E. G. Williamson), symptom focused (e.g., behaviorism), or oriented to personality change (e.g., psychoanalysis). Rogers altered the counseling landscape with his initial emphasis on being nondirective and letting clients take the lead in directing change.

Rogers's approach to helping was revolutionary. He emphasized caring, empathy, understanding, and acceptance in ways that had never been tried before. He trusted that his clients would grow if the right conditions were established. His journey as a clinician, his development as a person, and the growth of his theory were all achieved despite resistance and, at times, adversity. The validity of the person-centered approach to counseling may seem obvious to people in the 21st century, but its therapeutic process and procedures were considered anything but routine when it emerged.

MAJOR THEORIST: CARL ROGERS

Carl Rogers, the individual most identified with person-centered counseling, was born in 1902 in Oak Park, Illinois, a suburb of Chicago. He was the fourth of six children. As fundamentalist Christians, his parents discouraged Rogers from forming friendships outside the family because of the bad influence others might have on him. Thus, Rogers (1980) describes his childhood as solitary, with "no close friend and only superficial personal contact" (p. 29). When he was 12, his family moved to a farm outside Chicago, where he developed a strong interest in science and reading. Among his early scientific experiments was one investigating a species of moth.

As a teenager Rogers read everything he could, including encyclopedias and dictionaries. However, his academic interests and abilities did not help him socially, and Rogers (1967a) describes himself as being generally inept in his interpersonal relations during his high school years. A major turning point occurred when Rogers enrolled at the University of Wisconsin in 1919 to study agriculture. There he became involved with a YMCA group and began to develop friendships. He also started dating and began to trust others. A life-changing event for him was a 6-month trip in 1922 as one of ten American students attending the World Student Christian Federation conference in Peking, China. The trip exposed him to people of other cultures, religions, and ways of thinking.

After his return Rogers broke away from the domination of his parents and changed his major to history, intending to become a minister. After graduation in 1924, he enrolled in New York's Union Theological Seminary but became discouraged 2 years later about the prospect of entering the ministry. Therefore, he transferred to Teachers College, Columbia University, "a hotbed of radical behavioristic thinking in the 1920s" (Bankart, 1997, p. 293). There he studied clinical and educational psychology, receiving an M.A. degree in 1928 and a Ph.D. in 1931. As a graduate student Rogers studied briefly with Alfred Adler, who was a visiting instructor at the Institute for Child Guidance in New York City, where Rogers was an intern (Watts, 1996).

After completing his studies, Rogers took a position with a child guidance agency in Rochester, New York. His 12-year tenure there was productive and greatly influenced his later theory of counseling. He found that the psychoanalytic approach, which was dominant in this work setting, was time-consuming and often ineffective. However, clients with whom Rogers formed an open and permissive relationship seemed to improve. During this time Rogers was reinforced in his clinical beliefs by the works of Otto Rank and his followers (Raskin & Rogers, 2000).

Rogers left Rochester in 1940 to accept a professorship at Ohio State University. Two years later he published his ideas on counseling in his first book on theory, *Counseling and Psychotherapy* (1942). He refined and revised those ideas during extensive research in the 1950s and 1960s at the universities of Chicago and Wisconsin. At Wisconsin Rogers first examined the effectiveness of his approach in a hospital setting with persons diagnosed as schizophrenic. In 1964 he became a resident fellow at the Western Behavioral Sciences Institute, and in 1968 he helped establish the Center for the Study of Persons in La Jolla, California.

A prolific writer, Rogers published more than 200 articles and 15 books (Heppner, Rogers, & Lee, 1990). Among his most noteworthy books are *Counseling and Psychotherapy* (1942), which laid the foundation for person-centered counseling; *Client-Centered Therapy* (1951), which thrust him and his theory into national prominence; and *On Becoming a Person* (1961), which "solidified his reputation in his chosen profession" (Whiteley, 1987, p. 8) and with the public at large.

Rogers wrote five books after the age of 65, including *Freedom to Learn* (1969), *Carl Rogers on Encounter Groups* (1970), and *A Way of Being* (1980). He considered his theory to be constantly evolving, becoming relevant in groups, marriages, families, and international relations, especially the peace movement of the 1980s (Goodyear, 1987; Rogers, 1987). He died unexpectedly at the age of 85 on February 4, 1987, from complications following hip surgery.

VIEW OF HUMAN NATURE/PERSONALITY

Implicit in person-centered counseling is the view that people are essentially good (Rogers, 1961). Humans are characteristically "positive, forward-moving, constructive, realistic, and trustworthy" (Rogers, 1957, p. 199). From infancy on, each person is aware, inner-directed, and moving toward self-actualization.

- Whatever an infant perceives is that infant's reality. An infant's perception is an internal process of which no one else can be aware.
- All infants are born with a self-actualizing tendency that is satisfied through goal-directed behavior.
- An infant's interaction with the environment is an organized whole, and everything an infant does is interrelated.
- The experiences of an infant may be seen as positive or negative according to whether they enhance the actualization tendency.
- Infants maintain experiences that are actualizing and avoid those that are not. (Rogers, 1959)

According to Rogers, self-actualization is the most common and motivating drive of existence; it encompasses actions that influence the total person. "The organism has one basic tendency and striving, to actualize, maintain, and enhance the experiencing organism" (Rogers, 1951, p. 487). Person-centered theorists believe that each person is capable of finding a personal meaning and purpose in life.

Rogers views the individual from a *phenomenological perspective*: what is important is a person's perception of reality rather than an event itself (Rogers, 1955). This view is similar to Adler's, as is the concept of self. But for Rogers the concept is so central to his theory that his ideas are often referred to as *self theory*. The *self* is an outgrowth of what people experience, and an awareness of self helps individuals differentiate themselves from others (Nye, 2000).

For a healthy self to emerge, people need *positive regard*—love, warmth, care, respect, and acceptance. But in childhood, as well as in later life, individuals often receive conditional regard from parents and others. Conditional acceptance teaches persons to feel valued only when they conform to others' wishes. Thus, those persons may have to deny or distort a perception when others on whom they depend for approval see a situation differently. Individuals who are caught in such a dilemma become aware of incongruities between their self-perceptions and their experiences. If they conform, they open up a gap between the *ideal self* (what they are striving to become) and the *real self* (what they are). The further the ideal self is from the real self, the more alienated and maladjusted persons become.

ROLE OF THE COUNSELOR/THERAPIST

Person-centered counselors take on a holistic role in their work. They set up and promote a climate in which clients are free and encouraged to explore all aspects of their lives (Rogers, 1951, 1980). This atmosphere focuses on the counselor-client relationship, which Rogers describes as having a special "I-Thou" personal quality. Person-centered counselors are aware of the verbal and nonverbal language of their clients, and they reflect back what they hear or observe (Braaten, 1986). Neither clients nor counselors know what direction sessions will take or what goals will emerge in the process. Yet counselors trust clients to develop the agenda; counselors work as facilitators rather than as directors. In the person-centered approach counselors are process experts and expert learners. Patience is essential (Miller, 1996).

Person-centered counselors make limited use of psychological tests. Testing is usually done only at the request of clients and only after clients have had an opportunity to be reflective about their past decisions. If testing does take place, counselors focus on the meaning of the test for clients rather than on test scores. One innovative test occasionally used in evaluating clients is the Q Sort Technique (Hergenhahn & Olson, 2003). First, the client is given 100 cards, each of which contains a self-descriptive sentence, such as "I am intelligent" or "I despise myself." Next, the client is asked to place the cards in nine piles, from most-like-me to least-like-me. Then the client sorts the cards again according to how he or she would like to be. The final step of the process is correlating the degree of similarity between the two sortings before, during, and after counseling.

The use of diagnosis is eschewed in person-centered counseling because diagnosis is philosophically incompatible with the objectives of the approach. Diagnosis categorizes people, implying that each person is not unique. It also puts the counselor in charge because, once a diagnosis is made, a treatment plan follows. Thus, the *DSM* is not used by person-centered counselors.

GOALS

The goals of person-centered counseling are geared to clients as people, not to their problems. Rogers (1977) emphasizes that people need to be assisted in learning how to cope with situations so that they become fully functioning persons with no need to apply defense mechanisms to everyday experiences. Such individuals are increasingly willing to change and grow; they are more open to experience, more trusting of self-perception, and more engaged in self-exploration and evaluation (Rogers, 1961). Fully functioning persons develop a greater acceptance of themselves and others and become better decision makers.

Ultimately, person-centered counseling helps clients identify, use, and integrate their own resources and potential (Boy & Pine, 1982; Miller, 1996). Rogers (1961) holds that clients should become

> more realistic in their self-perceptions; more confident and self-directing; more positively valued by themselves; less likely to repress aspects of their experiences; more mature, socialized, and adaptive in their behavior; less upset by stress and quicker to recover from it; and more like the healthy integrated well functioning person in their personality structures. (p. 375)

Thus, a major goal of person-centered counseling is to bring about a harmony "between the client's real self-concept and his or her perceived self-concept" (Benjamin & Looby, 1998, p. 92).

PROCESS AND TECHNIQUES

Person-centered processes and techniques have evolved over the years. Hart (1970) identifies three periods of evolution, each of which was distinctively different in its emphasis.

- *Nondirective period (1940–1950).* During this period person-centered counselors emphasized forming a relationship with clients by creating a permissive atmosphere of nonintervention. Their main techniques were acceptance and clarification.
- *Reflective period (1950–1957).* This 7-year span was characterized by an emphasis on the creation of nonthreatening relationships. Techniques included responding to clients' feelings and reflecting underlying affect back to clients. During this period Rogers changed his terminology from *nondirective* to *client-centered* to deemphasize techniques and focus on the therapeutic relationship.
- *Experiential period (1957–1980).* This period began when Rogers (1957) issued his statement on the necessary and sufficient, or core, conditions of counseling: empathy; positive regard, or acceptance; and congruence, or genuineness (Gelso & Carter, 1985; Watts, 1996). *Empathy* is the ability to feel with clients and convey this understanding back to them. It is an attempt to think with, rather than for or about, them (Brammer, Abrego, & Shostrom, 1993). Rogers (1975) notes, "The research keeps piling up and it points strongly to the conclusion that a high degree of empathy in a relationship is possibly the most potent and certainly one of the most potent factors in bringing about change and learning" (p. 3). *Positive regard*, also known as acceptance, is a deep and genuine caring for clients as persons; that is, prizing people just for being (Rogers, 1961, 1980). *Congruence* is the condition of being transparent in the therapeutic relationship by giving up roles and facades (Rogers, 1980). This period helped make person-centered counseling more active and well defined.

Since 1980 person-centered counselors have tried a number of other procedures for working with clients, such as limited self-disclosure of counselors' feelings, thoughts, and values. However, because clients grow by experiencing themselves and others in relationships (Cormier & Cormier, 1998), Rogers (1967b) holds that "significant positive personality change" cannot occur except in relationships (p. 73). He lists six necessary and sufficient conditions for a counseling relationship:

1. Two persons are in psychological contact.
2. The first person, the client, is in a state of incongruence and is vulnerable or anxious.
3. The second person, the counselor, is congruent, or integrated, in the relationship.
4. The counselor experiences unconditional positive regard for the client.
5. The counselor experiences an empathic understanding of the client's internal frame of reference and attempts to communicate his or her experience to the client.

6. There is at least a minimal degree of communication to the client of the counselor's understanding and unconditional positive regard.

According to Rogers (1959) these six conditions exist on a continuum and, except for the first condition, are not on an all-or-nothing basis.

Methods that help promote the counselor-client relationship include, but are not limited to, the following: active and passive listening, accurate reflection of thoughts and feelings, clarification, summarization, confrontation, and general or open-ended leads (Poppen & Thompson, 1974). All of these techniques have been incorporated into other counseling approaches and systematic human-relations training courses.

Overall, person-centered counseling places minimal emphasis on formal techniques and maximal focus on creating a therapeutic relationship. A classic example of this emphasis can be seen in Rogers's (1965) interview with a client named Gloria, in which he focuses on her acceptance of herself and their relationship rather than on Gloria's problem.

MULTICULTURAL AND GENDER-SENSITIVE ISSUES

Person-centered counseling receives mixed reviews regarding its appropriateness in a multicultural context. On the positive side, this approach to therapy and human relationships has been used in a number of countries to promote cross-cultural communication and understanding. Rogers himself conducted many such workshops in countries as diverse as Japan, Mexico, China, Northern Ireland, and the former Soviet Union. That work continues, and as Spangenberg (2003) points out, person-centered counseling provides an excellent cross-cultural approach in South Africa, where there is a relationship between person-centered counseling and traditional African healing practices. In addition, person-centered theory has some similarities to Eastern philosophies and psychologies in which there is an openness to the development of people and the self is seen as a process rather than a fixed being (Sharf, 2004).

However, Rogers's beliefs about the necessary and sufficient conditions for therapy are not necessarily universal. Also, in some cultures help from others is valued if it is direct and comes from an authority—just the opposite of the person-centered approach.

Gender issues receive a mixed report as well. On the one hand, Rogers appears to be effective with Gloria, a young divorced woman in the film demonstrating his approach. A number of other incidents are documented in which person-centered therapy conducted by Rogers seems to be successful with both women and men, in groups and other settings. Gender-related concerns arise primarily because Rogers does not address them and some question whether one gender can truly empathize with and relate to the other.

EVALUATION OF THE THEORY

STRENGTHS AND CONTRIBUTIONS

Person-centered therapy revolutionized the counseling profession by linking counseling with psychotherapy and demystifying it in an actual transcript of a counseling session (Goodyear, 1987). Basically, Rogers "turned the field of counseling upside down" (Rogers, 1974, p. 115). Furthermore, he made the person-centered approach applicable to a wide range of human problems, including institutional changes, labor-management relationships, leadership development, career decision making, and international diplomacy. He summed up his view of the approach in this way: "I am no longer talking about psychotherapy, but about a point of view, a philosophy, an approach to life, a way of being, which fits any situation in which growth, of a person, a group, or a community is part of the goal" (Rogers, 1980, p. ix).

Besides transforming the therapeutic community, person-centered counseling has contributed to the profession by generating a great deal of research. Initially, it set the standard for doing research on counseling variables, especially those that Rogers (1957) deemed necessary and sufficient to bring about therapeutic change. In addition, Rogers was the first practitioner to make audiotape recordings of counseling sessions and insisted that the person-centered approach be compared only to theories that were as empirically verified (Rogers, 1986). "Above all, Rogers was the quintessential scientist practitioner. He continually put his formulations to the test of research. In fact, no model of therapy is more extensively researched than his own" (Goodyear, 1987, p. 523).

A third contribution of person-centered counseling is its focus on the open relationship established by counselors and clients. More than most, Rogers's theory emphasizes the importance of an accepting counselor-client relationship. Specific dimensions of that relationship have been examined for their impact on the total counseling process (Carkhuff, 1969a, 1969b).

Another strength of the person-centered approach is its effectiveness. It helps improve psychological adjustment, learning, and frustration tolerance and helps decrease defensiveness (Grummon, 1972). In addition, it is appropriate in treating mild to moderate anxiety states, adjustment disorders, and conditions not attributable to mental disorders, such as uncomplicated bereavement or interpersonal relations (Seligman, 1997).

A further strength of person-centered counseling is that the basics of the approach take a relatively short time to learn, although a lifetime to master. With its emphasis on relationship and listening skills, person-centered counseling becomes a foundation for training many professionals to work in varied settings (Glauser & Bozarth, 2001).

Yet another beneficial aspect of person-centered therapy is its positive view of human nature (Heppner et al., 1990), which is different from the more pessimistic and deterministic views that some theories hold. One of the strongest reasons that people change is the belief that they can change, and person-centered counselors are strong believers in the change process.

LIMITATIONS AND CRITICISMS

One initial drawback to person-centered therapy was that it provided few instructions for counselors on how to establish relationships with clients and bring about change. The work of Carkhuff (1969a, 1969b) and Gazda (1973) helped rectify this deficiency; however, person-centered theory is still sometimes viewed as an approach without clearly defined terms or techniques (Nye, 2000).

Another limitation of the person-centered approach is that it depends on bright, insightful, hard-working clients for best results. Thus, this theory of helping has limited applicability and is seldom employed with the severely handicapped or with young children (Thompson, Rudolph, & Henderson, 2004).

A third criticism of person-centered counseling is that it ignores diagnosis, the unconscious, and innately generated sexual and aggressive drives. Many critics think that it is overly optimistic. Even though Rogers compiled a great deal of data supporting his point of view, much of that research has been attacked as being simplistic and based on self-reports (Hergenhahn & Olson, 2003).

Finally, person-centered counseling is directed by clients and may thus deal only with surface issues. Believing that only deep change is lasting, critics charge that therapists do not challenge their clients to explore those deeper areas. Because person-centered counseling is relatively brief in nature and is not directed by an expert professional, critics claim that it cannot have a permanent impact on the client.

TREATING LINDA WITH PERSON-CENTERED THERAPY

CONCEPTUALIZATION

From a person-centered perspective what is important is that Linda has been accepted conditionally throughout her life. She has been valued as a daughter and a wife only when she has performed these roles as others have defined them. Linda's relationship with her ex-husband lasted only as long as she conformed to his wishes that she look and act in a certain way. Now she is searching to be accepted for herself unconditionally, and so far she has not found people that value her just for herself. She does not get close to her family members because they, too, judge her.

As Linda looks at life, she sees a rather hostile environment. Men are mean or sexist. Families do not offer support or comfort. Thus, it is little wonder that she has retreated to books, television, and movies as ways to escape and feel safe. On the other hand, Linda knows that she is more capable than she has been allowed to be.

TREATMENT PROCESS

As a person-centered therapist you immediately set up a therapeutic environment in which Linda is accepted and encouraged. You use yourself and the relationship you establish with her to help her see herself. You actively listen and reflect back to her what you hear her saying. You empathize, clarify, confront, and show her unconditional positive regard. You convey to her that you trust her to make observations, insights, and decisions. You are genuine in your statements and try to create an atmosphere in which Linda can be herself. In the process she begins to feel like a person capable of finding her own direction in life.

As Linda begins to disclose, she initially ventilates anger toward her father, her former husband, and individuals in her work environments. You self-disclose and reveal that you would be angry, too, if you had been through her experiences. After a while Linda shifts away from her anger and begins to concentrate on who she can be and how she can be. Her thoughts and feelings move into the present, and she recognizes that she has a quick mind and is capable of going back to school or finding a higher level job. She also realizes that all men are not like her father or her ex-husband and that she might be able to be in a relationship in which she is valued for herself.

With these ideas in mind, Linda begins to make plans that will expand her environment and her opportunities, such as taking a yoga class at the Y and joining a reading club at the library. After a few more sessions, Linda reveals that she is ready to trust herself to make other plans and arrangements. Thus, she leaves therapy with an optimistic sense of hope and a new perspective on herself.

SUMMARY AND CONCLUSION

The person-centered approach to counseling created a great deal of excitement and controversy when it was introduced to the therapeutic community in 1942 by Carl Rogers. It emphasized that clients could and would make important and needed changes in their lives if a proper relationship was set up and someone listened to them. The emphasis on being nondirective was just the opposite of prominent theories of the time that put therapists in charge of change. Yet this approach has prevailed because of research supporting its underlying tenets.

Even though person-centered counseling has undergone a number of changes since its introduction, it still places priority on creating a therapeutic relationship and fostering the conditions necessary and sufficient for change to take place. It continues to be one of the most popular theories of counseling and has been used both domestically and internationally in a number of venues, ranging from group work to peace talks.

SUMMARY TABLE: PERSON-CENTERED THERAPY

Major Theorists

Carl Rogers

View of Human Nature/Personality

Emphasis on the good and the positive

Phenomenological view of self
Self-direction and orientation toward growth

Role of the Counselor/Therapist

Stresses holism and I-Thou relationship
Facilitates
Focuses on client uniqueness
Conveys empathy, acceptance, genuineness

Goals

Promote self-exploration and openness
Emphasize self-direction and realistic orientation
Encourage acceptance of self and others
Focus on here and now

Process and Techniques

Includes six necessary and sufficient conditions for change
Involves varied techniques: acceptance, clarification, reflection, empathy, congruence
Uses active listening, self-disclosure, summarization, and unconditional positive regard

Multicultural and Gender-Sensitive Issues

Used in numerous countries
Similar to some Eastern philosophies and African healing practices
Inappropriate in some cultures
Successful with men and women
Questionable in closing gender gap through empathy

Strengths and Contributions

Credited with revolutionizing the world of therapy and helping it evolve
Applicable to varied problems and concerns
Effective with specific disorders
Short-term
Useful in training paraprofessional helpers
Positive in its view of people

Limitations and Criticisms

Lacks concrete direction in relationship formation
Depends on articulate and insightful clients
Ignores the unconscious and innate drives
May not resolve in-depth problems

LEARNING MORE

A limited number of periodicals are devoted to the theory, research, and practice of person-centered therapy. The best is probably *The Person-Centered Journal*, published by the Association for the Development of the Person-Centered Approach.

In addition, the *Journal of Counseling and Development* and other major counseling journals carry articles and research periodically on person-centered counseling.

Several training institutes offer clinicians a chance to learn more about person-centered counseling. Two of the best known are

Center for Studies of the Person
1150 Silverado, Suite #112
La Jolla, CA 92037
www.centerfortheperson.org

Association for the Development of the Person-Centered Approach
http://www.adpca.org/

CLASSROOM ACTIVITIES

1. How do you think a person-centered counselor would handle reluctant clients, such as an adolescent sent to the counselor or a person on probation who is court ordered to receive counseling? Discuss your ideas in pairs and then share them with the class as a whole.
2. Read *A Way of Being* (1980) by Carl Rogers. In small groups discuss how Rogers's theory was influenced by his personal development and how person-centered theory might be applied to educational, political, industrial, medical, recreational, and managerial settings. Be as specific as possible in relating the theory to these settings. After you have come to some conclusions, discuss your views with the class as a whole.
3. Compare the person-centered approach with psychoanalysis. How are the two similar? How do they differ? Without considering money or time, which do you think most clients would prefer and why?

REFERENCES

Bankart, C. P. (1997). *Talking cures*. Pacific Grove, CA: Brooks/Cole.

Benjamin, P., & Looby, J. (1998). Defining the nature of spirituality in the context of Maslow's and Rogers's theories. *Counseling and Values, 42*, 92–100.

Boy, A. V., & Pine, G. J. (1982). *Client-centered counseling: A renewal*. Boston: Allyn & Bacon.

Braaten, L. J. (1986). Thirty years with Rogers's necessary and sufficient conditions of therapeutic personality change. *Person-Centered Review, 1*, 37–49.

Brammer, L. M., Abrego, P. J., & Shostrom, E. L. (1993). *Therapeutic counseling and psychotherapy* (6th ed.). Upper Saddle River, NJ: Merrill/Prentice Hall.

Carkhuff, R. R. (1969a). *Helping and human relations* (Vol. 1). New York: Holt, Rinehart, & Winston.

Carkhuff, R. R. (1969b). *Helping and human relations* (Vol. 2). New York: Holt, Rinehart, & Winston.

Cormier, W. H., & Cormier, L. S. (1998). *Interviewing strategies for helpers* (4th ed.). Pacific Grove, CA: Brooks/Cole.

Gazda, G. M. (1973). *Human relations development: A manual for education*. Boston: Allyn & Bacon.

Gelso, C. J., & Carter, J. A. (1985). The relationship in counseling and psychotherapy: Components, consequences, and theoretical antecedents. *Counseling Psychologist, 13*, 155–243.

Glauser, A. S., & Bozarth, J. D. (2001). Person-centered counseling: The culture within. *Journal of Counseling and Development, 79*, 142–147.

Goodyear, R. K. (1987). In memory of Carl Ransom Rogers. *Journal of Counseling and Development, 65*, 523–524.

Grummon, D. L. (1972). Client-centered therapy. In B. Stefflre & W. H. Grant (Eds.), *Theories of counseling* (2nd ed.). New York: McGraw-Hill.

Hart, J. (1970). The development of client-centered therapy. In J. T. Hart & T. M. Tomlinson (Eds.), *New directions in client centered therapy*. Boston: Houghton Mifflin.

Heppner, P. P., Rogers, M. E., & Lee, L. A. (1990). Carl Rogers: Reflections on his life. In P. P. Heppner (Ed.), *Pioneers in counseling and development* (pp. 54–59). Alexandria, VA: American Counseling Association.

Hergenhahn, B. R., & Olson, M. H. (2003). *An introduction to theories of personality* (6th ed.). Upper Saddle River, NJ: Prentice Hall.

Miller, M. J. (1996). Client-centered reflections on career decision making. *Journal of Employment Counseling, 33*, 43–46.

Nye, R. D. (2000). *Three psychologies* (6th ed.). Pacific Grove, CA: Brooks/Cole.

Partenheimer, D. (1990). Teaching literature toward a humanistic society. *Journal of Humanistic Education and Development, 29*, 40–44.

Poppen, W. A., & Thompson, C. L. (1974). *School counseling: Theories and concepts*. Lincoln, NE: Professional Educators Publications.

Raskin, N. J., & Rogers, C. R. (2000). Person-centered therapy. In R. J. Corsini & D. Wedding (Eds.), *Current psychotherapies* (6th ed., pp. 133–167). Itasca, IL: Peacock.

Rogers, C. R. (1942). *Counseling and psychotherapy*. Boston: Houghton Mifflin.

Rogers, C. R. (1951). *Client-centered therapy*. Boston: Houghton Mifflin.

Rogers, C. R. (1955). Persons or science? A philosophical question. *American Psychologist, 10*, 267–278.

Rogers, C. R. (1957). The necessary and sufficient conditions of therapeutic personality change. *Journal of Consulting Psychology, 21*, 95–103.

Rogers, C. R. (1959). A theory of therapy, personality, and interpersonal relationships, as developed in the client-centered framework. In S. Koch (Ed.), *Psychology: A study of science* (Vol. 3, pp. 184–256). New York: McGraw-Hill.

Rogers, C. R. (1961). *On becoming a person*. Boston: Houghton Mifflin.

Rogers, C. R. (1965). Client-centered therapy: Part I. In E. Shostrom (Producer), *Three approaches to psychotherapy* [film]. Santa Anna, CA: Psychological Films.

Rogers, C. R. (1967a). Autobiography. In E. G. Boring & G. Lindzey (Eds.), *A history of psychology in autobiography* (Vol. 5, pp. 341–384). New York: Appleton.

Rogers, C. R. (1967b). The conditions of change from a client-centered viewpoint. In B. Berenson & R. Carkhuff (Eds.), *Sources of gain in counseling and psychotherapy* (pp. 71–86). New York: Holt, Rinehart, & Winston.

Rogers, C. R. (1969). *Freedom to learn*. Upper Saddle River, NJ: Prentice Hall.

Rogers, C. R. (1970). *Carl Rogers on encounter groups*. New York: Harper & Row.

Rogers, C. R. (1974). In retrospect: Forty-six years. *American Psychologist, 29*, 115–123.

Rogers, C. R. (1975). Empathic: An unappreciated way of being. *Counseling Psychologist, 5*, 2–10.

Rogers, C. R. (1977). *Carl Rogers on personal power: Inner strength and its revolutionary impact*. New York: Delacorte.

Rogers, C. R. (1980). *A way of being*. Boston: Houghton Mifflin.

Rogers, C. R. (1986). Rogers, Kohut, and Erickson: A personal perspective on some similarities and differences. *Person-Centered Review, 1*, 125–140.

Rogers, C. R. (1987). The underlying theory: Drawn from experience with individuals and groups. *Counseling and Values, 32*, 38–46.

Seligman, L. (1997). *Diagnosis and treatment planning in counseling*. New York: Plenum.

Sharf, R. S. (2004). *Theories of psychotherapy and counseling* (3rd ed.). Pacific Grove, CA: Brooks/Cole.

Spangenberg, J. J. (2003). The cross-cultural relevance of person-centered counseling in postapartheid South Africa. *Journal of Counseling and Development, 81*, 48–54.

Thompson, C., Rudolph, L., & Henderson, D. A. (2004). *Counseling children* (6th ed.). Pacific Grove, CA: Brooks/Cole.

Watts, R. E. (1996). Social interest and the core conditions: Could it be that Adler influenced Rogers? *Journal of Humanistic Education and Development, 34*, 165–170.

Whiteley, J. M. (1987). The person-centered approach to peace. *Counseling and Values, 32*, 5–8.

Gestalt Therapy

CHAPTER 6

They wait stiff and still
  in the summer sun
    for the boys who loved them
      to return
But those boys,
  now grown to an age
    where swing sets
      are only a part of their history
Sit on front porch steps
  talking and waiting for the cool of evening
    when the once-upon-a-time girls they knew,
      now women,
        will walk by, perhaps speak,
          and send their hearts into orbit.

Note: "Time and Motion" by S. T. Gladding. Copyright 2003 by Samuel T. Gladding.

Gestalt therapy is associated with Gestalt psychology, a school of thought that stresses the perception of completeness and wholeness. In fact, the term *gestalt* literally translated means "whole figure." Gestalt therapy arose as a reaction to the reductionist emphasis in other schools of counseling and psychotherapy, such as psychoanalysis and behaviorism, which tried to break down the personality or client behaviors into explainable parts. In contrast, Gestalt theory emphasizes how people function in their totality.

Gestalt therapy was popularized in the 1960s by Fritz Perls, who focused on helping individuals become more aware of the many aspects of their personhood. Laura Perls, Fritz's wife, and Paul Goodman helped Perls write, enlarge, and refine his original ideas. Other theorists, particularly Joen Fagan and Irma Lee Shepherd (1970), developed the model still further. However, since Fritz Perls is the best known of these, he is highlighted here.

MAJOR THEORIST: FRITZ PERLS

Frederick Salomon Perls was born in 1893 into a middle-class Jewish family in Berlin. He had a younger and an older sister. Even though his parents fought bitterly and Perls disliked his older sister, he remembered his childhood as happy. Initially, he loved to read and was a top student in his grade school. However, in secondary school Perls encountered difficulty because of a conservative learning environment and his own rebellious spirit. He had difficulty obeying authorities and failed the 7th grade twice. Nevertheless, he completed his secondary education once placed in a more liberal environment and was later awarded a medical degree from Frederich Wilhelm University in 1920. His schooling was interrupted by World War I and his service as a medic with the German army.

Perls trained as a psychoanalyst in both Vienna and Berlin. Wilhelm Reich and Karen Horney each participated in Perls's analysis as part of his training. Subsequently he took a position in Frankfurt at the Institute for Brain Injured Soldiers. There Perls became associated with Kurt Goldstein, from whom he learned to view humans as complete, or holistic, entities rather than as individuals made of separate parts.

In 1933 Perls fled Nazi Germany, first to Holland and then to Johannesburg, South Africa, where he and his wife, Laura Posner Perls, built a strong psychoanalytic practice, just as they had previously done in Germany. In 1936 Perls sailed his private yacht 4,000 miles from South Africa to Germany to attend an international psychoanalytic congress in Czechoslovakia. There he arranged an audience with Freud, which left Perls feeling humiliated. Having been frequently humiliated by his father, Perls dedicated himself to proving Freud and psychoanalysis wrong.

Perls immigrated to the United States in 1946. Although his ideas were not readily accepted, he gained prominence through the publication of *Gestalt Therapy* (1951), which he coauthored with Hefferline and Goodman. Perls also established the Institute for Gestalt Therapy in New York City in 1952 and offered lectures and workshops around North America. In 1960 he moved to the Esalen Institute in Big Sur, California. Perls was an actor at heart and loved to parade his ideas before the public at Esalen. Laura Perls, long separated from Fritz, continued to be supportive of her husband until his death in 1970 in British Columbia at the Gestalt kibbutz, a commune he had founded (Bankart, 1997). Perls recounted many of the more personal moments of his life in his autobiographical book, *In and Out of the Garbage Pail*, published posthumously in 1972.

VIEW OF HUMAN NATURE/PERSONALITY

Gestaltists believe that human beings work for wholeness and completeness in their lives. Each person has a self-actualizing tendency that emerges through the beginning of self-awareness and personal interaction with the environment. *Self-actualization* is centered in the present; it "is the process of being what one is and not a process of striving to become" (Kempler, 1973, p. 262). The Gestalt view of human nature places trust in the inner wisdom of people, much as person-centered counseling does. Each person seeks to live integratively and productively, striving to coordinate the various parts of the person into a healthy, unified whole. From a Gestalt perspective, persons are more than a sum of their parts (Perls, 1969).

The Gestalt view is antideterministic: each person is able to change and become responsible (Hatcher & Himelsteint, 1997). Thus, individuals are actors in the events around them, not just reactors to events. Overall, the Gestalt point of view is existential, experiential, and phenomenological: the now is what really matters. People discover different aspects of themselves through experience rather than talk, and individuals' own assessment and interpretation of their lives at any given moment are what matter most.

According to Gestalt therapy, many troubled persons have an overdependency on intellectual experience (Simkin, 1975). Such an emphasis diminishes the importance of emotions and the senses, limiting people's abilities to respond to various situations. Another frequent problem is the inability to identify and resolve *unfinished business;* that is, earlier thoughts, feelings, and reactions that still affect personal functioning and interfere with living life in the present. The most common unfinished business is the failure to forgive parents for their mistakes. Gestaltists do not attribute either of these difficulties to any unconscious force within persons but rather to a lack of awareness, "the ability of the client to be in full mental and sensory" contact and to be "experiencing the now" (Gilliland & James, 1998, p. 142).

Every person operates on some conscious level, ranging from very aware to very unaware. Healthy individuals are those who are most aware. Such people realize that body signs, such as headaches or stomach pains, may indicate a need to change behaviors. They are also aware of personal limitations. For instance, in conflicts with others they may be able to resolve the situation or they may have to dismiss it. Healthy people avoid complicating such situations, refusing to embellish them with fantasy. Instead, they focus "sharply on one need (the figure) at a time while relegating other needs to the background. When the need is met—or the Gestalt is closed or completed—it is relegated to the background and a new need comes into focus (becomes the figure)" (Thompson, Rudolph, & Henderson, 2004, p. 185). Such functioning requires that persons recognize internal needs and learn how to manipulate those needs and the environment (Perls, 1976).

According to Gestaltists, persons experience difficulties in several ways.

1. They may lose contact with the environment and the resources in it.
2. People may become overinvolved with the environment and thus grow out of touch with themselves.
3. Individuals may fail to put aside unfinished business.
4. They may become fragmented or scattered in many directions.
5. Persons may experience conflict between the *top dog* (what they think they should do) and the *underdog* (what they want to do).
6. People may have difficulty handling the dichotomies of life, such as love/hate, masculinity/femininity, and pleasure/pain (Assagioli, 1965).

Individuals who become neurotic try to attend to too many needs at one time and therefore do not take care of any one need fully. They also depend on others for care instead of caring for themselves, as they are capable of doing.

ROLE OF THE COUNSELOR/THERAPIST

The role of the Gestalt counselor or therapist is to create an atmosphere that encourages clients to explore what they need to grow. Counselors provide such an atmosphere by being intensely and personally involved with clients and by being honest. Therapists must be exciting, energetic, and fully human (Polster and Polster, 1973). Involvement occurs in the *now*, which is a continuing process (Perls, 1969) in which counselors help clients learn to redirect energy in positive and adaptive ways (Zinker, 1978). The now also entails helping clients recognize patterns in their lives (Fagan, 1970).

Gestalt therapists follow several rules in helping clients become more aware of the now (Levitsky & Perls, 1970):

- *The principle of now*—always using the present tense
- *An I-and-thou* relationship—always addressing someone directly instead of talking about him or her

- *The use of I*—substituting the word *I* for *it*, especially when talking about one's body
- *The use of an awareness continuum*—focusing on how and what rather than why
- *The conversion of questions*—asking clients to convert questions into statements

Gestalt counselors do not use standardized assessment instruments, such as psychological tests. Furthermore, they do not diagnose their clients according to *DSM* classification standards.

GOALS

The goals of Gestalt therapy are well-defined. They include an emphasis on the here and now and a recognition of the immediacy of experience (Bankart, 1997). The importance of these first two goals can be seen in the fact that the term *contact* is used to refer to the sensory and motor immediacy that can be experienced when the environment is met directly (Perls et al., 1951). Further goals include a focus on both nonverbal and verbal expression and on the concept that life involves making choices (Fagan & Shepherd, 1970).

The Gestalt approach concentrates on helping clients become integrated by resolving the past, completing the process of growing up mentally and becoming mature (Perls, 1969). It emphasizes the coalescence of the emotional, cognitive, and behavioral aspects of a person. A primary focus is the acceptance of polarities within the person (Gelso & Carter, 1985).

As a group, Gestalt therapists stress action, pushing their clients to experience feelings and behaviors. They also emphasize the meaning of the word *now*. Perls (1970) developed a formula that expresses the word's essence: "Now = experience = awareness = reality. The past is no more and the future not yet. Only the now exists" (p. 14).

To be mature in the now, a person must often shed neurotic tendencies. Perls (1970) identifies five layers of neurosis that interfere with being authentically in touch with oneself.

- The *phony layer* consists of pretending to be something that one is not, often involving game playing and fantasy enactment. When persons become more aware of the games they are playing, they can be more honest, open, and in touch with unpleasantness and pain.
- The *phobic layer* is an attempt to avoid recognizing aspects of one self that an individual would prefer to deny. People at this layer of awareness are afraid that they will be rejected if they acknowledge who they are and present that to others.
- The *impasse layer* has no sense of direction. Individuals wonder how they are going to make it in the environment and are adrift in a sea of helplessness and dread.

- The *implosive* and *explosive layers* are often grouped together; people at these layers frequently feel vulnerable to feelings. As they peel back the layers of defensiveness built up over the years (the implosive layer), they may explode in intense feelings of joy, sorrow, or pain (the explosive layer). When persons reach this point, they can become authentic with themselves and others.

PROCESS AND TECHNIQUES

Some of the most innovative counseling techniques ever developed are found in Gestalt therapy (Harman, 1997). These techniques take two forms—exercises and experiments. *Exercises* are ready-made techniques, such as the enactment of fantasies, role-playing, and psychodrama (Covin, 1977). They are employed to evoke a certain response from clients, such as anger or exploration. *Experiments,* on the other hand, are activities that grow out of the interaction between counselors and clients. They are not planned, and what is learned is often a surprise to both participants. Even though many of the techniques of Gestalt therapy do take the form of unplanned experiments (Zinker, 1978), the concentration here is on exercise-oriented techniques.

One common exercise is *dream work.* Perls describes dreams as messages that represent a person's place at a certain time (Bernard, 1986). Unlike psychoanalysts, however, Gestalt counselors do not interpret; instead, clients present dreams and are then directed to experience what it is like to be in each part of the dream—a type of dramatized free association. In this way clients get more in touch with the multiple aspects of themselves. Individuals with repetitive dreams are encouraged to realize that unfinished business is being brought into their awareness and that they need to take care of the message being delivered.

Another effective technique is the *empty chair* (see Figure 6.1). In this procedure clients focus on an empty chair and talk to the various parts of their personality, such as the part that is dominant and the part that is passive. Clients may use the chair as a representative of the self or may use different chairs to represent different parts of themselves. In this dialogue both rational and irrational parts of the client come into focus, and the client becomes able to deal with the inner dichotomies. Overall, the empty chair technique is a three-stage model: opposition, merging, and integration. It works well with many clients, such as those who may be in a predivorce situation (Mackay, 2002), but it is not recommended for the severely emotionally disturbed (Bernard, 1986).

One of the most powerful Gestalt exercises is *confrontation.* In confrontation, counselors point out to clients incongruent behaviors and feelings, such as smiling when nervous. Confrontation involves asking clients *what* and *how* questions. *Why* questions are avoided because they lead to intellectualization. Therapists may purposely frustrate their clients to help them move beyond present states of denial

FIGURE 6.1 The empty chair

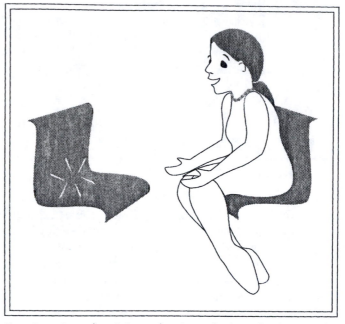

Note: From *Counseling: A Comprehensive Profession* (5th ed., p. 207) by Samuel T. Gladding. Copyright 2004. Reprinted by permission of Pearson Education, Inc., Upper Saddle River, NJ.

(Harman, 1975), hoping that clients will make valuable interpretations when confronted. Techniques that center on working in the here and now help clients focus on breaking out of old habits and becoming more in touch with themselves.

Other powerful Gestalt exercises that are oriented to individuals are often used in groups (Harman, 1997).

- *Making the rounds.* Counselors use this exercise when a particular theme or feeling should be faced by every person in the group. For instance, one client may say, "I can't stand anyone" and is then instructed to repeat this sentence to each person in the group, adding some remarks about each group member. The exercise is flexible and may include nonverbal as well as positive feelings. It helps clients become more aware of inner feelings.
- *I take responsibility.* In this exercise clients make statements about perceptions and close each statement with the phrase "and I take responsibility for it." The exercise helps clients integrate and own their perceptions and behaviors.
- *Exaggeration.* Clients accentuate their own unwitting movements or gestures and in the process make the inner meaning of these behaviors more apparent.
- *May I feed you a sentence?* Aware of implicit attitudes or messages in what a client is saying, the counselor asks whether the client will repeat a certain sentence that makes the client's thoughts explicit. If the counselor is correct about the underlying message, the client will gain insight as the sentence is repeated.

MULTICULTURAL AND GENDER-SENSITIVE ISSUES

Gestalt therapy is widely used throughout the world. For example, in a recent survey of European psychotherapy training, Gestalt therapy was one of only four modalities practiced in the majority of the 32 countries polled (Zerbetto & Tantam, 2001). One reason for this popularity may be that Gestalt experiments can be used "to help individuals deal with and perceive their own culture" (Sharf, 2004, p. 269). Gestalt experiments may also help clients recognize polarities between cultures in which they live, such as a minority culture within a majority culture.

However, because Gestalt therapy is very individualistic, it contrasts sharply with cultures that are more oriented to group values and traditions. Thus, for Gestalt therapy to be practiced effectively and ethically in such communities, it needs to focus more attention on the importance of human interconnectedness (Ivey, D'Andrea, Ivey, & Simek-Morgan, 2002).

Gestalt therapy is probably as open to sensitive gender issues as any other counseling modality. At its conception and during its formative years, the approach was influenced strongly by women, such as Laura Perls, Joen Fagan, and Irma Lee Shepherd.

EVALUATION OF THE THEORY

STRENGTHS AND CONTRIBUTIONS

One strength of Gestalt therapy is its emphasis on helping people incorporate and accept all aspects of their lives. An individual cannot be understood outside the context of the whole person, who is choosing to act on the environment in the present (Passons, 1975). The Gestalt approach also helps clients focus on resolving areas of unfinished business so that their lives can be lived productively.

A third contribution of Gestalt therapy is that it places primary emphasis on doing rather than talking. Activity helps individuals experience what the process of change is about and thus make more rapid progress. In addition, the change is likely to be enduring (Melnick, 2003).

Furthermore, the Gestalt approach is flexible and is not limited to a few techniques (Yontef & Jacobs, 2000). Any activity that helps clients become more integrative can be employed in Gestalt therapy. Such activities are readily available in the *Gestalt Journal*, "the literary organ that disseminates research, theory, and innovative techniques of the approach" (Gilliland & James, 1998, p. 137).

A final strength of Gestalt therapy is its appropriateness for certain affective disorders, anxiety states, somatoform disorders, adjustment disorders, and *DSM-IV* diagnoses, such as occupational problems and interpersonal problems (Glinnwater, 2000; Seligman, 1997). In short, Gestalt therapy is versatile.

LIMITATIONS AND CRITICISMS

Gestalt therapy lacks a strong theoretical base. In fact, some critics view Gestalt counseling as all experience and technique—that is, too gimmicky (Corey, 2001). They maintain that it is antitheoretical and often cite a line from Fritz Perls: "Lose your mind and come to your senses."

A second limitation of Gestalt therapy is that it deals strictly with the now and how of experience (Perls, 1969). Thus, it does not allow for passive insight and internal change, which some clients are more likely to use.

Still another criticism of Gestalt therapy is that it eschews diagnosis and testing. Some individuals need to be screened before they experience such an intense method of counseling. Although Gestalt therapists do screen their clients for appropriateness, some critics argue that the process needs to be more thorough and uniform.

Finally, Gestalt therapy is too concerned with individual development and a self-centered approach to helping; it focuses primarily on feelings and personal discovery. Although many other counseling theories are also centered on individual development, Gestalt therapy is considered extreme by some. An example of its self-centeredness is seen in the Gestalt prayer:

> *I do my thing and you do your thing.*
> *I am not in this world to live up to your expectations*
> *And you are not in this world to live up to mine.*
> *You are you and I am I,*
> *And if by chance we find each other, it's beautiful.*
> *If not, it cannot be helped. (Perls, 1969, p.4)*

TREATING LINDA WITH GESTALT THERAPY

CONCEPTUALIZATION

From the perspective of Gestalt therapy, Linda is having relationship problems but her difficulties are as much internal as they are external. Linda is not aware of how fragmented she is as a person and how much unfinished business she has in regard to her family of origin and her former husband. Although Linda did some mild acting out as a teenager, she was mostly submissive, as her father insisted. Instead of breaking away from family constraints by going to college, she denied herself that opportunity and instead earned a 2-year degree locally in an area in which she was not even interested. As a result, Linda has hopped from one glorified secretarial position to another because of boredom. Externally she blames the situation on her bosses, but internally she blames herself.

In addition to her resentment about the past, Linda is angry about her present situation. She is lonely and does not have a support system. Consequently, she reads fantasy novels and watches exciting movies and instructional television programs. All of this activity is an attempt to escape rather than construct a productive life.

TREATMENT PROCESS

As a Gestalt therapist you establish rapport with Linda and then begin to challenge her in regard to what she is aware of and what she is doing now. At first Linda wants to guide you back into the past and discuss what has been, but you insist on staying in the present, even if it involves dealing with unfinished business. You direct Linda to be an actor as opposed to a reactor. You are also adamant that she use *I* messages to promote responsibility and that she focus on *how* rather than *why* questions. You notice that Linda sometimes smiles when she talks about being abused by her husband or put down by her father. To get her to be more aware, you call her on this action, saying that she is playing games and being phony. Linda becomes angry with you in the process but continues in therapy.

In order to help Linda become more congruent and real, you ask her to engage in some anger exercises with you. In one of these she shows you, by hitting a pillow with her hand, how angry certain events, people, or situations make her. As Linda completes this exercise, she starts growling spontaneously each time she hits the pillow. You then move her into a chair and have her talk as the more active person she is now to the inactive, passive side of herself. She switches chairs as she switches from active to passive. This empty chair technique helps her to integrate her life. As homework you ask her to keep a diary of her dreams and to bring it with her each time so that she can reenact and understand the messages that her unconscious is sending her.

As Linda continues to be active in therapy, she begins to gain insight into what she is doing and feels more empowered. She realizes she cannot dwell on what has been but can live in the now. She decides to complete a 4-year degree, join a women's support group, and participate in several community clubs that engage in interesting activities, such as biking and cooking. She lets her family know what she is doing and talks with them about how she is changing. She resists their attempts to pull her back and continues to develop greater self-awareness as she begins to accomplish new tasks.

SUMMARY AND CONCLUSION

Gestalt therapy has been a force in the field of counseling and therapy since the 1950s. It was initially associated primarily with Fritz Perls; but since Perls's death in 1970, a number of other proponents—including Laura Perls, Joen Fagan, and Irma Lee Shepherd—have been its main developers as well as its strong advocates.

As a therapeutic modality Gestalt therapy is action oriented. It stresses acting in the present, that is, the now. Basically, changes in thoughts and feelings follow changes in behaviors. Gestalt therapy uses both structured exercises and spontaneous experiments. Exercises are planned, whereas experiments grow out of client/counselor relationships. Both may lead clients to greater awareness of themselves and others, which is a primary goal.

Although the Gestalt approach does help individuals and groups act differently, it has been criticized for not having a strong theoretical base and for dealing too much with the here and now, eschewing diagnosis and testing, and being too self-centered, that is, focused on the individual. Nevertheless, Gestalt therapy is quite flexible and holistic, helps clients resolve unfinished business, and is appropriate for certain affective disorders.

SUMMARY TABLE: GESTALT THERAPY

Major Theorists

Fritz Perls	Joen Fagan
Laura Perls	Irma Lee Shepherd

View of Human Nature/Personality

Emphasizes wholeness and completeness
Focuses on the inner wisdom of individuals
Is phenomenological and antideterministic
Stresses human change through action

Role of the Counselor/Therapist

Must be authentic, exciting, energetic
Emphasizes the here and now
Helps clients resolve unfinished business
Assists clients in using I messages

Goals

Focus on the here and now
Attend to both nonverbal and verbal expression
Recognize that life presents choices
Help clients become more integrated and mature
Bring together emotion, cognition, and behavior
Help clients accept internal polarities and shed neurotic tendencies

Process and Techniques

Exercises, or planned interactions: e.g., dream work, empty chair, confrontation
Experiments, or spontaneous interactions
Group exercises: e.g., making the rounds, taking responsibility, exaggerating, repeating a sentence

Multicultural and Gender-Sensitive Issues

Used worldwide
Inappropriate for some cultures
Open to sensitive gender issues

Strengths and Contributions

Incorporates all parts of life
Resolves the past

Stresses doing and acting
Helps in the treatment of certain affective disorders
Is flexible in using exercises and experiments

Limitations and Criticisms

Lacks a strong theoretical base
May become gimmicky
Does not allow for passive learning
Eschews testing and diagnosis
Is too self-centered

LEARNING MORE

A number of periodicals devoted to Gestalt therapy and theory might prove helpful in exploring this approach to counseling.

International Gestalt Journal
Gestalt Review
Gestalt Journal

In addition to journals, several training institutes and professional associations offer clinicians an opportunity to learn more about Gestalt therapy.

The Association for the Advancement of Gestalt Therapy
http://www.aagt.org/

The Gestalt Therapy Page
http://www.gestalt.org/index.htm

Gestalt Theory: Society for Gestalt Theory and Its Applications
www.enabling.org./ia/gestalt/gerhards/

CLASSROOM ACTIVITIES

1. Approximately 50 Gestalt institutes exist in the United States. With the help of your instructor or a librarian, locate as many of them as you can and find out what types of training programs they offer. If possible, interview a professional who practices Gestalt, and ask how he or she compares the Gestalt approach to other ways of counseling.
2. In a small group make a list of questions that people might direct to others, such as, "Why are you smiling?" Then convert the questions into statements, such as, "I see you are smiling." Note the differences in your group between questions and statements. Share your impressions with your classmates.

3. In a group of five discuss and then act out how a counselor and a client might devise an experiment to depict anger. How easy or difficult did you find this experiment? What advantages do you think an experiment like this has over a more formalized exercise? What are the disadvantages?

REFERENCES

Assagioli, R. (1965). *Psychosynthesis*. New York: Viking.

Bankart, C. P. (1997). *Talking cures*. Pacific Grove, CA: Brooks/Cole.

Bernard, J. M. (1986). Laura Perls: From ground to figure. *Journal of Counseling and Development, 64,* 367–373.

Corey, G. (2001). *Theory and practice of counseling and psychotherapy* (6th ed.). Pacific Grove, CA: Brooks/Cole.

Covin, A. B. (1977). Using Gestalt psychodrama experiments in rehabilitation counseling. *Personnel and Guidance Journal, 56,* 143–147.

Fagan, J. (1970). The task of the therapist. In J. Fagan & I. L. Shepherd (Eds.), *Gestalt therapy now* (pp. 88–106). Palo Alto, CA: Science and Behavior Books.

Fagan, J., & Shepherd, I. L. (1970). Theory of Gestalt therapy. In J. Fagan & I. L. Shepherd (Eds.), *Gestalt therapy now* (pp. 1–7). Palo Alto, CA: Science and Behavior Books.

Gelso, C. J., & Carter, J. A. (1985). The relationship in counseling and psychotherapy: Components, consequences, and theoretical antecedents. *Counseling Psychologist, 13,* 155–243.

Gilliland, B. E., & James, R. K. (1998). *Theories and strategies in counseling and psychotherapy* (4th ed.). Boston: Allyn & Bacon.

Glinnwater, J. T. (2000). Gestalt therapy: Treatment of the affective self. *Gestalt Journal, 23,* 81–97

Harman, R. L. (1975). A Gestalt point of view on facilitating growth in counseling. *Personnel and Guidance Journal, 53,* 363–366.

Harman, R. L. (1997). *Gestalt therapy techniques: Working with groups, couples, and sexually dysfunctional men.* Northvale, NJ: Aronson.

Hatcher, C., & Himelsteint, P. (Eds.). (1997). *The handbook of Gestalt therapy.* Northvale, NJ: Aronson.

Ivey, A. E., D'Andrea, M., Ivey, M. B., & Simek-Morgan, L. (2002). *Theories of counseling and psychotherapy* (5th ed.). Boston: Allyn & Bacon.

Kempler, W. (1973). Gestalt therapy. In R. Corsini (Ed.), *Current psychotherapies* (pp. 251–286). Itasca, IL: Peacock.

Levitsky, A., & Perls, F. S. (1970). The rules and games of Gestalt therapy. In J. Fagan & I. L. Shepherd (Eds.), *Gestalt*

therapy now (pp. 140–149). Palo Alto, CA: Science and Behavior Books.

Mackay, B. (2002). Effects of Gestalt therapy two-chair dialogue on divorce decision making. *Gestalt Review, 6,* 220–235.

Melnick, J. (2003). Making the learning last. *Gestalt Review, 7,* 1–4.

Passons, W. R. (1975). *Gestalt approaches to counseling.* New York: Holt, Rinehart, & Winston.

Perls, F. (1969). *Gestalt therapy verbatim.* Lafayette, CA: Real People Press.

Perls, F. (1970). Four lectures. In J. Fagan & I. L. Shepherd (Eds.), *Gestalt therapy now* (pp. 14–38). Palo Alto, CA: Science and Behavior Books.

Perls, F. (1972). *In and out of the garbage pail.* New York: Bantam.

Perls, F. (1976). *The Gestalt approaches and eye witnesses to therapy.* New York: Bantam.

Perls, F., Hefferline, R. F., & Goodman, P. (1951). *Gestalt therapy.* New York: Dell.

Polster, E., & Polster, M. (1973). *Gestalt therapy integrated: Contours of theory and practice.* New York: Brunner/Mazel.

Seligman, L. (1997). *Diagnosis and treatment planning in counseling.* New York: Plenum.

Sharf, R. S. (2004). *Theories of psychotherapy and counseling* (3rd ed.). Pacific Grove, CA: Brooks/Cole.

Simkin, J. S. (1975). An introduction to Gestalt therapy. In F. D. Stephenson (Ed.), *Gestalt therapy primer* (pp. 3–12). Springfield, IL: Thomas.

Thompson, C. D., Rudolph, L. B., & Henderson, D. (2004). *Counseling children* (6th ed.). Pacific Grove, CA: Brooks/Cole.

Yontef, G., & Jacobs, L. (2000). Gestalt therapy. In R. J. Corsini & D. Wedding (Eds.), *Current psychotherapies* (6th ed., pp. 303–339). Itasca, IL: F. E. Peacock.

Zerbetto, R., & Tantam, D. (2001). The Survey of European Psychotherapy Training 3: What psychotherapy is available in Europe? *European Journal of Psychotherapy, Counselling and Health, 4,* 397–405.

Zinker, J. (1978). *Creative process in Gestalt therapy.* New York: Random House.

Reality Therapy

CHAPTER 7

When I leave the office with a headache
I know I have done your work
and you are without a plan.
When I go home with a heartache
it is because I have seen you fail
to capture your dreams in reality.
Give me heartaches any day
for embedded in them is the pain
that often leads to change.

Note: "Headaches and Heartaches" by S. T. Gladding. Copyright 2003 by Samuel T. Gladding.

Reality therapy was formulated by William Glasser in the early 1960s. It began as a major theoretical approach in 1965 with the publication of Glasser's book *Reality Therapy* (1965). This approach emphasizes choices that people can make to change their lives and focuses on two general concepts: the environment necessary for conducting counseling and the procedures leading to change (Wubbolding, 1998). It is usually essential to establish a safe environment before change can occur.

Reality therapy is a flexible, friendly, and firm approach to working with clients, it is also action oriented. Overall, it emphasizes the fulfillment of psychological needs, the resolution of personal difficulties, and the prevention of future problems.

MAJOR THEORIST: WILLIAM GLASSER

William Glasser was born in Cleveland, Ohio, in 1925, the third and youngest child in a close-knit family. He describes his childhood as happy and uneventful but like his theory he does not emphasize the past. In school he played in the band and developed a strong interest in sports. After graduating at the age of 19 from the Case Institute of Technology with a degree in chemical engineering, he began graduate work in clinical psychology. He finished work for a master's degree in 1948, but his doctoral dissertation was rejected. He then entered medical school at Western Reserve University, graduating with a medical degree in 1953.

Glasser moved to California with his wife, Naomi Judith Silver, for a psychiatric residency at UCLA, which he completed in 1957. Although he hoped to establish a private psychiatric practice, he found that referrals were slow in coming because of his open resistance to traditional psychoanalytic treatment. Therefore, he took a position as head psychiatrist at the Ventura School for Girls, a state-operated facility for juvenile delinquents.

At Ventura in the 1960s Glasser began to formalize his approach to counseling. As a resident his doubts about the effectiveness of classical psychoanalysis had been supported by one of his faculty supervisors, G. L. Harrington. Harrington helped Glasser develop some of the basic tenets of reality therapy and even assisted Glasser in verifying these primary concepts. Glasser's first book, *Mental Health or Mental Illness?* (1961), contained many of the ideas that were later more formally expressed in *Reality Therapy: A New Approach to Psychiatry* (1965). Glasser developed reality therapy because he thought "conventional psychiatry wastes too much time arguing over how many diagnoses can dance at the end of a case history" (1965, p. 49). He wanted an approach that was practical and more easily understood by both clinicians and the public. By using the basic principles of reality therapy, he was able to cut recidivism at the Ventura School to only 20 percent.

Shortly after the publication of *Reality Therapy*, Glasser founded the Institute of Reality Therapy in Canoga Park, California, where he did some of his most creative work. He applied reality therapy to school settings in *Schools Without Failure* (1969) and to areas of identity in *The Identity Society* (1972). In *Positive Addiction* (1976) he asserted that individuals can become stronger instead of weaker from so-called addictive habits; for example, jogging and meditation improve physical and mental health.

In 1981 Glasser linked his original ideas with control theory, which argues that all behavior is generated internally. Thus, the only thing that people obtain from the outside world is information (Glasser, 1988). Two of Glasser's books, *Stations of the Mind* (1981) and *Control Theory: A New Explanation of How We Control Our Lives* (1984), reflect this theoretical stance and emphasize how the brain influences inner perceptions. However, Glasser abandoned control theory as a part of his approach in 1996 and incorporated choice theory in its place, asserting that people choose to be the way they are. This tenet is reflected in Glasser's most recent books.

VIEW OF HUMAN NATURE/PERSONALITY

Reality therapy does not include a comprehensive explanation of human development, as Freud's system does. Instead, it offers practitioners a focused view of some important aspects of human life and human nature. One major tenet of reality therapy is its focus on consciousness: human beings operate on a conscious level and are not driven by unconscious forces or instincts (Glasser, 1965, 1988).

A second belief about human nature is that a health/growth force exists within everyone (Glasser & Wubbolding, 1995). This force is manifested on two levels—the physical and the psychological. Physically, there is the need to obtain and use life-sustaining necessities such as food, water, and shelter. According to Glasser, human behavior was once controlled by the physical need for survival. He associates behaviors such as breathing, digesting, and sweating with physical, or *old-brain*, needs because they are automatically controlled by the body. In modern times most important behavior is associated with psychological, or *new-brain*, needs. The four primary psychological needs include the following:

- *Belonging*—the need for friends, family, and love
- *Power*—the need for self-esteem, recognition, and competition
- *Freedom*—the need to make choices and decisions
- *Fun*—the need for play, laughter, learning, and recreation (see Figure 7.1)

Associated with these psychological needs is the need for identity, that is, a psychologically healthy sense of self. Identity needs are met when a person is accepted by others. Especially important in this process is the experience of love and worth. When

FIGURE 7.1 Basic needs according to reality therapy

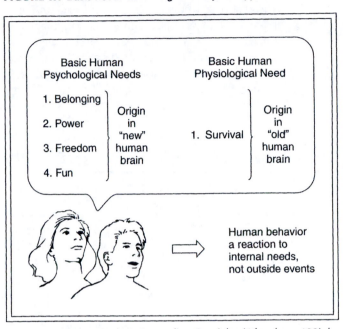

Note: From *Group Work: A Counseling Specialty* (4th ed., p. 402) by Samuel T. Gladding. Copyright 2003. Reprinted by permission of Pearson Education, Inc., Upper Saddle River, NJ.

these needs are met, people achieve a *success identity*; those whose needs are not met establish a *failure identity*, a maladjusted personality characterized by a lack of confidence and a tendency to give up easily. Because "almost everyone is personally engaged in a search for acceptance as a person rather than as a performer of a task," personal identity precedes performance (Glasser, 1972, p. 10).

In regard to identity Glasser thinks there are two critical periods in children's lives. First, between the ages of 2 and 5, children learn early socialization skills—such as how to relate to their parents, siblings, and friends—and they begin to deal with frustrations and disappointments. During this period children especially need the love, acceptance, guidance, and involvement of their parents. If that is not forthcoming, a child may begin to establish a failure identity. Second, between the ages of 5 and 10, children are involved with school, where they gain knowledge and self-concept. Many children establish a failure identity during this period because of socialization difficulties or learning problems (Glasser, 1969).

Reality therapy proposes that human learning is a lifelong process based on choice. If individuals do not learn something early in life, such as how to relate to others, they can choose to learn it later. In the process they may change their identity and the way they behave (Glasser & Wubbolding, 1995).

A final tenet of reality therapy is a new psychology of personal freedom called *choice theory* (Glasser, 1998, 2000). The idea is that people have mental images of their needs and behave accordingly; thus, individuals are ultimately self-determining (Glasser, 1984;

Wubbolding, 1994). Individuals can choose to be miserable or mentally disturbed; they may also choose to behave in positive ways and give up trying to control others. People who are mentally healthy are in noncontrolling relationships with significant others, such as a parent, a child, a spouse, or an employee/employer. They choose to "care, listen, support, negotiate, encourage, love, befriend, trust, accept, welcome, and esteem" rather than "coerce, force, compel, punish, reward, manipulate, boss, motivate, criticize, blame, complain, nag, badger, rank, rate, and withdraw" (Glasser, 1998, p. 21).

ROLE OF THE COUNSELOR/THERAPIST

Reality therapists serve primarily as teachers and models, accepting their clients in a warm, involved way and creating an environment in which counseling can take place. Therapists immediately seek to build relationships with clients by developing trust through friendliness, firmness, and fairness (Wubbolding, 1998, 2000). Counselors use *ing* verbs, such as *angering* or *bullying*, to describe clients' thoughts and actions. Thus, there is an emphasis on choice, on what clients choose to do. Counselor-client interactions focus on behaviors that clients would like to change and ways to go about achieving these desires. Positive, constructive actions are emphasized (Glasser, 1988), with special attention paid to metaphors and themes that clients verbalize.

There is little attempt in reality therapy to test, diagnose, interpret, or otherwise analyze clients' actions, except to ask questions such as, "What are you doing now?" "Is it working?" and "What are the consequences?" Reality therapists do not concentrate on early childhood experiences, clients' insights, aspects of the unconscious, mental illness, blame, or stimulus-response perception of interaction. They emphasize aspects of the clients' lives that can be controlled and little or no use is made of the latest edition of the *DSM*.

GOALS

The primary goal of reality therapy is to help clients become psychologically strong and rational and realize that they have choices in how they treat themselves and others. If this goal is reached, individuals become autonomous and responsible (Wubbolding, 1988, 1991; Wallace, 1986). Responsible behavior allows individuals to take charge of their actions and obtain their goals; it also keeps them from interfering with others or getting into trouble. In addition, it leads to the formation of a success identity, which enables clients to live more productive and harmonious lives. Glasser (1981) contends that to help people "we must help them gain strength to do worthwhile things with their lives and at the same time become warmly involved with the people they need" (p. 48). Reality therapy strives to prevent problems from occurring.

A second goal is to help clients clarify what they want in life; it is vital for individuals to be aware of their life goals if they are to act responsibly. In assessing goals, reality therapists help their clients examine personal assets as well as environmental supports and hindrances. It is then the responsibility of clients to choose behaviors that fulfill personal needs. Glasser (1976) lists six criteria with which to judge whether a person is choosing a suitable and healthy behavior.

1. The behavior is noncompetitive.
2. The behavior is easily completed without a great deal of mental effort.
3. The behavior can be done by oneself.
4. The behavior has value for the person.
5. The client believes that improvements in lifestyle will result from the behavior.
6. The client can practice the behavior without being self-critical.

Another goal of reality therapy is to help clients formulate a realistic plan to achieve personal needs and wishes. Poor mental health is sometimes the result of not knowing how to achieve what has been planned. Glasser advocates that plans be as specific and concrete as possible. Once a plan is formulated, alternative behaviors, decisions, and outcomes are examined; often a contract is written. The focus is on helping individuals become more responsible and realize that no single plan is absolute.

An additional goal of reality therapy is to have counselors establish meaningful relationships with their clients (Glasser, 1980, 1981). Such relationships are based on understanding, acceptance, empathy, and a willingness to express faith in a client's ability to change. Counselors help their clients establish boundaries for behaviors but do not give up on their clients if they are unable to complete a behavior. Often, to facilitate effective relationships, therapists risk disclosing personal information to clients.

Another goal of reality therapy is to focus on behavior and the present. Glasser (1988) believes that behavior—that is, thought and action—is interrelated with feeling and physiology. Thus, a change in behavior also brings about other positive changes. Basically, Glasser emphasizes now activities because they can be controlled by clients, who have no control over the past.

Finally, reality therapy aims to eliminate both fear of punishment and excuses from clients' lives. Clients often use the excuse that they cannot formulate and carry out a plan because they fear being punished by either their counselors or outside people if they fail. Reality therapy helps clients formulate new plans if old ones do not work. The emphasis is on planning, revision, and eventual success, regardless of setbacks. The entire procedure empowers clients and enables them to be more productive.

PROCESS AND TECHNIQUES

Reality therapy relies on action-oriented techniques that help clients realize that they have choices in how they respond to events and people and that others do not control them any more than they control others (Glasser, 1998). Some of the more effective and active techniques are teaching, employing humor, confronting, role playing, giving feedback, formulating specific plans, and making contracts.

Reality therapy relies heavily on teaching as a primary technique. Glasser (1965) states that "the specialized learning situation . . . is made up of three separate but interwoven procedures" (p. 21). First, there is involvement between counselors and clients in which clients begin to face reality and see that a behavior is unrealistic. Second, therapists reject the unrealistic behavior of their clients without rejecting the clients as persons. Finally, counselors teach clients better ways to fulfill needs within the confines of reality. One strategy that counselors use is *positiveness*, in which they talk about, focus on, and reinforce positive and constructive planning and behaving (Gilliland & James, 1998).

In reality therapy, humor is the ability to see the absurdity within a situation and view matters from a different and amusing perspective. It is an appropriate technique if used sparingly. Most clients do not instinctively see difficult situations as funny; yet if counselors offer a well-timed remark, clients may come to see some silliness in their behavior. The ability to laugh at oneself promotes the ability to change because the situation can be seen in a new and often insightful way. Never should humor be used as a sarcastic put-down, which would likely deteriorate the counseling relationship and adversely affect the process of change.

In confrontation, counselors challenge clients about certain behaviors as a way of helping clients accept responsibility for their actions. This procedure does not differ much from the confrontation used in other approaches. Role-playing in reality therapy is also similar to that employed in other counseling approaches. However, its purpose in reality therapy is to help clients bring the past or future into the present and assess how life will be different when they start behaving differently. Role plays are almost always followed by counselor feedback. After specific plans are formulated for improving their lives, clients develop contracts to carry out these plans in a timely and systematic way.

Reality therapy uses the *WDEP system* as a way of helping counselors and clients make progress. In this system the *W* stands for wants; at the beginning of the counseling process, counselors find out what clients want and what they have been doing to get it (Wubbolding, 1988, 1991, 2000). Counselors, in turn, share their wants for and perceptions of clients' situations. The *D* in WDEP involves clients' exploration of the direction of their lives. The effective and ineffective self-talk that clients use is discussed. Strategically incorporated in these two steps are establishing a relationship and focusing on present behavior.

The *E* in the WDEP process stands for evaluation, which is the cornerstone of reality therapy. In this procedure clients are helped to evaluate their behaviors and determine how responsible their personal behaviors are. Behaviors that do not contribute to meeting client needs often alienate clients from themselves and significant others. If clients recognize a behavior as unproductive, they may be motivated to change. But if there is no recognition, the therapeutic process may break down. It is crucial, therefore, that clients, not counselors, do the evaluation.

The final letter *P*, of the WDEP system stands for plan, which clients make to change behaviors. The plan stresses actions that clients will take, not behaviors that they will eliminate. The best plans are simple, attainable, measurable, immediate, and consistent (Wubbolding, 1998, 2000). They are also controlled by clients and are often supported by written contracts in which responsible alternatives are spelled out.

Clients are then requested to make a commitment to the action plans. Therapists make it clear that no excuses will be accepted for failing to carry out plans of action; neither will counselors blame or punish. Thus, responsibility is placed entirely on clients. If they fail to accomplish their plans, Glasser thinks they should suffer the natural or reasonable consequences of that failure (Evans, 1982).

According to Glasser (1965, 1980), counselors should not give up on their clients even if they fail to accomplish their goals. Instead, counselors should stubbornly and tenaciously encourage their clients to make new plans or revise old ones. Most clients, who are used to being put down or abandoned when goals are not achieved, find in Glasser's approach an opportunity to alter that cycle of failure.

MULTICULTURAL AND GENDER-SENSITIVE ISSUES

Reality therapy respects cultural differences. Clients "decide on the changes they wish to make that are consistent with their own cultural values" (Sharf, 2004, p. 431). Thus, reality therapy focuses on the responsibility of clients to themselves, others, and society. This emphasis puts it "in accord with Native American Indian and Asian and Asian-American value systems" (Ivey, D'Andrea, Ivey, & Simek-Morgan, 2002, pp. 220–221). In addition, reality therapy has actually been used with a wide range of people from varied cultures, including African-American, Korean, Latino, and Saudi Arabian. However, reality therapy "does not take into account environmental forces such as discrimination and racism that affect people from different cultures" (Sharf, 2004, p. 430).

In regard to gender issues, reality therapy emphasizes the empowerment of clients to make choices regardless of their gender. This approach may be especially good for men who are achievement oriented because it concentrates on specific plans and behaviors without broaching the area of feelings and emotions, which many men eschew. However, this therapy may be limited in what it can do for women because it does not advocate for social change or address societal ills, such as sexism.

EVALUATION OF THE THEORY

STRENGTHS AND CONTRIBUTIONS

First of all, reality therapy is versatile. It can be applied to many different disorders and populations; it is especially appropriate in treating conduct disorders, substance-abuse disorders, impulse-control disorders, personality disorders, and antisocial behavior. It can also be employed in individual counseling with children, adolescents, adults, and the aged as well as in group, marriage, and family counseling. This approach has such flexibility that it is helpful in almost any setting that emphasizes mental health and adjustment, such as hospitals, mental health clinics, schools, prisons, rehabilitation centers, and crisis centers (Glasser, 1986, 2000; Seligman, 1997).

A second advantage of reality therapy is its concreteness. Both counselors and clients are able to assess how much progress is being made and in what areas, especially if a goal-specific contract is drawn up. When clients are doing well in modifying one behavior but not another, increased attention can be given to the underdeveloped area.

Another advantage of reality therapy is that it promotes responsibility and freedom within individuals without blaming or criticizing or attempting to restructure entire personalities. To act in a responsible manner is "to fulfill one's needs, and to do so in a way that does not deprive others of the ability to fulfill their needs" (Glasser, 1965, p. 13). Many individuals need help in becoming responsible, and reality therapy provides this assistance.

Reality therapy also addresses the resolution of conflict. Glasser (1984) believes that conflict occurs on two levels, true and false. On the true level, conflict develops over interpersonal disagreements about change. In such cases no single solution exists, and people should expend their energy in other, nonconflict areas. In false conflict, however, such as losing weight, change is possible if persons are willing to give the effort. Responsible behavior in such situations can bring resolutions.

An additional strength of reality therapy is its stress on the present; current behavior is most amenable to clients' control. Reality therapists are not interested in the past.

Furthermore, reality therapy emphasizes short-term treatment. It is usually limited to a relatively few sessions, which focus on present behaviors. Clients work with conscious and verifiable objectives that can be achieved quickly. This approach is especially valuable in a time-limited, managed care environment.

One other strength of reality therapy is that it has national training centers. The Institute for Reality Therapy in Los Angeles and the Center for Reality Therapy in Cincinnati promote a uniform educational experience among practitioners employing this theory. The centers also publish professional literature.

Finally, reality therapy has contributed to counseling by successfully challenging the medical model of client treatment. The rationale and positive emphasis of this approach are refreshing alternatives to pathology-centered models (James & Gilliland, 2003).

LIMITATIONS AND CRITICISMS

By emphasizing so strongly the here and now of behavior, reality therapy tends to ignore other concepts, such as the unconscious and personal history. However, people may sometimes be informed by the unconscious, for example, in dreams; or persons may need to relive and resolve past traumas. Reality therapy makes little allowance for these situations.

A second limitation of reality therapy is its belief that all forms of mental illness are attempts to deal with external events (Glasser, 1984). Mental illness does not just happen, Glasser contends; persons choose mental illness to help control their world. Thus, Glasser ignores biology as a factor in mental illness, a stance considered by some critics to be naive and irresponsible.

Reality therapy is also criticized for being too simple because it has few theoretical constructs. Even though it is becoming more sophisticated by virtue of its link to choice theory, reality therapy does not deal with the full complexity of human life, preferring to ignore most developmental stages. Thus, its critics state that the theory behind the therapy lacks comprehensiveness.

Another limitation is that reality therapy is susceptible to becoming overly moralistic, a potential difficulty rather than a certain disadvantage. Glasser (1972) asserts that reality therapy was never intended to function in this way. Therapists who practice reality therapy are not to judge clients' behaviors; clients judge their own behaviors. The role of therapists is to support their clients in a personal exploration of values. Nonetheless, overzealous practitioners may impose their values on clients.

Yet another limitation of reality therapy is its dependence on establishing a good counselor-client relationship. Without sufficient involvement, counselors may settle for general client goals, force a plan, or proceed too quickly to commitment (Wubbolding, 1975).

A related limitation of reality therapy is its dependence on verbal interaction and two-way communication. As a consequence, it may falter in helping clients who, for any reason, cannot adequately express their needs, options, and plans (James & Gilliland, 2003).

Finally, reality therapy keeps changing its focus and emphasis, despite an initial denial of that charge by Glasser (1976). Acceptance is now emphasized more than it previously was. Furthermore, the integration of control theory and then its replacement by choice theory as the bedrock of the approach necessarily altered the theory's earlier focus. Thus far there has been no attempt to document these changes and to note which emphases are most essential to the practice, leaving reality therapy less well understood and utilized than it might otherwise be.

TREATING LINDA WITH REALITY THERAPY

CONCEPTUALIZATION

From the perspective of reality therapy Linda is avoiding making choices. She has let others decide for her, such as whether to have a baby. Thus, she has a number of excuses as to why her life has been relatively unproductive. In addition, Linda has not taken care of her psychological need for belonging, power, freedom, and fun. By neglecting these needs, Linda has taken on a failure identity.

However, Linda can choose to be different. She can choose to be in noncontrolling relationships with her family and friends. Furthermore, she can choose to take other constructive action and stop failing and depressing herself. If she makes these choices, Linda can become more autonomous, responsible, and successful. She can also clarify what she wants in life and find internal and external support for realistic pursuit of her goals. Thus, her mental health can improve, and she will be able to live in the present in a productive way.

TREATMENT PROCESS

As a reality therapist, you are active in Linda's treatment process. You base your work on a good, strong, and trusting client-counselor relationship. You try to teach her how she can reject unrealistic behaviors without rejecting herself or being rejected by you. And you reinforce her positive and constructive plans and behaviors.

You use humor with Linda as she gains insight into herself and sees the folly of her ways. However, you are mostly serious and confront Linda with the fact that she is responsible for her actions, especially now in the present. You role-play with her how she can act responsibly.

After you confront, you use the WDEP acronym to help Linda articulate her wants and the direction she wishes to travel. You help her evaluate behaviors that will contribute to her growth, and then you support her in formulating a plan for moving on. As a part of this process, you draw up a contract with Linda to help her see how she is carrying out her ambitions. Even though Linda has been discriminated against in the past and treated in sexist ways, you do not dwell on what has been or what might recur. Instead, you encourage and support her as she begins anew.

When Linda fails to carry out some part of her plan, such as returning to college, you do not blame or punish her. Instead, you help her formulate another plan. For Linda the ultimate achievement is to become more responsible and free and to accomplish that within a relatively brief period of time.

SUMMARY AND CONCLUSION

Reality therapy is an ever-evolving system of counseling that began with William Glasser in the 1960s. It focuses on present situations that clients wish to modify or change. Counselors work to establish collaborative relationships with their clients and use those relationships to help clients develop plans involving choices that are concrete and goal oriented. Excuses and blame are not a part of the process, and counselors do not give up on their clients.

Counselors use a number of techniques to help clients reach their goals. Besides strong relationships and persistence, counselors also teach, use humor, confront, and role-play with clients. Wubbolding's WDEP system—wants, direction, evaluation, plan—is sometimes used as a guide to help counselors evaluate what they need to do to help their clients be successful. If all goes well, clients become more focused and skilled in reaching realistic and productive goals.

SUMMARY TABLE: REALITY THERAPY

Major Theorists

William Glasser
Robert Wubbolding

View of Human Nature/Personality

A health/growth force in all individuals
Problems arise from failure to take responsibility for behavior
Lifelong learning
A need for love, worth, success, and control

Role of the Counselor/Therapist

Teacher and model
Collaborative relationship with client
Active, direct, practical, didactic style

Goals

Become psychologically strong and rational
Take responsibility
Clarify goals
Formulate a realistic plan, focused on behavior
Accept no punishment, offer no excuses
Develop new plans when needed

Process and Techniques

Help clients see choices
Use action-oriented techniques: teaching, employing humor, confronting,
    role-playing, giving feedback, formulating specific plans, making contracts
Use Wubbolding's *WDEP system*

Multicultural and Gender-Sensitive Issues

Respects cultural differences
Does not address environmental forces
Emphasizes the empowerment of clients
Does not deal with societal ills, such as sexism

Strengths and Contributions

Is versatile, concrete, short-term
Promotes responsibility and freedom
Addresses conflict resolution
Stresses the present
Has national training centers
Challenges medical model of client treatment

Limitations and Criticisms

Ignores some concepts (e.g., the unconscious and personal history)
Sees no biological aspect in mental illness
Has few theoretical constructs
Does not deal with full complexity of human life
Can become overly moralistic
Depends on good counselor-client relationship
Keeps changing focus

LEARNING MORE

Articles on the theory, research, and practice of reality therapy are found in a number of counseling and therapy publications. Probably the best journal devoted exclusively to reality therapy is published by the William Glasser Institute—*International Journal of Reality Therapy*.

That institute also maintains an international resource library, both at its headquarters in California and at Northeastern University in Boston.

For more information on reality therapy organizations and institutes, contact the following:

William Glasser Institute
22024 Lassen Street, Suite #118
Chatsworth, California 91311-3600
818-700-8000 or 800-899-0688
http://www.wglasser.com/

Center for Reality Therapy
7672 Montgomery Road
Cincinnati, Ohio 45236-4258
513-561-1911
http://home.fuse.net/3dtemplar/

William Glasser Institute Ireland
http://www.socc.ie/~wgii/whatirti.htm

CLASSROOM ACTIVITIES

1. Discuss with another classmate how you meet each of the four primary psychological needs in your life—belonging, power, freedom, and fun.
2. Write down what you think of choice theory and the idea that we choose how we are and how we behave. How do you see choice theory working in your life? What do you think are the weaknesses in choice theory?
3. Explore the Web sites mentioned in this text for training in reality therapy. How do they compare? What do you see as the strengths and limitations of each center?

REFERENCES

Evans, D. (1982). What are you doing? An interview with William Glasser. *Personnel and Guidance Journal, 60,* 460–464.

Gilliland, B. E., & James, R. K. (1998). *Theories and strategies in counseling and psychotherapy* (4th ed.). Boston: Allyn & Bacon.

Glasser, W. (1961). *Mental health or mental illness.* New York: Harper & Row.

Glasser, W. (1965). *Reality therapy: A new approach to psychiatry.* New York: Harper & Row.

Glasser, W. (1969). *Schools without failure*. New York: Harper & Row.

Glasser, W. (1972). *The identity society*. New York: Harper & Row.

Glasser, W. (1976). *Positive addiction*. New York: Harper & Row.

Glasser, W. (1980). Reality therapy: An explanation of the steps of reality therapy. In W. Glasser (Ed.), *What are you doing? How people are helped through reality therapy*. New York: Harper & Row.

Glasser, W. (1981). *Stations of the mind*. New York: Harper & Row.

Glasser, W. (1984). *Control theory: A new explanation of how we control our lives*. New York: Harper & Row.

Glasser, W. (1986). *Control theory in the classroom*. New York: Harper & Row.

Glasser, W. (1988). Reality therapy. Workshop presented at the Alabama Association for Counseling and Development, Fall Conference, November, Birmingham.

Glasser, W. (1998). *Choice theory*. New York: HarperCollins.

Glasser, W. (2000). *Counseling with choice theory*. New York: HarperCollins.

Glasser, W., & Wubbolding, R. (1995). Reality therapy. In R. Corsini & D. Wedding (Eds.), *Current psychotherapies* (5th ed., pp. 293–321). Itasca, IL: Peacock.

Ivey, A. E., D'Andrea, M., Ivey, M. B., & Simek-Morgan, L. (2002). *Theories of counseling and psychotherapy* (5th ed.). Boston: Allyn & Bacon.

James, R. K., & Gilliland, B. E. (2003). *Theories and strategies in counseling and psychotherapy* (5th ed.). Boston: Allyn & Bacon.

Seligman, L. (1997). *Diagnosis and treatment planning in counseling*. New York: Plenum.

Sharf, R. S. (2004). *Theories of psychotherapy and counseling* (3rd ed.). Pacific Grove, CA: Brooks/Cole.

Wallace, W. A. (1986). *Theories of counseling and psychotherapy*. Boston: Allyn & Bacon.

Wubbolding, R. E. (1975). Practicing reality therapy. *Personnel and Guidance Journal, 53*, 164–165.

Wubbolding, R. E. (1988). *Using reality therapy*. New York: HarperCollins.

Wubbolding, R. E. (1991). *Understanding reality therapy*. New York: HarperCollins.

Wubbolding, R. E. (1994). The early years of control theory: Forerunners Marcus Aurelius & Norbert Wiener. *Journal of Reality Therapy, 13*, 51–54.

Wubbolding, R. E. (1996). *Basic concepts of reality therapy*. Los Angeles: Institute for Control Theory, Reality Therapy and Quality Management.

Wubbolding, R. E. (1998). *Cycle of managing, supervising, counseling, and coaching using reality therapy*. Cincinnati: Center for Reality Therapy.

Wubbolding, R. E. (2000). *Reality therapy for the 21st century*. Philadelphia: Brunner-Routledge.

CHAPTER 8

Behavioral Therapy

She was lonely so she cut herself
  to get her friends' attention,
He was scared so he hit someone
  and now he has detention,
Neither one knew what to do
  so they did their best,
The trouble is now they wear labels:
  "Different from the rest!"

Note: "Different" by S. T. Gladding. Copyright 2003 by Samuel T. Gladding.

Behavioral theories and the origins of behavioral therapy date back to the beginning of the 20th century. They focused on how to reinforce, extinguish, or modify a broad range of behaviors. Over the years these approaches have become very popular because people who seek counseling often have difficulties that are due to a behavioral deficit or excess or to a repertoire of inappropriate behaviors.

The term *behavioral* encompasses a wide range of ideas, practices, and theories. In its infancy (1900s–1930s), behaviorism was concerned almost entirely with external observations and was promoted as a scientific approach to the study of human life. The first major advocate for behaviorism was John B. Watson (1913, 1925), who used his work with a child named Little Albert to demonstrate that human emotions are amenable to conditioning (Watson & Raynor, 1920). After World War I, behaviorist ideas were explored by researchers such as Mary Cover Jones (1924), who demonstrated how a process known as counterconditioning can be employed to help people overcome phobic reactions.

In the 1940s and 1950s behaviorism achieved even more prominence. In this time period behavioral therapists were seen as scientific practitioners who based their work on research. Prominent scientist-practitioners included B. F. Skinner (1953) and his work in operant conditioning, Joseph Wolpe (1958) and his study of respondent conditioning, Hans Eysenck (1960) and his treatment of abnormal behavior, and Albert Bandura (Bandura & Walters, 1963) and his study of the effects of vicarious learning. During the 1950s the term *behavior therapy* was introduced to describe diverse behavioral approaches to resolving client problems (Yates, 1970).

John Krumboltz (1966) is credited as being one of the major personalities to popularize behaviorism in counseling. He drew upon Bandura's earlier work and revolutionized the counseling profession (Hosford, 1980). Krumboltz's ideas, as well as behaviorism in general, gained widespread acceptance in the 1970s. By the late 1980s behavioral approaches to therapy had generally split into three main theories: the stimulus-response model, applied behavior analysis, and social-cognitive theory.

This chapter examines the dominant forms of behavioral counseling approaches, except cognitive-behaviorism, which is covered in the next chapter. As a school of thought, behaviorists "stress instrumental rationality, control over emotions, enhanced human liberty, efficiency in ways of achieving self-defined goals, and opposition to irrational authority or arbitrary privilege" (Christopher, 1996, pp. 19–20).

MAJOR THEORIST: B. F. SKINNER

B. F. (Burrhus Frederick) Skinner was born in Susquehanna, Pennsylvania, in 1904. He was the older of two sons, but his younger brother died at the age of 16. Skinner's home environment was warm, comfortable, and stable, imbued with the virtues of small-town, middle-class America at the turn of the century (Skinner, 1976). His parents did not use corporal punishment.

Skinner's father, a wealthy attorney, wanted his son to become an attorney also; but Skinner showed skills in other areas, such as an early facility with mechanical devices. The young Skinner made roller skate scooters, blow guns, model airplanes, and a flotation system to separate green from ripe elderberries (Skinner, 1967). These inventions were precursors of later devices, such as the infant air crib and the Skinner Box. Skinner was also interested in animal behavior and was highly impressed by a troupe of performing pigeons at a country fair. He later used pigeons to demonstrate aspects of his theory, teaching them to do a variety of tasks. In addition, Skinner enjoyed music and played the saxophone in a jazz band.

As a young adult, Skinner wanted to be a writer. He majored in English literature at Hamilton College, where he earned Phi Beta Kappa honors and graduated in 1926. Back home he set about the task of writing, having been encouraged in his efforts by Robert Frost. After a year he moved to New York's Greenwich Village to live among writers and benefit from a stimulating environment. There he discovered the works of Ivan Pavlov and John B. Watson, as well as those of Bertrand Russell and Francis Bacon. Soon he gave up his writing ambitions to become a psychologist, although he had never taken a psychology course in college. He was accepted for graduate study at Harvard, where he received a master's degree in 1930 and a Ph.D. in 1931. After another 5 years of postdoctoral training, he joined the faculty of the University of Minnesota in 1936, the same year in which he married Yvonne Blue.

Skinner's first book, *The Behavior of Organisms* (1938), was followed by other major works, and he rapidly developed a national reputation. He left Minnesota for the University of Indiana in 1945, where he chaired the department of psychology until he returned to Harvard in 1948. At Indiana he wrote perhaps his most influential book, *Walden Two* (1948), which describes a utopian society functioning without punishment and following the principles of learning.

The writing process itself was a remarkable experience for Skinner, filled with much emotion (Elms, 1981). At Harvard he was prolific. His best book on theory, *Science and Human Behavior* (1953), was published while he was there; it describes how learning principles can be applied to all areas of society. *Beyond Freedom and Dignity* (1971), also influential, outlined the steps necessary for civilization to survive and flourish. In the early 1980s Skinner wrote about how behavioral principles could be applied to problems of the aged (Skinner & Vaughan, 1983).

Overall, Skinner can be classified as a behavioral determinist because of his emphasis on learning as the primary determinant of human actions. He died at the age of 86 on August 18, 1990, a much admired and respected pioneer in the helping professions (Fowler, 1990).

VIEW OF HUMAN NATURE/PERSONALITY

Despite the great diversity of thought among behaviorists, certain characteristics are basic to their overall view of human nature and the development of personality. Rimm and Cunningham (1985) list some commonalities that behaviorists share.

- Behaviorists assume that all behavior is learned, whether it is adaptive or maladaptive.
- Behaviorists believe that learning can be effective in changing maladaptive behavior or acquiring new behavior.
- Behaviorists reject the idea that the human personality is composed of traits.

As mentioned earlier, the three main approaches in contemporary behavioral therapy are the stimulus-response model, applied behavior analysis, and social-cognitive theory. These ways of learning are used by all organisms, although only human learning is addressed here.

THE STIMULUS-RESPONSE MODEL

The stimulus-response (S-R) model applies *classical conditioning,* sometimes called *respondent learning.* In this model the person need not be an active participant to learn because learning occurs through the association of two stimuli, also known as the *conditioning of involuntary responses.*

The best-known example of S-R learning is Pavlov's famous experiments with his laboratory dogs. Pavlov found that when a dog's food was paired with the sound of a bell, the dog would associate the bell with food and would begin to salivate in response to the bell before the food was served. The bell, initially a neutral stimulus, became a conditioned, or learned, stimulus (CS) because of its association with an unconditioned, or natural, stimulus (UCS), that is, the food. Salivating at the sound of the bell became a conditioned, or learned, response (CR), as opposed to the uncond-itioned response (UCR) of naturally salivating when presented with food. S-R learning in this case is represented in the following sequence (Holden, 1993b):

CS does not initially elicit CR
UCS elicits UCR
CS + UCS elicit UCR
 CS + UCS presented simultaneously or
 CS followed immediately by UCS
CS + UCS repeated several times
CS elicits CR

In a similar way many human emotions, such as phobias, arise because of paired associations. For example, a person may have an accident after eating a certain food. The association of the food with the accident, even though the two are unrelated, may result in that person's eventual fear or avoidance of the food. Clients often associate feelings with certain events and vice versa. The sound of music, the smell of certain odors, the sight of certain colors, and the touch of a stranger are experiences to which individuals may react emotionally because of S-R learning. Once learned, these associations can be unlearned and replaced in a process known as *counterconditioning*.

APPLIED BEHAVIOR ANALYSIS

Applied behavior analysis, "a direct extension of Skinner's (1953) radical behaviorism" (Wilson, 1995, p. 198), is based on operant conditioning. According to that theory, learning occurs only when a person is involved as an active participant with the environment. *Operant conditioning*—along with its successor, applied behavior analysis—focuses primarily on how individuals operate in the environment. In general, the idea is that a person learns to discriminate between behaviors that bring rewards and those that do not and is then likely to increase behavior that is rewarded and decrease behavior that is either punished or not reinforced. Thus, "applied behavior analysis makes use of reinforcement, punishment, extinction, stimulus control, and other procedures derived from laboratory research" (Wilson, 1995, p. 198).

Skinner's (1953) basic premise is the foundation on which applied behavior analysis is built: when a certain behavior is followed closely by a reinforcer, or reward, chances increase that the behavior will recur in similar or identical circumstances. Thus, individuals do not shape their environments as much as they are shaped by them through rewards and punishments. In other words, the consequences of a behavior determine whether that behavior will be learned or repeated.

SOCIAL-COGNITIVE THEORY

In social-cognitive learning, people acquire new knowledge and behavior by observing other people and events without engaging in the behavior themselves and without any direct consequences to themselves. Synonyms for social-cognitive theory include *observational learning, imitation, social modeling*, and *vicarious learning*.

"The social-cognitive approach depends on the theory that behavior is based on three separate but interacting regulatory systems (Bandura, 1986). They are (a) external stimulus events, (b) external reinforcement, and (c) cognitive mediational processes" (Wilson, 1995, p. 198). In social-cognitive learning "the behavior of an individual or a group, the model, acts as a stimulus for similar thoughts, attitudes, or behavior on the part of another individual who observes" (Perry & Furukawa, 1980, p. 131). Learning to drive a car, use the correct fork at a dinner party, give oneself positive messages, and react appropriately to a new client are often learned in this way. Learning through social-cognitive processes emphasizes the self-regulation of behavior and deemphasizes the importance of external reinforcers. Thus, learning may be independent of reinforcement (Hergenhahn & Olson, 2003). The advantages of social-cognitive learning are many, but chief among them is saving time, energy, and effort in acquiring new skills. In addition, social-cognitive theory is easily administered and is directed toward positive behavioral change. It is visually appealing and is of little or no risk to clients.

Bandura (1969) finds that models closest to the observer's age, gender, race, and attitude have the greatest impact. Live models, symbolic models (i.e., those on films and videos), and multiple models (i.e., groups of people) are equally effective in producing desired behavior change. In addition, covert models are quite effective, whereby a client imagines a model performing a socially desired activity (Cautela, 1976).

ROLE OF THE COUNSELOR/THERAPIST

Behaviorists concentrate on behavioral processes, that is, processes closely associated with overt behavior. Counselors who take a behavioral approach help clients learn new, appropriate ways of acting or modify or eliminate excessive actions; adaptive behaviors replace those that are maladaptive. Generally, behaviorally based counselors are active in counseling sessions and serve as learning specialists (Krumboltz, 1966) so that clients can learn, unlearn, or relearn specific ways of behaving. In this process counselors function as consultants, teachers, advisers, reinforcers, and facilitators (James & Gilliland, 2003). They may also instruct or supervise support people in a client's environment who are assisting in the change process. An effective behavioral counselor operates from a broad perspective, involving the client in every phase of the counseling. Counselors who are oriented toward social-cognitive learning serve as models for emulation, whereas those who lean toward S-R or applied approaches are more direct and prescriptive in offering assistance.

Counselors using a behavioral approach differ widely in their use of psychological tests and diagnoses. Most employ some form of client assessment device, but often these instruments measure behavior and action. Rarely do counselors use paper-and-pencil personality tests. For diagnosis they describe clients according to the behaviors they display, many of which are listed in the *DSM*.

GOALS

Behaviorists focus on changing, modifying, or eliminating behaviors; they set up well-defined therapy goals with their clients. Basically, behavioral counselors want to help clients achieve personal and professional objectives that are definable. Thus, the focus is on helping clients acquire healthy, constructive ways of acting. Just eliminating a behavior is not enough; unproductive actions must be replaced with productive responses.

In reaching mutually agreed-upon goals, counselors and clients follow four specific steps (Blackham & Silberman, 1979):

1. *Define the problem.* If a problem is to be solved, it must be stated concretely. Therefore, clients are asked to specify when, where, how, and with whom the problem arises. Counselors may benefit from actually observing the problem behavior.

2. *Take a developmental history.* It is useful for both clients and counselors to know whether the presenting problem is organically based and how clients have handled past circumstances.

3. *Establish specific goals.* Behavioral therapists help clients break down goals into small, achievable units. Counselors also set up learning experiences for clients to develop any needed skills (Krumboltz & Thoresen, 1976). For example, if a woman wishes to complete college, she must first select and then pass courses during a school term. She may also need to learn new study habits and new ways of interrelating with others, such as roommates.

4. *Determine the best methods for change.* Usually several behavioral methods can help clients reach desired goals. If one method does not work, it can be modified, or a new one can be generated and tried. Continual assessment of the effectiveness of methods is critical.

In general, behavioral counselors specialize in helping clients learn how to set up and achieve specific goals and the subgoals that go with them. Counselors are concrete, objective, and collaborative in their work in order to help clients define and reach the goals they are seeking.

PROCESS AND TECHNIQUES

Behavioral therapy is a process; it takes time and dedication. Accentuating, eliminating, adding, or modifying behaviors requires a collaborative effort between therapist and client. Behaviorists concentrate on the here and now as opposed to the then and there of behavior. Therefore, they focus on presenting symptoms and concerns and ways in which they can be immediately treated.

Behavioral counselors have at their disposal some of the best-researched and most-effective counseling techniques available. They stress the importance of obtaining empirical evidence and scientific support for any techniques they use. A sample of behavioral procedures is discussed here, although behaviorally oriented publications offer many additional techniques.

GENERAL BEHAVIORAL TECHNIQUES

General behavioral techniques are applicable to all behavioral theories, although a given technique may be more applicable to a particular approach at a given time or in a specific circumstance.

Use of Reinforcers.   *Reinforcers* are those events that, when they follow a behavior, increase the probability of the behavior's recurring. A *positive reinforcer* is valued and considered pleasurable by the person affected. Certain events and objects frequently serve in this capacity, such as social recognition, money, and food. A *negative reinforcer* is an aversive stimulus, the removal of which is contingent upon performance of a

desired action; that removal is reinforcing for the person involved. For example, when a mother nags her son until he washes the dishes, the nagging could be viewed as a negative reinforcer, especially if the son values peace. In behavioral counseling, positive reinforcers are used more frequently than negative ones.

A reinforcer may also be either primary or secondary. A *primary reinforcer* is one that is valued intrinsically, such as food. A *secondary reinforcer*—for example, money or some other token—acquires its value by being associated with a primary reinforcer. Clients know best what activities or items are most reinforcing for them.

Schedules of Reinforcement. When a behavior is first being learned, it should be reinforced every time it occurs—that is, by *continuous reinforcement*. After a behavior is established, however, it should be reinforced less frequently—that is, by *intermittent reinforcement. Schedules of reinforcement* operate according to either *ratio* (the number of responses between reinforcers) or *interval* (the length of time between reinforcers). Both ratio and interval schedules are either fixed or variable. A *fixed-ratio schedule* delivers reinforcement based on the number of responses made, for instance, being paid for the number of items produced. A *fixed-interval schedule* occurs on a regular time schedule, such as a salary payment every 2 weeks. A *variable-ratio schedule* offers reinforcement irregularly, as a slot machine does, but averages out to a given figure. A *variable-interval schedule* follows an irregular time schedule so that reinforcement takes place unpredictably; for example, the boss might congratulate an employee twice in one day and then not again for a month. A counselor who knows what type of schedule a client prefers can set up reinforcers accordingly.

Shaping. *Shaping* occurs when behavior is learned gradually in steps through successive approximation. When clients are learning new skills, counselors may help break down behavior into manageable units. Clients may actually practice a behavior or may imagine doing more of a task than they had previously done (i.e., focused imagery). Before undertaking shaping, however, counselors and clients need to be aware of the specific response sequence they wish to establish—that is, what follows what and how, a process known as *chaining.* When carefully planned, such a procedure usually leads to new or improved behaviors.

Generalization. *Generalization* involves the display of behaviors in environments other than those in which the behaviors were originally learned. Generalizing behaviors and transferring them to another setting require a number of procedures, including the assignment of behavioral homework, training significant others to reinforce appropriate behaviors, and consulting with clients about particular problems in making behavioral switches (Rose, 1983).

Maintenance. *Maintenance* is defined as consistent performance of desired actions without depending on anyone else for support. Maintenance emphasizes increasing a clients' self-control and self-management (Thoresen & Mahoney, 1974). When clients learn to modify their own behaviors, self-monitoring occurs in two related processes: self-observation and self-recording (Goldiamond, 1976). *Self-observation* requires that clients notice particular behaviors that they exhibit; *self-recording* focuses on keeping track of these behaviors. Self-monitoring interferes with learned habits by having clients count the occurrences of specific behaviors, which are normally done without thought. Such self-monitoring increases client awareness of targeted behaviors and the ways in which they occur. In the management of weight control, for example, individuals monitor their calorie intake and their reactions to eating certain foods.

Extinction. *Extinction* is the elimination of a behavior by withdrawal of its reinforcement. Few individuals continue doing something that is not rewarding. For example, when clients are no longer reinforced for talking about the past, they stop bringing it up. Thus, talking about that subject has disappeared and is said to be extinct.

Punishment. *Punishment* presents an aversive stimulus in order to suppress or eliminate a behavior. A counselor might punish a client with a critical statement, such as, "I don't want to hear you talk like that." Usually, however, behavior therapists do not use punishment in their treatment of clients. Holden (1993a) identifies the differences in behavioral consequences, which are summarized in Table 8.1.

SPECIFIC BEHAVIORAL TECHNIQUES

Specific behavioral techniques are refined behavioral methods that combine general techniques in precise ways. They are found in different behavioral approaches but are used only after rapport and trust have been established between counselors and clients.

Behavioral Rehearsal. *Behavioral rehearsal* consists of practicing a desired behavior until it is performed in the way a client wishes (Lazarus, 1985). The process involves gradually shaping a behavior and getting corrective feedback. It is frequently used

TABLE 8.1	Use of Pleasurable Stimulus	Use of Aversive Stimulus	Effect
The effect of behavioral consequences on behavior	Positive reinforcement (response followed quickly by pleasurable stimulus)	Negative reinforcement (response followed quickly by termination of aversive stimulus or response precludes aversive stimulus)	Increased rate or strength of response
	Extinction (response no longer followed by pleasurable stimulus)	Punishment (response followed quickly by aversive stimulus)	Decreased rate or strength of response

Note: From *Counseling: A Comprehensive Profession* (4th ed., p. 267) by Samuel T. Gladding. Copyright 2000. Reprinted by permission of Pearson Education, Inc., Upper Saddle River, NJ.

after clients have viewed a model enacting the desired behavior. In such cases, especially with complex behavior, clients who wish to acquire the behavior will practice in a counselor's presence what they have observed. Clients then receive feedback and suggestions and make modifications accordingly. Clients also receive homework designed to help them practice the new behavior outside the counselor's office. Practice in real-life conditions often leads to success and generalization; if not, modifications can be made during the next counseling session (Kipper, 1986). Behavioral rehearsal is sometimes called *role-playing* because clients are practicing new roles. Improvisational role-playing of new behavior is an effective mechanism for change (Zimbardo & Leippe, 1991).

Environmental Planning. In *environmental planning* a client sets up part of the environment to promote or limit certain behaviors (Krasner & Ullmann, 1973). For example, if a client associates painful memories with a certain place, a daily schedule might be designed to avoid that setting. Similarly, to control a situation and therefore promote desirable interaction, a client might arrange a room or chairs in a certain way.

Systematic desensitization. *Systematic desensitization* is designed to help clients overcome anxiety in particular situations. Clients are asked first to describe a situation that causes anxiety and then to rank this situation and related events on a hierarchical scale, from aspects that cause no concern (0) to those that are most troublesome (100) (see Table 8.2). The higher up the scale an event or situation is, the more anxious clients are about it. To help clients avoid anxiety and face situations, counselors teach them to relax physically or mentally. Then the hierarchy is reviewed, starting with low-anxiety items. When clients' anxieties begin to mount, they are helped to relax again. The underlying

TABLE 8.2	Amount of Anxiety (%)	Event
Joe's anxiety hierarchy	90	Relating to my spouse
	85	Relating to my in-laws
	80	Relating to my newborn child
	75	Relating to my dad
	70	Relating to my mother
	65	General family relations and responsibilities
	60	Being a project manager at work
	50	Work in general
	40	Coming to counseling
	35	Personal finances
	20	Having fun (being spontaneous)
	10	Going to sleep

Note: From *Counseling: A Comprehensive Profession* (5th ed., p. 217) by Samuel T. Gladding. Copyright 2004. Reprinted by permission of pearson Education, Inc., Upper Saddle River, NJ.

idea is that people cannot feel anxious and relaxed at the same time, a phenomenon called *reciprocal inhibition* (Wolpe, 1958).

Assertiveness training. The major tenet of *assertiveness training* is that people should be free to express thoughts and feelings appropriately without feeling undue anxiety (Alberti & Emmons, 1996). The technique consists of counterconditioning anxiety and reinforcing assertiveness. Clients are taught that everyone has the right, not the obligation, of self-expression. Clients then learn the differences among aggressive, passive, and assertive actions. Clients tell their counselors at the beginning of the counseling relationship what their objectives are, such as being able to speak out at public meetings. Counselors then give their clients feedback, both positive and negative, about present behaviors. The next steps involve modeling the desired behaviors and having clients role-play them. Counselors reinforce these behaviors and help shape their clients' actions. Finally, clients receive homework to be completed between sessions (Bellack & Hersen, 1998). Assertive behaviors should be shaped gradually to keep clients encouraged and on track. The objective is for individuals to feel good about their ability to express themselves, not for them to become aggressive and manipulative.

Contingency Contracts. *Contingency contracts* spell out the behaviors to be performed, changed, or discontinued; the rewards associated with the achievement of these goals; and the conditions under which rewards are to be received. Most often contracts are used with children rather than adults, who may find them offensive (see Figure 8.1). The contracts are frequently written out as quasi-formal documents.

Implosion and Flooding. *Implosive therapy* involves desensitizing clients to a situation by having them imagine an anxiety-producing situation that may have dire consequences, without having been taught to relax first (as in systematic desensitization). This technique should not be used by beginning counselors or with clients who

FIGURE 8.1 Contingency contract

	make bed	clean room	hang up clothes	pick up toys	set table	read a book	Goal
George	✓	✓		✓	✓	✓	Pizza
Will		✓		✓			Baseball game
Ann	✓	✓	✓	✓	✓	✓	Spend-the-night party

Contingency Contract
week one
(must earn 5 points for a reward)

Note: From *Family Therapy: History, Theory, and Practice* (3rd ed., p. 183) by Samuel T. Gladding. Copyright 2002. Reprinted by permission of Pearson Education, Inc., Upper Saddle River, NJ.

have heart conditions. In *flooding*, which is less traumatic, the imagined anxiety-producing scene does not have dire consequences. Instead, clients are overwhelmed with images of anxiety-producing stimuli.

Aversive Techniques. Although most behaviorists recommend that positive techniques be employed first, sometimes it is necessary to use *aversive techniques*, such as punishment. Such techniques, which vary in their severity, are useful when one behavior must be eliminated before another can be taught. *Time-out* separates clients, usually children, from the opportunity to receive positive reinforcement. It is a mild aversive technique that requires careful monitoring and is most effective when employed for short periods of time, such as 5 minutes. One example is separating a child from classmates when he or she misbehaves. *Overcorrection* is a technique in which clients first restore the environment to its natural state and then make it better. For example, children who throw food in the lunchroom might be required to clean up their mess and then wax the floor. *Covert sensitization* eliminates undesirable behavior by associating it with unpleasantness. It is used in treating clients who have problems with smoking, obesity, substance abuse, and sexual deviation.

In the long run, aversive stimuli are usually not effective by themselves:

- their negative emotional effects soon dissipate
- they may interfere with the learning of desired behaviors
- they may encourage escape, which, when successful, becomes a positive reinforcement

Furthermore, ethical and legal concerns are associated with all aversive techniques. Before administering them, counselors and therapists should obtain written permission for their use, especially if minors are involved.

MULTICULTURAL AND GENDER-SENSITIVE ISSUES

Like most approaches, behavioral therapy has strengths and weaknesses when it comes to working with clients from cultures that differ from that of the counselor. A behavioral approach may help clients be more specific about what they want to do within their subcultures and larger cultural groups. Thus, clients in a behavioral orientation may define more precisely the behaviors that are oppressive for them and may then be better able to address these behaviors, especially if they learn new ways of responding. The drawback to such work, however, is that counselors must become even more attuned to culture-specific behaviors and ways to address them appropriately.

In regard to gender, behavior therapy "terms and techniques are free of reference to gender" (Sharf, 2004, p. 310). In addition, the behavioral approach allows clients to acquire new skills that may enhance their status across gender lines. Observational learning may be especially powerful in helping clients make changes related to nontraditional gender-role behavior, such as that involved in careers (Bussey & Bandura, 1999).

EVALUATION OF THE THEORY

STRENGTHS AND CONTRIBUTIONS

Behavioral therapy works well with clients who are predominantly goal and action oriented, with a need for achievement and results. It is also a good approach with clients who are interested in changing either a discrete response or a limited number of behaviors.

A second strength of behavioral therapy is that it deals directly with symptoms; it is objective in defining and addressing problems. Thus, it demystifies the process of counseling and makes it possible for clients and outside evaluators to assess levels of change in a measurable way. Moreover, by working directly with symptoms, counselors are often able to assist clients immediately. Because behavioral approaches focus on the here and now, clients do not have to examine the past to obtain help in the present, thus saving time and money.

Another positive aspect of behavioral counseling is its appropriateness in working with certain disorders, for example, attention deficit disorders, conduct disorders, eating disorders, substance abuse disorders, psychosexual dysfunction, impulse control disorders, and phobic disorders (Seligman, 1997). Behavioral approaches are also useful in addressing difficulties associated with anxiety, stress, assertiveness, parenting, and social interaction (Hackney & Cormier, 2002; Seligman, 1997).

In addition, behavioral therapy offers numerous techniques for counselors to use. Behavioral techniques, which more than doubled from 1969 to 1976, continue to increase. And therapists can employ these techniques in numerous settings, including institutions such as mental hospitals or sheltered workshops. Many behaviorally oriented counseling journals are also available, such as the *Journal of Applied Behavior Analysis*.

Yet another strength of behavioral therapy is that it is based on learning theory, which is a well-formulated way of documenting how new behaviors are acquired (Krumboltz & Thoresen, 1976; Thoresen, 1969). Furthermore, learning theory continues to evolve and generate pragmatic applications for treatment in a wide variety of areas (Rescorla, 1988).

Behavioral therapy is also buttressed by the Association for the Advancement of Behavior Therapy (AABT), which publishes ethical guidelines for its members (Azrin, Stuart, Risely, & Stolz, 1977). The AABT promotes the practice of and education about behavioral counseling methods, while protecting the public from unscrupulous practitioners.

Finally, behaviorism is supported by exceptionally good research on how techniques and processes affect the process of counseling. Thus, novice counselors can follow one of many research designs. A common denominator among all behavioral approaches is a commitment to objectivity and evaluation.

LIMITATIONS AND CRITICISMS

Behavioral therapy does not deal with the total person, just with explicit behaviors. Critics contend that many behaviorists, such as B. F. Skinner, have taken the person out of personality and replaced it with an emphasis on laws that govern actions in specific environments. This emphasis may be too simplistic in explaining complex human interaction (Hergenhahn & Olson, 2003).

A second criticism is that behaviorism is sometimes applied mechanically. Goldstein (1973) notes that "the most common error of neophyte behavior therapists is to start employing techniques too quickly" (p. 221). Even though most behaviorists are careful to establish rapport with their clients and make counseling a collaborative effort, those who do not initially stress the counselor-client relationship have hurt the approach's image.

A third limitation of the behavioral approach is that it is best demonstrated under controlled conditions that are difficult to replicate in normal counseling situations. Implicit in this criticism is an uneasiness that much of behavioral theory has been formulated using other animal forms, such as rats and pigeons. Many counselors wonder whether a behavioral approach can work with human clients who operate in less than ideal environments.

Another weakness of behaviorism is that techniques may be ahead of theory (Thoresen & Coates, 1980). A proliferation of new methods has been generated by behavioral counselors, yet the theory that should underlie these methods has not kept pace.

Yet another criticism is that behaviorism ignores clients' past histories and unconscious forces. Although it may work quite well with someone who clearly has a behavioral concern, those who wish to resolve past issues or deal with insight from the unconscious may not be helped.

A related concern is that behaviorism does not consider developmental stages (Sprinthall, 1971). Skinner (1974) notes that a child's world does develop, but he and many other behaviorists think that developmental stages do little to explain overt behavior.

Finally, critics charge that behaviorists program clients for minimum or tolerable levels of behavior, reinforce conformity, stifle creativity, and ignore client needs for self-fulfillment, self-actualization, and feelings of self-worth (James & Gilliland, 2003).

TREATING LINDA WITH BEHAVIORAL THERAPY

CONCEPTUALIZATION

From a behaviorist point of view Linda has been reinforced for being passive, dependent, depressed, and submissive. She has been punished when assertive. Thus, the behaviors Linda has learned have prevented her from utilizing many of her talents and have resulted in her now being isolated, relying on things she can manipulate, such as the pages of books and the remote control of the television.

Linda has lacked models of strong and competent women in her life. Her mother was rather withdrawn, her sisters have achieved very little, and Linda has never had a woman supervisor. Overall, Linda lacks the behaviors that would help make her successful as a person and a professional.

TREATMENT PROCESS

As a behavioral therapist, you want to help Linda learn new, appropriate ways of acting, replacing maladaptive behaviors with adaptive ones. Thus, you function as a consultant, teacher, adviser, reinforcer, and facilitator. Initially, you work with Linda to identify behaviors she wants to acquire and those she wants to eliminate. For instance, Linda reveals that she would like to be more assertive instead of passively accepting the dictates of others and then getting angry about it. Linda also wants to explore how to make the most of her talents and possibly gain new job skills.

You set up specific and mutually agreed-upon goals by concretely defining the problem (i.e., a lack of adequate social and vocational skills), taking a developmental history, establishing specific goals, and determining the best method for change. In Linda's case you believe that an assertiveness training course offered by a community agency would be helpful, as would an assessment of her vocational interests and skills. As an active learning specialist you set up both experiences.

During therapy sessions you discover what are reinforcers for Linda and begin to help her shape and generalize the assertive behavior she wants by role-playing different scenarios with her. You also set up a self-observation and self-monitoring schedule for Linda to use outside counseling sessions so that she becomes ever more aware of her behavior. In addition, you encourage Linda to reinforce herself when she realizes that she is speaking up for herself or when she takes positive steps to acquire additional vocational skills.

As therapy continues, Linda becomes more independent and joins a number of community organizations in which she has an interest. She finds out how best to use the business skills she already has and takes some additional courses at a nearby college. Without being aggressive or passive, she lets her family know how she wants to relate to them and even plans some of the regular Sunday outings so that they are fun for her and educational for her family. Overall, behavioral therapy helps Linda become a more accomplished person.

SUMMARY AND CONCLUSION

Behavior therapy is a diverse way of working with clients to help them improve their personal and interpersonal skills. Through behavioral therapy, individuals learn how to manage excessive behaviors, extinguish unwanted behaviors, and learn new behaviors. The three primary approaches to behavioral change are the stimulus-response model, applied behavior analysis, and the social-cognitive theory. Behaviorists employ many general techniques with their clients, including the use of reinforcement, shaping, generalization, extinction, and problem-solving rehearsals. They also use specialized and refined techniques such as environmental planning, systematic desensitization, assertiveness training, contracts, implosion, flooding, time-out, and overcorrection.

A real strength of behavioral therapy is its solid learning theory base; excellent research supports the behavioral approaches. In addition, behavioral therapy is extolled for dealing directly with symptoms and behaviors, working in the present, being relatively brief, demystifying the counseling process, having a plethora of available techniques, and being buttressed by a professional association of practitioners and researchers in the field—the Association for the Advancement of Behavior Therapy. On the other hand, behaviorism is limited by conducting some of its research with animals, ignoring clients' histories and the unconscious, dismissing developmental stages as unimportant, and reinforcing conformity.

SUMMARY TABLE: BEHAVIORAL THERAPY

Major Theorists

John B. Watson	Mary Cover Jones
B. F. Skinner	Joseph Wolpe
Albert Bandura	John Krumboltz

View of Human Nature/Personality

All behavior is learned
There are no human personality traits
Learn through respondent learning, operant conditioning, social modeling

Role of the Counselor/Therapist

Teacher, director, expert
Active participant in counseling sessions
Aide in clarifying goals and modifying behaviors

Goals

Extinguish or adjust behavior
Learn productive responses
Establish and achieve behavioral goals

Process and Techniques

Reinforcement: positive/negative, primary/secondary, continuous/intermittent
Shaping and extinction
Environmental planning and systematic desensitization
Implosion and flooding
Time-out and overcorrection

Multicultural and Gender-Sensitive Issues

May be applied in every culture
Requires sensitivity to cultural context
Cuts across gender lines

Strengths and Contributions

Focused on symptom removal in the present
Supported by many behavioral procedures
Based on learning theory and well researched

Effective for certain disorders
Increasing in sophistication and effectiveness
Able to be combined with other theoretical positions

Limitations and Criticisms

Does not focus on the whole person
May be applied too mechanically
Cannot replicate lab conditions in the field
Ignores past history and the unconscious
Does not consider developmental stages

LEARNING MORE

A number of periodicals devoted to behavioral therapy may prove helpful in exploring this approach.

Advances in Behaviour Research and Therapy
Behavior Analysis
Behavior Modification
Behavior Therapy, Cognitive and Behavioral Practice
Behavior Therapist
Behavioral Assessment
Journal of Applied Behavior Analysis
Journal of Behavior Therapy and Experimental Psychiatry
Progress in Behavior Modification

In addition to journals, several training institutes and professional associations offer clinicians a chance to learn more about behavior therapy and its uses in therapeutic settings.

Association for Advancement of Behavior Therapy
305 Seventh Avenue
New York, NY 10001-6008
212-647-1890 or 800-685-AABT
www.aabt.org/aabt

Behavior OnLine: The Mental Health and Behavioral Science Meeting Place
www.behavior.net

CLASSROOM ACTIVITIES

1. With another classmate discuss your own positive and negative reinforcers. How has punishment affected your life, especially in regard to learning?
2. As a class discuss how and what you have learned in life by way of each of the three behavioral models: stimulus-response conditioning, applied behavior analysis, and social-cognitive learning.

3. Find examples of behaviors that have either generalized or been extinguished in society. As a class discuss these behaviors and the impact their generalization or extinction has had.

REFERENCES

Alberti, R. E., & Emmons, M. L. (1996). *Your perfect right: A guide to assertive behavior* (7th ed.). San Luis Obispo, CA: Impact.

Azrin, N. H., Stuart, R. B., Risely, T. R., & Stolz, S. (1977). Ethical issues for human services. *AABT Newsletter, 4*, 11.

Bandura, A. (1969). *Principles of behavior modification.* New York: Holt, Rinehart & Winston.

Bandura, A. (1986). *Social foundations of thought and action: A social cognitive theory.* Upper Saddle River, NJ: Prentice Hall.

Bandura, A., & Walters, R. H. (1963). *Social learning and personality development.* New York: Holt, Rinehart & Winston.

Bellack, A. S., & Hersen, M. (1998). *Behavioral assessment: A practical handbook.* Boston: Allyn & Bacon.

Blackham, G. J., & Silberman, A. (1979). *Modification of child and adolescent behavior.* Belmont, CA: Wadsworth.

Bussey, K., & Bandura, A. (1999). Social cognitive career theory of gender development and differentiation. *Psychological Review, 106,* 676–713.

Cautela, J. R. (1976). The present status of covert modeling. *Journal of Behavior Therapy and Experimental Psychiatry, 6,* 323–326.

Christopher, J. C. (1996). Counseling's inescapable moral vision. *Journal of Counseling & Development, 75,* 17–25.

Elms, A. C. (1981). Skinner's dark year and Walden Two. *American Psychologist, 36,* 470–479.

Eysenck, H. J. (1960). *Behavior therapy and the neuroses.* New York: Pergamon.

Fowler, R. D. (1990, October). B. F. Skinner: Farewell, with admiration and affection. *APA Monitor, 21*(10), 2.

Goldiamond, I. (1976). Self-reinforcement. *Journal of Applied Behavior Analysis, 9,* 509–514.

Goldstein, A. (1973). Behavior therapy. In R. Corsini (Ed.), *Current psychotherapies* (pp. 207–249). Itasca, IL: Peacock.

Hackney, H., & Cormier, L. S. (2002). *The professional counselor* (4th ed). Boston: Allyn & Bacon.

Hergenhahn, B. R., & Olson, M. H. (2003). *An introduction to theories of personality* (6th ed.). Upper Saddle River, NJ: Prentice Hall.

Holden, J. (1993a). *Behavioral consequences on behavior.* Unpublished manuscript, University of North Texas, Denton.

Holden, J. (1993b). *Respondent learning.* Unpublished manuscript.

Hosford, R. E. (1980). The Cubberley conference and the evolution of observational learning strategies. *Personnel and Guidance Journal, 58,* 467–472.

James, R. K., & Gilliland, B. E., (2003). *Theories and strategies in counseling and psychotherapy* (5th ed.). Boston: Allyn & Bacon.

Jones, M. C. (1924). The elimination of children's fears. *Journal of Experimental Psychology, 7,* 383–390.

Kipper, D. A. (1986). *Psychotherapy through clinical role playing.* New York: Brunner/Mazel.

Krasner, L., & Ullmann, L. P. (1973). *Behavior influence and personality: The social matrix of human action.* New York: Holt, Rinehart & Winston.

Krumboltz, J. D. (1966). Behavioral goals of counseling. *Journal of Counseling Psychology, 13,* 153–159.

Krumboltz, J. D., & Thoresen, C. E. (1976). *Counseling methods.* New York: Holt, Rinehart & Winston.

Lazarus, A. A. (1985). Behavior rehearsal. In A. S. Bellack & M. Hersen (Eds.), *Dictionary of behavior therapy techniques* (p. 22). New York: Pergamon.

Perry, M. A., & Furukawa, M. J. (1980). Modeling methods. In F. H. Kanfer & A. P. Goldstein (Eds.), *Helping people change* (pp. 131–171). New York: Pergamon.

Rescorla, R. A. (1988). Pavlovian conditioning: It's not what you think it is. *American Psychologist, 43,* 151–160.

Rimm, D. C., & Cunningham, H. M. (1985). Behavior therapies. In S. J. Lynn & J. P. Garske (Eds.), *Contemporary psychotherapies: Models and methods* (pp. 221–259). Upper Saddle River, NJ: Prentice Hall.

Rose, S. D. (1983). Behavior therapy in groups. In H. I. Kaplan & B. J. Sadock (Eds.), *Comprehensive group psychotherapy* (2nd ed.). Baltimore: Williams & Wilkins.

Seligman, L. (1997). *Diagnosis and treatment planning in counseling.* New York: Plenum.

Sharf, R. S. (2004). *Theories of psychotherapy and counseling* (3rd ed.). Pacific Grove, CA: Brooks/Cole.

Skinner, B. F. (1938). *The behavior of organisms: An experimental analysis.* Upper Saddle River, NJ: Prentice Hall.

Skinner, B. F. (1948). *Walden Two.* New York: Macmillan.

Skinner, B. F. (1953). *Science and human behavior.* New York: Macmillan.

Skinner, B. F. (1967). Autobiography. In E. G. Boring & G. Lindzey (Eds.), *A history of psychology in autobiography* (Vol. 5, pp. 387–413). New York: Appleton-Century-Crofts.

Skinner, B. F. (1971). *Beyond freedom and dignity*. New York: Knopf.

Skinner, B. F. (1974). *About behaviorism*. New York: Knopf.

Skinner, B. F. (1976). *Particulars of my life*. New York: McGraw-Hill.

Skinner, B. F., & Vaughan, M. E. (1983). *Enjoy old age*. New York: Norton.

Sprinthall, N. A. (1971). A program for psychological education: Some preliminary issues. *Journal of School Psychology, 9*, 373–382.

Thoresen, C. E. (1969). The counselor as an applied behavioral scientist. *Personnel and Guidance Journal, 47*, 841–848.

Thoresen, C. E., & Coates, T. J. (1980). What does it mean to be a behavior therapist? In C. E. Thoresen (Ed.), *The behavior therapist* (pp. 1–41). Pacific Grove, CA: Brooks/Cole.

Thoresen, C. E., & Mahoney, M. J. (1974). *Behavioral self-control*. New York: Holt, Rinehart, & Winston.

Watson, J. B. (1913). Psychology as a behaviorist views it. *Psychological Review, 20*, 158–177.

Watson, J. B. (1925). *Behaviorism*. New York: Norton.

Watson, J. B., & Raynor, R. (1920). Conditioned emotional reactions. *Journal of Experimental Psychology, 3*, 1–14.

Wilson, G. T. (1995). Behavior therapy. In R. J. Corsini & D. Wedding (Eds.), *Current psychotherapies* (5th ed., pp. 197–228). Itasca, IL: Peacock.

Wolpe, J. (1958). *Psychotherapy by reciprocal inhibition building*. Stanford, CA: Stanford University Press.

Yates, A. J. (1970). *Behavior therapy*. New York: Wiley.

Zimbardo, P. G., & Leippe, M. R. (1991). *The psychology of attitude change and social influence*. Philadelphia: Temple University Press.

Cognitive and Cognitive-Behavioral Therapy

Sweet Mary sits in her chair all day
  rocking back and forth pretending it's a sleigh
She seldom talks for that would give it away
  that within her mind she hears voices.

Note: "Sweet Mary" by S. T. Gladding. Copyright 2003 by Samuel T. Gladding.

Cognitions are thoughts, beliefs, and internal images that people have about events in their lives. Cognitive counseling theories focus on mental processes and their influence on mental health. A common premise of all cognitive approaches is this: How people think largely determines how they feel and behave (Beck & Weishaar, 2000). As Burns (1980) points out, "Every bad feeling you have is the result of your distorted negative thinking" (p. 28). Therefore, most cognitive theorists agree with the Biblical verse Proverbs 23:7, "As people think, so shall they be," and with Shakespeare's Hamlet, who said, "There's nothing either good or bad but thinking makes it so." In short, cognitive theorists and clinicians believe that if individuals change their ways of thinking, their feelings and behaviors will be modified as a result.

Cognitive approaches to counseling are relatively new; they came into prominence in the 1970s and have remained influential. Among the best-known cognitive theories are Aaron Beck's cognitive therapy and David Burns's new mood therapy. Cognitive-behavioral therapeutic approaches emerged slightly later, using behavioral tasks to modify faulty perceptions and interpretations of important life events (Bankart, 1997). Researchers and practitioners Donald Meichenbaum (1977, 1985) and Neil Jacobson have been among the most prominent cognitive-behaviorists. Their work emphasizes the importance of mental processes in human behavior and views thoughts as a type of behavior. The essence of the cognitive-behavioral approach is the blending of behavioral and cognitive strategies to help people make needed changes in their lives. Thus, cognitive-behaviorists form a bridge between counselors who are exclusively focused on either cognitive or behavioral changes.

MAJOR THEORISTS: AARON BECK AND DONALD MEICHENBAUM

A prolific writer of more than 400 articles and 15 books, Aaron T. Beck is a Philadelphia psychiatrist who was originally trained as a psychoanalyst. He developed a cognitive approach to mental disorders in the late 1950s and early 1960s, emphasizing the importance of cognitive thinking, especially dysfunctional thoughts, which are unproductive and unrealistic (Weinrach, 1988).

A professor emeritus now, Beck served for many years as the director of the Center for Cognitive Therapy at the University of Pennsylvania's Department of Psychiatry. There he refined his theory and rigorously tested it (see Beck, 1991; Rush & Beck, 2000). In the process he found that cognitive therapy is effective as a short-term treatment for a number of problems and disorders, especially for depression and general anxiety. In these maladies there are "interpretations and expectations that lead to the painful effects of sadness and anxiety, to avoidance and inhibition" (Weinrach, 1988, p. 161). Thus, cognitive counselors trained in Beck's methodology try to help clients become more realistic in their interpretation of events by generalizing less in the case of depression or projecting less in the case of anxiety. This approach uses a Socratic method that is problem oriented, educational, brief, and collaborative. In short, Beck's approach emphasizes that affect and behavior are determined by the ways in which people mentally structure their worlds.

Donald Meichenbaum (1995, 1997) is one of the founders of cognitive-behavior therapy (CBT). He was born and reared in New York City, where he observed many people talking to themselves. He concluded that helping people talk to themselves differently and constructively might be an excellent goal for therapy and might bring about behavioral changes.

Meichenbaum is the author of numerous articles, chapters, and books, some of which are now considered classics in the field of therapy, such as *Cognitive-Behavioral Modification: An Integrated Approach* (1977) and *Stress Inoculation Training* (1985). He is especially noted for his work on treating individuals with anger and aggressive behavior and adults with post-traumatic stress disorder. In a survey reported in the *American Psychologist*, North American clinicians voted Meichenbaum one of the ten most influential psychotherapists of the 20th century. He has served on the editorial boards of numerous journals and has lectured and consulted worldwide. Prior to retirement Meichenbaum was a professor of psychology at the University of Waterloo in Waterloo, Canada, where he also had a private practice as a clinical psychologist.

VIEW OF HUMAN NATURE/PERSONALITY

A particular concern of cognitive and cognitive-behavioral therapies is the impact of thinking on personality. These counseling approaches are usually employed with individuals who are not visibly impaired but who suffer from dysfunctional automatic thoughts specific to an event and *schemata*, which are general rules about themselves or the world associated with an event (Holden, 1993b). These individuals often engage in self-statements that affect their behaviors "in much the same way as statements made by another person" (Corey, 2001, p. 318). For instance, a guest who is slighted at a party may automatically think, "That person is a jerk!" The schema that follows may be "I'm offended" or "I'm hurt."

For Beck, and cognitive therapists in general, there are a number of cognitive distortions to which a counselor should be attuned. These include at least nine ways of mentally assessing a situation (Arnkoff & Glass, 1992; DeRubeis, Tang, & Beck, 2001; Sharf, 2004).

- *All-or-nothing thinking* (also known as *dichotomous thinking*) occurs when people think they must do something a certain way or else they are failures. For example, in giving a speech, if all-or-nothing thinkers do not say every word written, they believe they will be seen as incompetent.
- *In selective abstraction,* individuals pick out an idea or fact to support their negative thinking. For instance, if a person who usually makes straight A's in school suddenly makes a B, that person might use the B to conclude, "I'm not really very smart."
- *Overgeneralization* makes a rule based on a few incidences or events. For example, someone may think that all white people are insensitive because of encounters with some white people who were rude and uncaring.
- *Magnification* and *minimization* are two sides of the same thought process. In magnification a cognitive distortion occurs when an imperfection is exaggerated beyond reality. For instance, a high school student could fail a test and conclude, "I will never be able to get into a good college." In minimization a person downplays good points or notable achievements. The student who makes almost straight A's may not apply to appropriate colleges, thinking, "I am not up to the quality of these colleges."
- *Personalization* occurs when an event that is unrelated to a person is distorted and made to appear as if it is related. For example, a woman may begin to think that just the elevators in her office complex are slow even though she uses them only at peak times.
- *Labeling* and *mislabeling* are common cognitive distortions that arise when people characterize themselves in certain ways. For instance, a man who goes to a batting cage to hit balls and misses most of them during his first visit may label or mislabel himself as a poor hitter, instead of a person needing more practice.
- *Catastrophizing* is similar in both Beck's and Ellis's theories. Basically, it involves mentally distorting an event so that one becomes fearful of it. For example, if a shy, awkward, and homely young man is attracted to an outgoing, sophisticated, and good-looking young woman, he may say to himself, "She is far superior to me in every way. I cannot ever talk to her, let alone ask her out for a date." Thus, he precludes any possible relationship and becomes completely discombobulated any time he is near her.
- *Mind reading* refers to the tendency of some people to guess what others are thinking about them. An older adult may believe that others who see him think, "There is an incompetent old fool who is good for nothing." Therefore, he shies away from interactions and becomes a recluse.
- *Negative predictions* are beliefs that something bad is going to happen. They may have little basis in fact, but they influence a person's actions just the same. For instance, a person may believe, "I will get sick if I eat chicken, because I once got sick after a meal that included chicken." Thus, the prediction keeps that person from eating chicken, which, in reality, would have no negative impact.

ROLE OF THE COUNSELOR/THERAPIST

The role of cognitively oriented counselors is to collaborate with clients (Beck, 1976), sharing the responsibility to select goals and bring about change. In this relationship, counselors function as experts on cognitions, behaviors, and emotions and as educators also. Clients collaborate by participating in assignments. Initially, counselors do not try to disprove beliefs but let clients examine the functionality of their beliefs. Beck's model is exploratory in working with clients and Socratic in letting them assess what is correct and incorrect in their belief systems (Holden, 1993a). Thus, cognitive therapy is ever evolving so that as new data come in, the counselor-client team can make new strategies.

Overall, cognitively based counseling requires empirical testing on the part of clients to understand how functional or dysfunctional their beliefs are. Counselors, especially those who are cognitive-behavioral, may use diagnoses, such as those in the *DSM*, in working with clients. However, diagnoses are employed only as a way of working with clients to overcome a disorder, such as post-traumatic stress.

GOALS

Both cognitive and cognitive-behavioral approaches to counseling employ specific learning experiences to help counselors teach clients ways to monitor their negative or automatic thoughts. Clients are taught to recognize the relationship between these thoughts and their emotions and behaviors. In addition, counselors help clients compile evidence for and against their distorted automatic thoughts. Ideally, clients are freed to alter their distorted beliefs and to substitute reality-based interpretations for unrealistic thoughts.

In order to help clinicians achieve these goals, profiles and treatment plans have been developed, especially by Beck, for disorders such as depression (Beck, Rush, Shaw, & Emery, 1979), suicide, and anxiety (Dattilio & Padesky, 1990). However, goals are constantly reexamined and modified to fit particular clients; cognitive approaches are personally tailored to individual situations.

PROCESS AND TECHNIQUES

Cognitive and cognitive-behavioral therapy are specific and goal directed (Sharf, 2004), emphasizing the modification of thoughts to bring about therapeutic change. One way to organize thoughts is in three categories: cold, warm, and hot cognitions. A *cold cognition* is basically descriptive and nonevaluative, such as "I lost my job." A *warm cognition* emphasizes preferences and nonpreferences, such as "I lost my job and I really don't want to have to start looking for another one." *Hot cognitions* "are heavily laden emotional-demand statements" (James & Gilliland, 2003, p. 238) that may reveal varied distortions, such as overgeneralizing, catastrophizing, magnification, and all-or-nothing thinking—for example, "I must get a job just like the one I lost." Hot cognitions usually lead to dysfunctional behaviors because they are filled with both demands and distortions.

A cognitive approach to change must first establish a relationship between client and counselor and then implement cognitive strategies in a basic four-step procedure (Burns, 1989; Schuyler, 1991). These four steps and the premises behind them are at the heart of change.

The first step is to use standardized guidelines for understanding in a concrete manner the events in clients' lives, that is, what is happening in their environments. The second step is to set up a way of recording or reflecting clients' thoughts about these events in order to understand their cognitions in a clear, precise way. Often thoughts are written down so that they can be seen in as concrete a manner as possible.

In the third step, counselors and clients work to find a means to identify and challenge distorted thoughts. For instance, if a client believes that no one likes her, an empirical test might be set up whereby she records all positive as well as negative interactions. The final step is to implement new ways of thinking that are realistic and productive. Thus, the client might change her thinking from "Nobody likes me" to "Some people like me and some do not." This process frees her to act more positively with specific individuals and with people in general.

COGNITIVE TECHNIQUES

The following are among the most prevalent cognitive techniques in use.

- **Specifying automatic thoughts.** As mentioned earlier, automatic thoughts are cognitions that occur without effort. They are usually distorted and lead to emotional responses that are not healthy. Therefore, a major focus of cognitive therapy is to identify—that is, specify—and then correct such thoughts.
- **Homework.** As with other types of therapy, much change that occurs in cognitive therapy happens outside actual counseling sessions. Thus, clients may practice giving themselves different thoughts at home, on the job, or in particular settings. Such practice makes it easier for clients to achieve the desired changes in their thinking.
- **Cognitive interventions.** A number of processes occur under the heading of cognitive interventions. All of them focus on bringing cognitive distortions into greater awareness—for example, challenging absolutes, reattribution, labeling of distortions, and challenging all-or-nothing thinking
- **Cognitive rehearsals.** Because practice makes perfect, it is important for clients to consistently rehearse healthy thoughts. They may do so covertly or overtly, privately through mental rehearsal, or publicly, as in a gathering of friends. Cognitive rehearsals ensure that clients will say to themselves and others the right words in the right way—at least most of the time.
- **Scriptotherapy.** In the process of writing, which is scriptotherapy, individuals improve their thoughts by expressing them concretely. Pennebaker (1990),

among others, has noted both mental and physical changes in clients who write about stressful situations in their lives.

COGNITIVE-BEHAVIORAL TECHNIQUES

Some of the most exciting new techniques in counseling have been originated by cognitive-behaviorists (Craighead, Craighead, Kazdin, & Mahoney, 1994; Mahoney, 1995). Cognitive-behavioral techniques are "usually active, time-limited, and fairly structured. They are designed to enlist the client" and others in "a collaborative process" (Meichenbaum, 1986, p. 147). Although "there is no single definition of cognitive-behavioral theory . . . the individual theories are tied together by common assumptions, techniques, and research strategies" (Kalodner, 1995, p. 354). Thus, CBT approaches maintain a diversity of views about the role that cognitions play in behavior change, but all agree that cognitions play a part in such change.

CBT procedures emphasize the present, the environment, and learning. Common to cognitive-behavioral intervention is "a directive style; structured, goal-directed, and time-limited treatment; use of homework assignments and skill practice; and a focus on problem-solving ability" (Kalodner, 1995, p. 364). Dozens of interventions can be included under the cognitive-behavioral banner—for example, "cognitive restructuring, problem-solving, relaxation training, behavioral and imaginal rehearsal, self-monitoring, self-reinforcement, and efforts at environmental change" (Meichenbaum, 1985, p. 21). Following are some of the interventions most common to cognitive-behavioral counseling.

- **Self-instructional training.** One of the best methods for changing clients' cognitions and behaviors is a process known as *self-instructional training* (Meichenbaum, 1977). In this procedure counselors perform a task or engage in appropriate behaviors while verbalizing aloud through self-talk the reasons behind what they are doing. Clients then do the same task or behavior and also give themselves instructions aloud. Next, they engage in these actions while whispering self-instructions and then finally perform the behaviors while silently repeating the reasons behind what they are doing. These covert messages thus become the basis for the clients' behaviors, and in the future they may communicate with themselves in this manner. As a strategy self-instructional training is especially powerful and popular in working with impulsive, defiant, or attention-deficit children and adolescents (Barkley, 1987, 1991; Kendall & Braswell, 1992).
- **Stress-inoculation training.** *Stress inoculation* is a preventive technique, like medical inoculation, in which individuals are taught sets of coping skills to help them handle stressful events. First, clients are helped to understand the nature of stress and coping. Second, clients learn specific coping skills and are reinforced for using the ones they already possess. The final phase emphasizes practice: Clients use coping skills in clinical settings and real situations. Overall, stress inoculation involves focusing on what lies ahead, grouping stressful events into manageable doses, thinking of ways to handle small stressful events, and practicing coping skills (Meichenbaum, 1985, 1986). The major drawback to this procedure is that its initial results sometimes do not generalize into

permanent behavior changes (Arnkoff & Glass, 1992). Therefore, follow-up and booster sessions are often necessary.

- **Thought stopping.** *Thought stopping* helps clients who ruminate about the past or who have irrational thoughts to stop such self-defeating behavior and live more productively. Counselors initially ask their clients to think in the self-defeating manner and then, in the midst of such thoughts, suddenly yell, "Stop!" The shout interrupts the thought process and makes it impossible to continue. There are several components of the thought-stopping process (Cormier & Cormier, 1998); basically, it teaches clients to progress from outer to inner control of negative thought patterns. It also helps clients replace self-defeating thoughts with assertive, positive, or neutral ones.
- **Cognitive restructuring.** Among the most effective cognitive-behavioral techniques is *cognitive restructuring*, which includes stress inoculation and thought stopping. In cognitive restructuring clients are taught to identify, evaluate, and change self-defeating or irrational thoughts that negatively influence their behavior. This process is accomplished by getting them to vocalize their self-talk and then change it, when necessary, from negative to neutral or positive. This technique is similar to Ellis's (1962) and Beck's (1976) proposals for modifying thought processes.

MULTICULTURAL AND GENDER-SENSITIVE ISSUES

Cognitive counseling and CBT approaches are applicable to multicultural populations because they let clients take the lead in assessing whether their thoughts and beliefs are appropriate to their cultures. A number of studies have shown the positive use of cognitive counseling with African American and Latino men and with Malaysians (Sharf, 2004).

Cognitive and CBT approaches may also be appropriate for both men and women in dealing with gender-specific concerns. By examining their beliefs, men and women may come to better understand the cognitive distortions that hinder their overall functioning. The only major drawback in this regard is that some clients may become dependent on their counselors to structure sessions and help them examine their beliefs, thus failing to become empowered. This potential may be of special concern to women.

EVALUATION OF THE THEORIES

STRENGTHS AND CONTRIBUTIONS

Cognitive counseling and CBT are both focused on teaching clients how to identify and monitor their thoughts and behaviors and also to change or modify them. In addition, both approaches are proactive, providing training to clients that helps them prepare for and then successfully deal with a variety of specific and general problems.

Another contribution of these counseling theories is that they demystify the process and techniques associated with choice and change. Clients realize that in order to become someone different and act in a more functional manner, they have to think, behave, and feel in ways that are different from those of the past.

Cognitive counseling and CBT are also generally empowering for clients. When they learn new ways to think and behave, they are free to generalize their learning to new situations and end their treatment.

Furthermore, cognitive counseling and CBT are applicable to a wide range of client disorders, such as depression, guilt, phobias, distress, and pain. And because they work with children, adolescents, adults, and the aging, they are beneficial for a large group of clients.

LIMITATIONS AND CRITICISMS

In order to receive the maximum benefit from these approaches, clients need to have average to above-average intelligence. Individuals who fall too far below average in their cognitive abilities have more trouble using the various techniques. Furthermore, clients cannot be psychotic or disabled by present problems if they are to succeed with cognitive or cognitive-behavioral approaches. Both cognitive and CBT methods depend on clients being able to think clearly.

Another drawback is that clients must be willing and able to complete systematic homework assignments. Change comes about as a result of practice, and clients must be willing to work on their own as well as with their therapists.

In addition, clients must possess a repertoire of behavioral skills and responses or be able to learn such behaviors rapidly. Clients who cannot or will not apply what they know or learn are not good candidates for these approaches.

Finally, cognitive counseling and CBT do not explore to any great extent the past influences in clients' lives, including the unconscious or underlying conflicts. Even though surface thoughts and behaviors may be of greatest concern and may be most susceptible to change, previous difficulties and the history behind them may be pertinent as well.

TREATING LINDA WITH COGNITIVE AND COGNITIVE-BEHAVIORAL THERAPY

CONCEPTUALIZATION

From a cognitive and cognitive-behavioral perspective Linda is having difficulty with her life because of her thinking. She is using self-statements that are demoralizing or depressing. In many ways she is repeating in her own mind what her father, her former husband, and even some of her bosses have said to her, for example, "You are no good unless you obey us" or "Women are inferior and will never amount to anything." These thoughts have become automatic and have prevented Linda from doing anything constructive with her life. In fact, these thoughts have led her to contemplate suicide. Thus, Linda has labeled herself a failure and has acted accordingly. She has sabotaged her own life by not venturing out or speaking out. Indeed, she has engaged in catastrophizing and negative predictions to the point that these mental distortions now control her life.

TREATMENT PROCESS

As a cognitive or cognitive-behavioral therapist you work in collaboration with Linda to select goals and to bring about change. You encourage Linda to examine her beliefs functionally, using a Socratic method to determine which beliefs are correct and which are incorrect. For instance, in mulling over the idea that women are inferior and will never amount to anything, Linda quickly dismisses such a notion as she thinks of famous historical and contemporary women who have been high achievers. As you engage Linda in this way, you are also helping her see the link between thoughts and feelings; if she gives herself negative messages, she is going to depress herself. You urge Linda to keep a written record of her thoughts so that she can see what messages she is sending herself.

In addition to helping Linda decipher and challenge the automatic negative thoughts that are most pervasive in her life, you help her cognitively rehearse healthy thoughts. You use the CBT technique of self-instructional training, in which you perform a task or engage in appropriate behavior while verbalizing aloud the reasons behind what you are doing. Linda then does the same task or behavior, at first giving herself instructions aloud and then performing the action while whispering self-instructions. Finally, she does the task silently.

You also teach Linda stress inoculation as a preventive technique. In this procedure you teach her a set of coping skills to help her handle stressful events like interacting with sexist men and her father. In addition, you instruct Linda on how to thought stop so that she does not persist in her negative thinking. By the end of therapy, Linda is engaged in healthy thinking, and her actions reflect a woman who is much more self-confident and realistic about who she is and what she can do.

SUMMARY AND CONCLUSION

Cognitive and CBT approaches to treatment are some of the most creative and effective in counseling. They are based on the belief that cognitions are directly related to behaviors and, in the case of CBT, that beliefs are behaviors. As a rule, cognitive and cognitive-behavioral therapies are straightforward and successful with a wide variety of clients; the results can be seen in a timely and concrete way.

In addition, the number of sessions involved is usually minimal, and the outcomes are usually long lasting.

Although Beck's approach to cognitive therapy provides a common ground for linking psychodynamic and behavior therapies (Beck & Weishaar, 2000), cognitive counseling and CBT are distinct in their emphasis. They focus on the present as opposed to the past, and they target specific behaviors instead of general ways of acting. Furthermore, they continue to evolve in their techniques and processes. A common misconception of these approaches is that they neglect emotions; however, they do deal with the affective by attending to the cognitive and cognitive-behavioral aspects of life first.

Overall, Beck's cognitive approach and Meichenbaum's cognitive-behavioral therapy are among the most used and useful theories in practice today. They will most likely continue to gain in popularity because of their pragmatic nature and their applicability to the concerns of many clients. Their suitability for people of both genders, all ages and stages of life, and multiple cultures adds further to the prestige and practicality of these counseling approaches.

SUMMARY TABLE: COGNITIVE AND COGNITIVE-BEHAVIORAL THERAPY

Major Theorists

Aaron Beck
Donald Meichenbaum

View of Human Nature/Personality

Problems caused by dysfunctional automatic thoughts and schemata
Examples: all-or-nothing thinking, selective abstractions, overgeneralization, magnification and minimization, personalization, labeling and mislabeling, catastrophizing

Role of the Counselor/Therapist

Function as experts and educators on cognitions, behaviors, emotions
Allow clients to examine their beliefs
Collaborate in helping clients formulate new cognitive strategies

Goals

Monitor negative/automatic thoughts
Recognize relationship between thoughts, emotions, behaviors
Individualize approaches

Process and Techniques

Establish client-counselor relationship
Understand events, record thoughts, challenge distortions, implement new ways of thinking
Utilize varied techniques: specifying automatic thoughts, homework, cognitive interventions, cognitive rehearsals, and scriptotherapy; self-instruction training, stress inoculation, thought stopping, and cognitive restructuring

Multicultural and Gender-Sensitive Issues

Applicable to multicultural populations
Appropriate for gender concerns
Hindered by potential dependence

Strengths and Contributions

Teaches clients to identify and modify thoughts and behaviors
Approaches therapy proactively
Demystifies the process of choice and change
Empowers clients
Applies to a wide range of clients and disorders

Limitations and Criticisms

Requires average to above-average intelligence for maximum effectiveness
Excludes psychotic or mentally disabled clients
Necessitates systematic homework
Favors clients with behavioral skills and learning ability
Does not explore past influences or the unconscious

LEARNING MORE

A number of periodicals are devoted to the theory, research, and practice of cognitive and cognitive-behavioral therapy.

Journal of Cognitive Psychotherapy: An International Quarterly
Behavioural and Cognitive Psychotherapy
Cognitive & Behavioral Practice
Journal of Cognitive Psychotherapy
Cognitive Therapy and Research

In addition, several training institutes enable clinicians to learn cognitive and cognitive-behavioral processes and skills.

Beck Institute for Cognitive Therapy and Research
GSB Building
City Line and Belmont Avenues, Suite 700
Bala Cynwyd, PA: 19004-1610
http://www.beckinstitute.org

American Institute for Cognitive Therapy
136 East 57th Street, Suite 1101
New York, NY 10022
www.CognitiveTherapyNYC.com

National Association of Cognitive-Behavioral Therapy
http://www.nacbt.org

CLASSROOM ACTIVITIES

1. Think about the following situations and try to assess how distorted or realistic your thoughts are about each: a wedding, a funeral, the birth of a baby, a graduation, moving. How do your thoughts impact your feelings and behaviors?
2. Cognitive therapy and CBT have grown in their influence because of a strong research base. Find a journal article on either approach and critique it. Present to the class the findings of the article and your evaluation of how the research was conducted.
3. How are the cognitive and cognitive-behavioral counseling approaches similar? How do they differ? What do you think the future of each is likely to be, either separately or combined? Why?

REFERENCES

Arnkoff, D. B., & Glass, C. R. (1992). Cognitive therapy and psychotherapy integration. In D. K. Freedheim (Ed.), *History of psychotherapy: A century of change* (pp. 657–694). Washington, DC: American Psychological Association.

Bankart, C. P. (1997). *Talking cures.* Pacific Grove, CA: Brooks/Cole.

Barkley, R. A. (1987). *Defiant children: A clinician's manual for parent training.* New York: Guilford.

Barkley, R. A. (1991). *Attention-deficit hyperactivity disorder.* New York: Guilford.

Beck, A. T. (1976). *Cognitive therapy and emotional disorders.* New York: International Universities Press.

Beck, A. T. (1991). Cognitive therapy: A 30-year retrospective. *American Psychologist, 46,* 368–375.

Beck, A. T., Rush, A. J., Shaw, B. F., & Emery, G. (1979). *Cognitive therapy of depression.* New York: Guilford.

Beck, A. T., & Weishaar, M. E. (2000). Cognitive therapy. In R. J. Corsini & D. Wedding (Eds.), *Current psychotherapies* (6th ed., pp. 241–272). Itasca, IL: Peacock.

Burns, D. D. (1980). *Feeling good: The new mood therapy.* New York: Signet.

Burns, D. D. (1989). *The feeling good handbook: Using the new mood therapy in everyday life.* New York: Morrow.

Corey, G. (2001). *Theory and practice of counseling and psychotherapy* (6th ed.). Pacific Grove, CA: Brooks/Cole.

Cormier, W. H., & Cormier, L. S. (1998). *Interviewing strategies for helpers: A guide to assessment, treatment, and evaluation* (4th ed.). Pacific Grove, CA: Brooks/Cole.

Craighead, L. W., Craighead, W. E., Kazdin, A. E., & Mahoney, M. J. (1994). *Cognitive and behavioral interventions: An empirical approach to mental health problems.* Boston: Allyn & Bacon.

Dattilio, F. M., & Padesky, C. A. (1990). *Cognitive therapy with couples.* Sarasota, FL: Professional Resource Exchange.

DeRubeis, R. J., Tang, T.Z., & Beck, A. T. (2001). Cognitive therapy. In K. S. Dobson (Ed.), *Handbook of cognitive-behavioral therapies* (2nd ed., pp. 349–392). New York: Guilford.

Ellis, A. (1962). *Reason and emotion in psychotherapy.* New York: Stuart.

Hackney, H., & Cormier, L. S. (2002). *The professional counselor: A process guide to helping* (4th ed.). Boston: Allyn & Bacon.

Holden, J. (1993a). *Cognitive counseling* [Videotape]. Greensboro, NC: ACES/Chi Sigma Iota.

Holden, J. A. (1993b). *Learning module: Cognitive counseling.* Denton, TX: Author.

James, R. K., & Gilliland, B. E. (2003). *Theories and strategies in counseling and psychotherapy* (5th ed.). Boston: Allyn & Bacon.

Kalodner, C. R. (1995). Cognitive-behavioral theories. In D. Capuzzi & D. R. Gross (Eds.), *Counseling & psychotherapy* (pp. 353–384). Upper Saddle River, NJ: Merrill/Prentice Hall.

Kendall, P. C., & Braswell, L. (1992). *Cognitive-behavioral therapy for impulsive children* (2nd ed.). New York: Guilford.

Mahoney, M. J. (1995). *Cognitive and constructive psychotherapies: Theory, research, and practice.* New York: Springer.

Meichenbaum, D. (1977). *Cognitive-behavior modification: An integrated approach.* New York: Plenum.

Meichenbaum, D. (1985). *Stress inoculation training.* New York: Pergamon.

Meichenbaum, D. (1986). Cognitive behavior modification. In F. H. Kanfer & A. P. Goldstein (Eds.), *Helping people change: A textbook of methods* (pp. 346–380). New York: Pergamon.

Meichenbaum, D. (1995). Cognitive-behavioral therapy in historical perspective. In B. M. Bongar & L. E. Beutler (Eds.), *Comprehensive textbook of psychotherapy: Theory and practice* (Vol. 1, pp. 140–158). London: Oxford University Press.

Meichenbaum, D. (1997). The evolution of a cognitive-behavior therapist. In J. K. Zeig (Ed.), *The evolution of psychotherapy: The third conference* (pp. 95–104). Philadelphia: Brunner/Mazel.

Pennebaker, J. W. (1990). *Opening up: The healing power of confiding in others*. New York: Avon.

Rush, A. J., & Beck, A. T. (2000). Cognitive therapy. In H. I. Kaplan & B. J. Sadock (Eds.), *Comprehensive textbook of psychiatry* (7th ed.). Baltimore: Williams & Wilkins.

Schuyler, D. (1991). *A practical guide to cognitive therapy*. New York: Norton.

Sharf, R. S. (2004). *Theories of psychotherapy and counseling* (3rd ed.). Pacific Grove, CA: Brooks/Cole.

Weinrach, S. G. (1988). Cognitive therapist: A dialogue with Aaron Beck. *Journal of Counseling and Development, 67*, 159–164.

CHAPTER 10

Rational Emotive Behavior Therapy

He measured his words out carefully
  like a fine chef contemplating cups of confection
    for he wanted to be as perfect in his speech
      as he always was for the cakes
        he took to the Ritz
          for their grand celebrations.
But alas, as he spoke, he mumbled
  and his sentence structure crumbled
    as he awkwardly asked for a raise
      in a room that was much too hot.
Imperfection won the day
  but with a smile he walked away
    knowing he had done his best
      and that his mind deserved a rest
        before he practiced and tried again.

Note: "Imperfection" by S. T. Gladding. Copyright 2003 by Samuel T. Gladding.

Rational emotive behavior therapy (REBT) was originally known as rational-emotive therapy (RET) but changed its name when its founder, Albert Ellis (1995), decided that his approach needed to better reflect what the theory actually did, that is, focus on behavior as well as cognitions. Although the name change came in 1993, the various forms of REBT have been evolving for decades (Dryden, 1994).

REBT is sometimes considered a cognitive-behavioral therapy, even though it began to evolve long before the term *cognitive-behavioral* was formulated. Initially, it was more similar to the cognitive therapy of Aaron Beck than to any other counseling approach. However, because of its unique history, founder, and recent developments, it is treated on its own here.

MAJOR THEORIST: ALBERT ELLIS

Albert Ellis, the founder of rational emotive behavior therapy (REBT), has been described by Weinrach (1980) as "abrasive, impatient, and lacking in some of the basic social graces that my mother spent hours indoctrinating me with" but also as "brilliant, sensitive, perceptive, humorous, and stimulating" (p. 152). That Ellis fits both of these descriptions is partially the result of his life experience.

Albert Ellis was born in 1913 into a Jewish family in Pittsburgh, Pennsylvania; his parents eventually had a daughter and another son. Early in his life Ellis's family moved to New York City, where he has spent most of his time since then. Ellis describes his father in positive and neutral terms, although the elder Ellis was often absent from home. From his father Ellis believes he acquired his intelligence, drive, and persistence (Newhorn, 1978). His mother was quite independent for her time, often idiosyncratic in her behavior as well as happy and nonsmothering. Ellis describes her way of parenting as benign neglect (Dryden, 1989).

At the age of 5 Ellis almost died from tonsillitis and later suffered from acute nephritis and diabetes (Dryden, 1989; Morris & Kanitz, 1975). He thought most members of his family were pretty crazy and by the age of 7 was largely on his own (Weinrach, 1980). His parents' divorce when he was 12 years old caused him to give up plans to be a Hebrew teacher, and he became instead a self-described *probabilistic atheist*—someone who does not believe that God exists but would accept empirical evidence to the contrary.

Ellis's dream as an adolescent was to become a writer. He planned to make enough money to retire early in life and then devote his time to writing. In 1934 he graduated in business from the City College of New York and worked in the business world until the mid-1940s. When not working, he wrote fiction, but his literary efforts proved unsuccessful, and he decided to study psychology. From Columbia University, Ellis received a master's degree in 1943 and a Ph.D. in clinical psychology in 1947.

Ellis wanted to become a psychoanalytic clinical psychologist, a wish that was frustrated at first because institutions that specialized in such training admitted only medical professionals. He finally succeeded in obtaining his own analysis from the Karen Horney group and practiced classic psychoanalysis in the early 1950s. However, dissatisfied with that approach, Ellis began practicing his own theory in 1955.

Rational emotive behavior therapy was primarily a cognitive theory in the beginning. Its main tenets were first published in Ellis's *Reason and Emotion in Psychotherapy* (1962). REBT has since broadened its base considerably and now includes behavioral and emotional concepts.

Ellis has established a nonprofit institute to promote REBT—the Albert Ellis Institute. A prolific writer, he has produced more than 500 articles, some 50 books, and numerous films and tapes. Until recently Ellis's weekly schedule included as many as 80 clients for individual sessions and up to eight group sessions. Annually, he has given about 200 workshops and talks. Yet despite such a work load, Ellis does not consider himself a compulsive worker because he does not *have* to work or prove himself (Weinrach, 1980). He relaxes by reading, listening to music, and socializing.

Ellis has been married twice and states that he has learned something about himself and the nature of women from each marriage. Since 1964 he has had a solid love/companionship relationship with Janet Wolfe, who helped him build the Albert Ellis Institute (Dryden, 1989). Besides being a devout practitioner of his own theory, Ellis has been recognized in professional circles in many ways, including being named Humanist of the Year by the American Humanist Association. Although he is flamboyant in a humorous and startling manner, Ellis can be affectionate and warm (Dryden, 1989). Indeed, he is a man of contrasts who sees ways of combining ideas that, on the surface, might appear to clash, such as religion and REBT (Powell, 1976).

VIEW OF HUMAN NATURE/PERSONALITY

REBT assumes that people are both "inherently rational and irrational, sensible and crazy" (Weinrach, 1980, p. 154). According to Ellis (1995), this duality is biologically inherent and is perpetuated unless a new way of thinking is learned (Dryden, 1994). Irrational thinking, or as Ellis defines it, irrational Beliefs (iBs), may include the invention of upsetting and disturbing thoughts. These fallacies, which have been used in formulating various tests, have been correlated "with various kinds of emotional disturbance" (Ellis, 1984, p. 266). Ellis organizes irrational beliefs under three main headings:

1. "I *absolutely must* perform important tasks well and be approved by significant others, or else I am an *inadequate, pretty worthless person!*" Result: severe feelings of anxiety, depression, and demoralization, often leading to severe inhibition.
2. "Other people, especially my friends and relatives, *truly must* treat me kindly and fairly, or else they are *rotten, damnable people!*" Result: severe feelings of anger, rage, fury, often leading to fights, child abuse, assault, rape, murder, and genocide.
3. "The condition under which I live absolutely must be comfortable, unhassled, and enjoyable, or else it's *awful*, I *can't stand* it, and my life is hardly worth living!" Result: severe feelings of low frustration tolerance, often leading to compulsion, addiction, avoidance, inhibition, and public reaction. (Ellis, 1996b, p. 77)

Although Ellis (1973) does not deal with the developmental stages of individuals, he thinks that children are more vulnerable to outside influences and irrational thinking than adults are. He believes that human beings are by nature gullible, highly suggestible, and easily disturbed. Overall, people have within themselves the means to control their thoughts, feelings, and actions; but they must first realize what they are telling themselves (i.e., self-talk) to gain command of their lives (Ellis, 1962). This matter is one of personal, conscious awareness; the unconscious mind is not involved.

Ellis believes that it is a mistake for people to evaluate or rate themselves beyond the general idea that everyone is a fallible human being. He especially discourages the use of any form of the verb *to be* (e.g., *is, was, am, has been, being*) to describe a person. He reasons that human problems do not come from the id, as Freud envisioned, nor from the *what if*, but rather from the *is*; the verb *to be* makes it difficult to separate people from their actions. Therefore, Ellis advocates that individuals speak and think of their behavior as separate from their personhood—for example, "I act badly" rather than "I am bad" (Ellis & Harper, 1975). Avoiding the verb *to be* fosters a more rational thought process and gives a person the freedom to change, to focus on altering specific behaviors instead of overhauling personality.

ROLE OF THE COUNSELOR/THERAPIST

In the REBT approach counselors are active and direct; they are instructors who teach and correct clients' cognitions. Countering a deeply ingrained belief requires more than logic; it requires consistent attention and repetition (Krumboltz, 1992). Therefore, counselors must listen carefully for illogical or faulty statements from their clients and must challenge them. In the process they show concern and care for their clients by "attending to their behavior, by frequently asking questions for clarification, by recalling personal details about the client and his or her problems, by the use of gentle humor, and by active attempts to help the client solve difficult issues" (Vernon, 1996, p. 122).

Ellis (1980) and Walen, DiGuiseppe, and Dryden (1992) have identified several characteristics desirable for REBT counselors. They should be bright, knowledgeable, empathetic, respectful, genuine, concrete, persistent, scientific, interested in helping others, and involved in using REBT themselves. A counselor's main assessment instrument is the evaluation of a client's thinking. Some formal tests may be employed to measure rational and irrational thinking, but the evaluation process is primarily accomplished in counselor-client sessions. As a rule, REBT practitioners do not rely heavily on the diagnostic categories in the *DSM*.

GOALS

The primary goals of REBT focus on helping people realize that they can live more rational and productive lives. In general, rational emotive behavior therapy constitutes "an attempt to correct mistakes in a client's reasoning as a way of eliminating undesirable emotions" (Cohen, 1987, p. 37).

REBT is heavily influenced by stoic philosophy, and Ellis is fond of quoting a 1st-century stoic, Epictetus: "Men feel disturbed not by things, but by the views which they take of them." Thus, individuals often disturb themselves by changing wishes and desires into demands. Ellis points out that when people use words such as *must*, *should*, *ought*, *have to*, and *need*, they make demands of wishes and think irrationally. For individuals who think that wishes must or should occur, a wish unfulfilled results in a catastrophe. REBT helps clients stop catastrophizing and making such demands. Clients in REBT may express some negative feelings, but a major goal is to help them avoid a more emotional response than is warranted by the event.

Another goal of REBT is to help people change self-defeating habits of thought or behavior. One way this goal is accomplished is through the ABCs of REBT: *A* signifies an activating experience, *B* represents how the person thinks about the experience, and *C* is the emotional reaction to *B* (see Figure 10.1).

FIGURE 10.1 The ABC model of human interaction

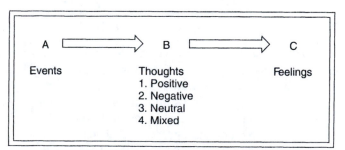

Note: From *Group Work: A Counseling Specialty* (4th ed., p. 439) by Samuel T. Gladding. Copyright 2003. Reprinted by permission of Pearson Education, Inc., Upper Saddle River, NJ.

Many clients believe that an experience directly causes feelings—a concept called *cognitive bypass*. Left out of this conceptualization is the thought process that leads to the development of emotions. For example, a person may lose a job or an opportunity and then assert that the experience caused depression. REBT helps people recognize their *emotional anatomy*, that is, how feelings are attached to thoughts.

Thoughts about experiences may be characterized in four ways: positive, negative, neutral, or mixed. A positive thought leads to positive feelings. For example, if a host at a party reminds a man that he has had too much to drink, the man may think about the host's care and concern on his behalf and have positive emotions. On the other hand, the man may think that the host is criticizing him and has no right to do so, resulting in negative feelings about that same experience. If the latter thought process occurs, the man becomes angry. With a neutral thought the man might simply note the host's actions and move on to another thought, having no emotional reaction. Mixed thoughts occur when a person has both negative and positive thoughts at once—for example, "I'm glad something was said, but I dislike the way it was said." The resulting feeling is ambivalence.

REBT encourages clients to be more tolerant of themselves and others, for everyone is a fallible human being. People are encouraged through REBT to achieve personal goals, rather than dwell on mistakes or miscues. Such goals are accomplished when individuals learn to think rationally in order to change self-defeating behavior.

PROCESS AND TECHNIQUES

The two primary emphases of REBT are teaching and disputing. Before any changes can be made, clients must learn the basic ideas of REBT and understand how thoughts are linked to emotions and behaviors. Consequently, REBT is highly didactic and very directive. In the first few sessions, counselors teach their clients the anatomy of an emotion; that is, feelings are a result of thoughts, not events, and self-talk influences emotions. This process, generally known as rational emotive education (REE), has had a high success rate with children, adolescents, and adults with a wide variety of problems and from a wide range of backgrounds (Wilde, 1996).

It is also critical in the REBT process that clients be able to dispute irrational thoughts. Disputing thoughts and beliefs takes one of three forms—cognitive, imaginal, or behavioral—and is most effective when all three forms are used (Walen et al., 1992). *Cognitive disputation* involves the use of direct questions, logical reasoning, and persuasion. Direct questions challenge clients to prove that their responses are logical. Sometimes these inquiries use the word *why*, which is seldom employed in other counseling approaches because it puts many people on the defensive and closes off exploration. However, *why* questions help REBT clinicians cut through defenses and educate clients to new ways of thinking, feeling, and behaving. For example, counselors might ask, "Why must you?" or "Why must that be so?" These inquiries help clients learn to distinguish between rational and irrational thoughts and appreciate the superiority of rational thoughts.

Another form of cognitive disputation involves the use of *syllogisms*, "a deductive form of reasoning consisting of two premises and a conclusion" (Cohen, 1987, p. 37). Syllogisms help clients and counselors more thoroughly understand inductive and deductive fallacies that underlie emotions. For example, in irrational can't-stand-it-ism the process might go as follows (Cohen, 1987, p. 39):

Major premise: "Nobody can stand to be lied to."
Minor premise: "I was lied to."
Conclusion: "I can't stand it."

Certainly, being lied to is not pleasant, but it is often a part of life, and concluding "I can't stand it" is silly, false, and illogical.

Imaginal disputation depends on a client's ability to imagine and employs a technique known as rational emotive imagery (REI) (Maultsby, 1984). REI may be used in one of two ways. First, a client may be asked to imagine a situation in which she is likely to become upset and to examine her self-talk during that imagined situation. Then she is asked to envision the same situation but to be more moderate in her self-talk this time. Second, a counselor may ask a client to imagine a situation in which he feels or behaves in a different way from that of a real occurrence. The client is then instructed to examine the self-talk he used in this imagined situation. REI does take practice.

The emotional control card (ECC) is a device that helps clients reinforce and expand the practice of REI (Sklare, Taylor, & Hyland, 1985). Wallet-sized ECCs list four emotionally debilitating categories—anger, self-criticism, anxiety, and depression (Ellis, 1986). Under each category is a list of inappropriate or self-destructive feelings and a parallel list of appropriate or nondefeating feelings (see Figure 10.2). In potentially troubling situations clients can refer to the cards and change the quality of their feelings about the situations. At their next counseling sessions the clients can discuss the use of the cards in cognitively restructuring their thoughts from irrational to rational.

Behavioral disputation involves behaving in a way that is the opposite of the client's usual way of acting. Sometimes behavioral disputation takes the form of bibliotherapy, in which clients read a self-help book such as those distributed by the Albert Ellis Institute. At other times behavioral disputation includes role-playing and completing a homework assignment in which clients do activities they previously considered impossible. In both cases clients bring their completed assignments to their scheduled counseling sessions and evaluate them with their counselors.

If disputation of irrational beliefs (iBs) is successful, a new and effective philosophy will emerge (Ellis, 2000). This philosophy will include a new cognitive Effect (cE), which is a restatement of original rational Beliefs (rBs). For example, "It is not awful, merely inconvenient, that I was rejected by a particular person."

Ellis (2000) has devised a number of homework assignments, such as *shame attack* exercises, to help clients learn to behave differently. These exercises usually include an activity that is harmless but dreaded, such as introducing oneself to a stranger or asking for a glass of water in a restaurant without ordering anything else. By participating in such exercises, clients learn the ABCs of REBT on a personal level and come to realize more fully that the world does not stop if a mistake is made or if a want remains unfulfilled. Clients also learn that others are fallible human beings and need not be perfect. And finally, clients learn that goals can be achieved without "awfulizing" or "terriblizing" personal situations.

FIGURE 10.2 Emotional control card

Inappropriate or Self-Destructive Feelings	Appropriate or Nondefeating Feelings
Anger Feelings of resentment, anger, madness, fury, rage	*Irritation* Feelings of (mild or intense) irritation, displeasure, annoyance, frustration; anger at people's acts but not at their persons
Self-criticism Feelings of humiliation, shame, embarrassment, inadequacy; discounting self as a person	*Criticism of one's behavior* Feelings of (mild or intense) regret, sorrow, displeasure, doubt; criticism of one's behavior but not of one's total self
Anxiety Feelings of anxiety, nervousness, hypertension, panic, helplessness, horror	*Concern* Feelings of (mild or intense) concern, caution, vigilance; tension about one's performance but not about one's self
Depression Feelings of depression, worthlessness, undeservingness, guilt, self-downing	*Sadness* Feelings of (mild or intense) sadness, sorrow, regret, discontentment, displeasure; feeling that one is a person who has performed badly but is not a bad person

Note: From "An Emotional Control Card for Inappropriate and Appropriate Emotions in Using Rational-Emotive Imagery" by A. Ellis, 1986, *Journal of Counseling and Development*, 65, p. 206. Copyright 1986 by ACA. Reprinted with permission. No further reproduction authorized without written permission of the American Counseling Association.

In addition, Ellis frequently uses puns and other humorous devices to help his clients see how irrational thinking develops and how silly the consequences of such thinking are. He cautions clients not to "should on themselves" and advises them to avoid "musterbation." He has even composed a number of songs to help remind himself and others to think rationally. For example, he penned the following words to the tune of the "Whiffenpoof Song":

> *I cannot have all of my wishes filled—*
> *Whine, whine, whine!*
> *I cannot have every frustration stilled—*
> *Whine, whine, whine!*
> *Life really owes me the things that I miss,*

Fate has to grant me eternal bliss!
And if I must settle for less than this—
Whine, whine, whine!

Note: From *Rational Humorous Songs: A Garland of Rational Songs* by A. Ellis, 1980, New York: Institute for Rational Emotive Therapy. Copyright 1980 by Institute for Rational Emotive Therapy. Reprinted with permission.

Other REBT counselors, such as Richard Watts (1996), have also written rational emotive behavior therapy songs to common tunes—"I've Been Working on the Railroad," "Jimmy Cracked Corn," "Twinkle, Twinkle, Little Star," and "O Suzannah." These songs address cognitively distorted thoughts in a humorous and therapeutic way.

Two other powerful REBT techniques are confrontation and encouragement. As previously noted, REBT counselors explicitly encourage their clients to abandon thought processes that are not working. Sometimes counselors challenge, or confront, clients who claim to be thinking rationally but who are not. At other times counselors encourage clients to continue working from an REBT base even when they are discouraged. Confrontation need not be done in the style of Ellis—that is, vigorously confronting and attacking a client's beliefs (Johnson, 1980). Instead, counselors can be empathetic and insistent at the same time.

MULTICULTURAL AND GENDER-SENSITIVE ISSUES

Almost from its beginning, REBT has been concerned with its effectiveness. In the 1970s Ellis (1977) provided research data on the effectiveness of REBT with different types of clients in specific settings across the life span. In addition, REBT counselors are generally sensitive to their clients' cultures and adjust their actions to respect those they are helping (Sharf, 2004). James and Gilliland (2003) summarize REBT effectiveness with minority culture clients and reveal that it is usually positive.

REBT is also sensitive to the needs and specific concerns of women. Because REBT practitioners realize that women may be stereotyped according to their gender and gender roles, REBT counselors give female clients a voice as to *what* they will work on (e.g., assertiveness, career, life change, stress) and *how* (e.g., in a group or individually).

EVALUATION OF THE THEORY

STRENGTHS AND CONTRIBUTIONS

One of the major strengths of REBT is that it is clear, easily learned, and effective. Most clients have few problems in understanding the principles or terminology of REBT. Furthermore, Roush (1984) reports that REBT is effective with many different types of individuals, including adolescents. And Seligman (2001) notes that it is appropriate for the treatment of affective disorders, anxiety disorders, and adjustment disorders.

A second strength of REBT is that it can easily be combined with other behavioral techniques to help clients experience more fully what they are learning (Ellis, 2002). REBT is like cognitive-behavioral counseling in that it borrows and integrates other techniques that are compatible with its theoretical foundation.

Another asset of REBT is that it is relatively short-term, usually lasting 10 to 50 sessions. Thereafter, clients can continue to use the approach on a self-help basis. Thus, the economy and efficiency of REBT are impressive (Ellis, 1996b).

Moreover, REBT has generated a great deal of literature and research for clients and counselors. Few other theories have developed as much bibliotherapy material; Ellis is a prolific writer and researcher, as are many other REBT practitioners. Each year the Albert Ellis Institute produces a catalog filled with an array of books, booklets, audiotapes, and videotapes on rational emotive behavior therapy. In addition, Ellis's institute is constantly engaged in empirical studies on the use of REBT with a wide variety of clients.

One final strength of REBT is that it has continued to evolve over the years as its processes and techniques have been refined. An example of this evolution is found in the difference between inelegant and elegant REBT. *Inelegant REBT,* which developed first, focuses on the activating event and the distortions that clients usually have about such events (Ellis, 1977, 1995, 2000). It does not give clients any coping strategies for dealing with situations in which perception matches reality. Instead, clients are encouraged to assure themselves that they will do better in the future or that they are good persons. *Elegant REBT,* on the other hand, concentrates on the beliefs of clients and focuses on their taking responsibility for their own feelings. In the process clients realize that success in everything is not essential and that catastrophe does not result from every unfulfilled want.

LIMITATIONS AND CRITICISMS

One drawback to REBT is that it cannot be used effectively with individuals who have mental problems or limitations, such as those with schizophrenia and those with severe thought disorders. Nor is it productive with people who are severely mentally impaired. A person who is intellectually bright benefits most from this approach.

Another limitation of REBT is that it may be too closely associated with its founder, Albert Ellis; many individuals have difficulty separating the theory from Ellis's eccentricities. Although Johnson (1980) urges counselors to adapt the theory and its techniques to their own personalities and individual styles of counseling, some therapists still eschew the approach because of its connection with Ellis.

REBT also has limited usefulness if its practitioners do not combine its cognitive base with more behavioral and emotive techniques. Ellis says that REBT has always been a diverse approach, and he advocates its use in various settings (Weinrach, 1980). Indeed, the theory is now much broader than it was originally, but some counselors still concentrate on the cognitive side of REBT, thus limiting its effectiveness.

Furthermore, REBT's direct and confrontive approach to clients may be a limitation for some individuals. There is the potential for counselors to be overzealous and pushy, with the result that clients may resist change more strongly than might otherwise be the case and/or drop out of treatment.

Finally, REBT's emphasis on changing thinking may not be the simplest way of helping clients change their behaviors or emotions. Gestalt theorists would challenge REBT and charge that emotions should be experienced before interventions are made.

TREATING LINDA WITH RATIONAL EMOTIVE BEHAVIOR THERAPY

CONCEPTUALIZATION

From the perspective of rational emotive behavior therapy (REBT), Linda is demonstrating her inherently rational and irrational sides through her thoughts, feelings, and behaviors. This duality is to be expected, but Linda is unduly upsetting herself with her irrational beliefs that life is not worth living and that she is worthless. Linda's negative self-talk is dangerous to her well being, as is her assessment of herself as inadequate.

TREATMENT PROCESS

As an REBT therapist, you work actively to teach Linda the ABCs of REBT. You show her that events do not cause feelings but thoughts do and she has a choice as to how she is going to think—with positive, negative, neutral, or mixed thoughts. Right now she is engaged almost exclusively in negative thinking. As a user of REBT yourself, you show genuine concern for Linda and build rapport with her by asking questions and using gentle humor. You even give her a personal example of how REBT has helped you.

You talk with Linda about how the use of words such as *must, should, ought, have to,* and *need* make demands of wishes and lead to irrational thinking. You also work with her on not responding more emotionally to an event than is warranted. You then teach Linda how to dispute thoughts—cognitively, imaginally, and behaviorally. She decides that she will dispute cognitively, and when things do not go her way, she will ask herself *why* questions, for example, "Why must things go my way?" By engaging herself in this way, she empowers herself.

To help Linda even more, you give her some of the bibliotherapy writings from REBT practitioners. You also encourage her to monitor her thoughts regularly and to challenge irrational ones. Treatment ends when Linda is more rational in her thinking and playful in her outlook. Through REBT she is able to see that the world will not end if her family does not become more functional or her workplace more friendly. On the other hand, she has become more aware that she can take control of her thoughts and the emotions and behaviors that go with them. She uses this knowledge to explore new vocational possibilities, new clubs and community activities in which she has an interest, and new and appropriate relationships with men.

SUMMARY AND CONCLUSION

Rational emotive behavior therapy is a popular approach in counseling and psychotherapy that makes use of affective, behavioral, and cognitive methods to help bring about change. A primary focus of this approach is teaching clients to realize that feelings are derived from thoughts, not events.

REBT stresses role play and homework assignments as well as recognition of thoughts. Disputations are employed to counteract faulty, irrational thinking and help clients take control of their lives. REBT is both a psychoeducational and a psychotherapeutic means of promoting change in clients.

SUMMARY TABLE: RATIONAL EMOTIVE BEHAVIOR THERAPY

Major Theorist

Albert Ellis

View of Human Nature/Personality

People are inherently rational and irrational
Disturbed by thoughts
Troubled by using verb *To be*

Role of the Counselor/Therapist

Teaches, confronts, corrects
Concentrates on clients' self-talk
Challenges irrational thinking
Encourages tolerance and acceptance of self and others

Goals

Live more rational and productive lives
Stop making demands of self and others
Recognize irrational thinking and its consequences
Change self-defeating habits
Become more tolerant of self and others

Process and Techniques

Teaching the anatomy of an emotion
Disputing thoughts and beliefs: cognitive, imaginal, and behavioral
    points of view
Using homework assignments

Multicultural and Gender-Sensitive Issues

Sensitive and adaptive to client cultures
Sensitive to women's needs and concerns

Strengths and Contributions

Is direct, clear, effective, and easily learned
Combines well with other theories
Is short-term
Has centralized training center
Continues to evolve

Limitations and Criticisms

Not applicable to all clients
Associated with unconventional theorist
Still primarily cognitive

LEARNING MORE

A number of journals publish articles on the theory, research, and practice of REBT. However, the best journal devoted solely to REBT is the *Journal of Rational Emotive and Cognitive Behavior Therapy.*

Further training in the clinical practice of REBT is available:

Albert Ellis Institute
45 East 65th Street
New York, NY 10021–6593
http://www.irebt.org

Rational-Emotive-Behavior Therapy
www.threeminutetherapy.com/rebt.html

CLASSROOM ACTIVITIES

1. Compare articles and books written by Albert Ellis in the 1970s and the late 1990s. What differences in emphasis do you notice? Share your findings and impressions with other classmates.
2. Using the ABC criteria, examine prominent thoughts you have about a person or an event. How were your thoughts modified using this method?
3. With a fellow classmate make up a humorous rational song set to a familiar and popular tune. Perform your song before the class. What is your underlying message? How do you think your song might help you be more rational in the future?

REFERENCES

Cohen, E. D. (1987). The use of syllogism in rational-emotive therapy. *Journal of Counseling and Development, 66,* 37–39.

Dryden, W. (1989). Albert Ellis: An efficient and passionate life. *Journal of Counseling and Development, 67,* 539–546.

Dryden, W. (1994). Reason and emotion in psychotherapy: Thirty years on. *Journal of Rational Emotive and Cognitive Behavior Therapy, 12,* 83–89.

Ellis, A. (1962). *Reason and emotion in psychotherapy.* New York: Stuart.

Ellis, A. (1973). Rational-emotive therapy. In R. Corsini (Ed.), *Current psychotherapies* (pp. 167–206). Itasca, IL: Peacock.

Ellis, A. (1977). The basic clinical theory of rational-emotive therapy. In A. Ellis and R. Grieger (Eds.), *Handbook of rational-emotive therapy* (pp. 3–34). New York: Springer.

Ellis, A. (1980). Foreword. In S. R. Walen, R. DiGiuseppe, & R. L. Wessler, *A practitioner's guide to rational-emotive therapy* (pp. vii–xii). New York: Oxford University Press.

Ellis, A. (1984). Rational-emotive therapy (RET) and pastoral counseling: A reply to Richard Wessler. *Personnel and Guidance Journal, 62,* 266–267.

Ellis, A. (1986). An emotional control card for inappropriate and appropriate emotions in using rational-emotive imagery. *Journal of Counseling and Development, 65,* 205–206.

Ellis, A. (1988). *How to stubbornly refuse to make yourself miserable about anything: Yes, anything!* Secaucus, NJ: Stuart.

Ellis, A. (1993). Changing rational emotive therapy (RET) to rational emotive behavior therapy (REBT). *Behavior Therapist, 16,* 257–258.

Ellis, A. (1995). Changing rational-emotive therapy (RET) to rational emotive behavioral therapy (REBT). *Journal of Rational Emotive and Cognitive Behavioral Therapy, 13,* 85–89.

Ellis, A. (1996a). *Better, deeper, and more enduring brief therapy: The rational emotive behavior therapy approach.* New York: Brunner/Mazel.

Ellis, A. (1996b). The humanism of rational emotive behavior therapy and other cognitive behavior therapies. *Journal of Humanistic Education and Development, 35,* 69–88.

Ellis, A. (2000). Rational-emotive therapy. In R. J. Corsini & D. Wedding (Eds.), *Current psychotherapies* (6th ed., pp.162–196). Itasca, IL: Peacock.

Ellis, A. (2002). *Overcoming resistance: A rational emotive behavior therapy integrated approach* (2nd ed.). New York: Springer.

Ellis, A., & Harper, R. A. (1975). *A new guide to rational living.* North Hollywood, CA: Wilshire.

James, R. K., & Gilliland, B. E. (2003). *Theories and Strategies in counseling and psychotherapy* (5th ed.). Boston: Allyn & Bacon.

Johnson, N. (1980). Must the RET therapist be like Albert Ellis? *Personnel and Guidance Journal, 59,* 49–51.

Krumboltz, J. D. (1992, December). Challenging troublesome career beliefs. *CAPS Digest,* EDO-CG-92-4.

Maultsby, M. C., Jr. (1984). *Rational behavior therapy.* Upper Saddle River, NJ: Prentice Hall.

Morris, K. T., & Kanitz, M. (1975). *Rational-emotive therapy.* Boston: Houghton Mifflin.

Newhorn, P. (1978). Albert Ellis. *Human Behavior, 7,* 30–35.

Powell, J. (1976). *Fully human, fully alive.* Niles, IL: Argos.

Roush, D. W. (1984). Rational-emotive therapy and youth: Some new techniques for counselors. *Personnel and Guidance Journal, 62,* 414–417.

Seligman, L. (2001). *Systems, strategies, and skills of counseling and psychotherapy.* Upper Saddle River, NJ: Prentice Hall.

Sharf, R. S. (2004). *Theories of psychotherapy and counseling* (3rd ed.). Pacific Grove, CA: Brooks/Cole.

Sklare, G., Taylor, J., & Hyland, S. (1985). An emotional control card for rational-emotive imagery. *Journal of Counseling and Development, 64,* 145–146.

Vernon, A. (1996). Counseling children and adolescents: Rational emotive behavior therapy and humanism. *Journal of Humanistic Education and Development, 35,* 120–127.

Walen, S. R., DiGiuseppe, R., & Dryden, W. (1992). *A practitioner's guide to rational-emotive therapy.* New York: Oxford University Press.

Watts, R. E. (1996). Some contemporary rational emotive behavior therapy songs. *Journal of Humanistic Education and Development, 35,* 117–119.

Weinrach, S. G. (1980). Unconventional therapist: Albert Ellis. *Personnel and Guidance Journal, 59,* 152–160.

Wilde, J. (1996). The efficacy of short-term rational-emotive education with e.g. fourth-grade students. *Elementary School Guidance & Counseling, 31,* 131–138.

CHAPTER 11

Transactional Analysis

He acted like a child
and ran wild up and down the halls
with a bottle in his hand
and liquor on his breath.
She was smart and played the part
of a grown-up
calming him down
and marching him back to his room
with a scolding.
In the middle of the night
amid what was chaos
quiet reigned again.

Note: "Chaos and Calm" by S. T. Gladding. Copyright 2003 by Samuel T. Gladding.

Some clinicians classify transactional analysis (TA) as an almost purely cognitive theory with a linkage to psychoanalysis. TA was formulated by Eric Berne in the early 1960s and rose to prominence after the publication of two best-selling books: Berne's *Games People Play* (1964) and Thomas Harris's *I'm OK, You're OK* (1967). Although Berne was fearful that the popularity of these books would undermine the seriousness of his work, they simply made the theory more attractive and familiar to the general public.

Since the 1970s, TA has not been as popular in the United States as it has been in some other countries. One explanation is that the theory has not continued to evolve and research supporting it has been sparse. In addition, TA has suffered from the rise of cognitive therapy and REBT, both of which have had strong proponents and a plethora of research supporting their use. Nevertheless, TA is still used by a number of practitioners and is important to understand.

MAJOR THEORIST: ERIC BERNE

Eric Berne was born in 1910 in Montreal, Canada, where his father was a doctor and his mother, a writer and an editor. Berne was 5 years older than his only sibling, a sister. He was close to his father, who died at the age of 38, when Eric was only 9 years old. Berne followed in his father's footsteps, earning a medical degree from McGill University in 1935. He then completed a psychiatric residency at Yale, set up a private practice in Connecticut and New York, became a U.S. citizen, and married. During World War II he served as an army psychiatrist in Utah, where he started practicing group therapy.

After the war Berne settled in Carmel, California, where he separated from his wife and completed his first book, *The Mind in Action* (1947), which was a critical survey of psychiatry and psychoanalysis. In California he resumed the psychoanalytic training he had started before the war, part of which was his own analysis, supervised by Erik Erikson. Erikson insisted that Berne not remarry until after the analysis was finished, and Berne complied. He remarried in 1949 and fathered two children, as he had in his first marriage. He built a study in his house away from the noise of the children and, in 1950, began a demanding schedule that included consultations and practice in Carmel, San Francisco, and Monterey. His only breaks occurred on Friday nights, when he played poker at his house.

In 1956 Berne was turned down for membership in the Psychoanalytic Institute, a rejection that proved to be a turning point in his life. He reacted by disassociating himself from psychoanalysis and devoting his time to the development of transactional analysis, which has a psychoanalytic aspect.

Dusay (1977) describes the formulation of TA in four phases. In the first (1955–1962), Berne developed the concept of ego states. His ideas were influenced by his clients' descriptions of behaving like a child, a parent, and an adult—the three ego states. In the second phase (1962–1966), Berne concentrated on transactions and games. The International Transactional Analysis Association was created in 1964, and Berne published the popular *Games People Play*. In the third phase (1966–1970), he emphasized the reasons some individuals choose to play certain games in life. In the fourth phase (from 1970 on), he and his followers emphasized action and energy distribution.

Berne was involved in the first three phases of TA development. After a second divorce in 1964, he spent a great deal of time writing; at one point he was working on the manuscripts of six books and editing the *Transactional Analysis Bulletin*. He also gave numerous lectures and seminars. Berne's third marriage was short-lived; he died of a heart attack in 1970 at the age of 60.

VIEW OF HUMAN NATURE/PERSONALITY

Transactional analysis is an optimistic theory: It assumes that people can change despite any unfortunate events of the past. TA is also antideterministic, proposing that people have choices in their lives and that what was once decided can be redecided at a later date. As James and Jongeward (1971) emphasize, "Transactional analysis is a rational approach to understanding behavior and is based on the assumption that all individuals can learn to trust themselves, think for themselves, make their own decisions, and express their feelings" (p. 12).

TA focuses on four major methods of understanding and predicting human behavior:

- *Structural analysis*—understanding what is happening within the individual
- *Transactional analysis*—describing what happens between two or more people
- *Game analysis*—understanding transactions that lead to bad feelings
- *Script analysis*—understanding an individual's life plan

STRUCTURAL ANALYSIS

In structural analysis each person is considered to have three functional ego states—child, parent, and adult. Berne (1964) defines an *ego state* as "a consistent pattern of feeling and experience directly related to a corresponding consistent pattern of behavior" (p. 364). He notes that the findings of Wilder Penfield and his associates (1952, 1954) support this definition. Penfield, a neurosurgeon, found that an electrode applied to different parts of the brain evokes memories and feelings long forgotten by the person. The implication is that the brain functions like a tape recorder to preserve complete experiences in a sequential form recognizable as ego states.

The *child ego state*, the first to develop, is that part of the personality characterized by childlike behaviors and feelings. Childlike behavior might be described as inquisitive, affectionate, selfish, mean, playful, whiny, manipulative. The child ego state consists of two subdivisions—the natural, or free, child and the adaptive child. The *natural child* is the part of the person that is spontaneous, impulsive, feeling oriented, and often self-centered and pleasure loving. The natural child is also intuitive, creative, and responsive to nonverbal messages. The *adaptive child* is the compliant part of the personality that conforms to the wishes and demands of parental figures. These adaptations of natural impulses occur in response to traumas, natural life experiences, and training.

The *parent ego state* incorporates the attitudes and behaviors of parental figures—that is, the dos, shoulds, and oughts. Outwardly, these messages are expressed through critical or nurturing behavior. Parental messages are present throughout a person's life; any response to a thoughtful question that occurs within 10 seconds usually comes from the parent ego state. This ego state also consists of two subdivisions. The *nurturing parent* is the part that comforts, praises, and aids others. The *critical parent* is the part that finds fault, displays prejudices, disapproves, and prevents others from feeling good about themselves. These two parts are revealed in nonverbal behaviors such as pointing a finger at someone and in verbal statements such as, "That's too bad, but don't worry."

The *adult ego state* is not subdivided or related to a person's age. It is the objective, thinking, data-gathering part of a person. The adult ego state tests reality, much as the ego does in Freud's system. The adult is rational and organized, functioning in some ways like a computer by processing data without feelings and expressing itself through phrases such as, "I understand" and "I'm going to."

Sometimes the different ego states operate simultaneously. For example, a woman may observe an attractive man and go through the following self-dialogue: "He is really good looking and well spoken [adult], but he's probably stuck up [critical parent], although I've heard he's very sensitive [nurturing parent]. I wonder how I could attract him and get him to notice me [natural child]. Oops! I'd better stop looking and get back to work, or my boss will get mad at me [adaptive child]."

A major focus of transactional analysis is determining which ego state(s) a person is using. Although TA does not favor one ego state over another, the theory stresses the importance of being able to balance responses when necessary and appropriate. Those who constantly exhibit just one ego state do not function as well as those who are more flexible.

One way of assessing which ego state(s) a person employs most is through the use of an *egogram* (Dusay & Dusay, 1989). An egogram remains fixed unless an individual invests energy in changing response patterns. The egogram of a person who responds primarily from the adult ego state is shown in Figure 11.1.

TRANSACTIONAL ANALYSIS

The second way of understanding and predicting human behavior involves ego state transactions. In contrast to the intrapersonal focus of structural analysis, transactional analysis is interpersonal. Transactions may occur on one of three levels: complementary,

FIGURE 11.1 An egogram

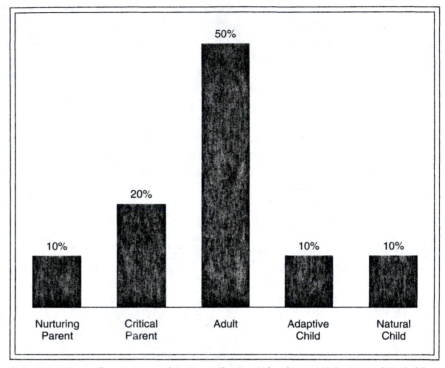

Note: From *Counseling: A Comprehensive Profession* (4th ed., p. 248) by Samuel T. Gladding. Copyright 2000. Reprinted by permission of Pearson Education, Inc., Upper Saddle River, NJ.

crossed, or ulterior. In a *complementary transaction* both persons are operating either from the same ego state (e.g., child to child, adult to adult) or from complementary ego states (e.g., parent to child, adult to parent). In such cases responses are predictable and appropriate. An adult-to-adult transaction might look like this:

PERSON 1: What time is it?

PERSON 2: It's 7 o'clock.

A child-to-child transaction would involve more playfulness:

PERSON 1: Let's go play with Billy.

PERSON 2: Yeah! We could have lots of fun with him!

A parent-to-parent transaction, however, would be more nurturing or critical:

PERSON 1: You never do anything right.

PERSON 2: The problem is that you're always finding fault with my work.

In a *crossed transaction* an inappropriate ego state is activated, producing an unexpected response. Crossed transactions hurt, prompting individuals to withdraw from each other or switch topics. In a crossed transaction one person might be operating from a child ego state and hoping for a complementary parent ego state response but might receive instead a comment from the other person's adult ego state:

PERSON 1: Can you help me carry these bags? They must weigh a ton.

PERSON 2: Those bags weigh approximately twenty pounds, and you're capable of carrying them.

An *ulterior transaction* is one in which two ego states operate simultaneously and one message disguises the other. Ulterior transactions appear to be complementary and socially acceptable even though they are not. For example, at the end of a date one person might say to the other, "Do you want to come in and listen to a little music?" On the surface this question might seem to be coming from an adult ego state but in reality is masking a child ego state: "Want to come in and have some fun together?"

GAME ANALYSIS

Games are ulteriorly motivated transactions that appear complementary on the surface but end in bad feelings. People play games to structure time, achieve recognition, make others predictable, and prevent intimacy. Because intimacy involves risks, games keep people safe from exposing their thoughts and feelings. There are first-degree, second-degree, and third-degree games; and all have predictable ends. Berne (1964) offers examples of each degree.

First-degree games are played in social circles with anyone who is willing to participate. They generally lead to mild upsets. An example of a first-degree game is Seducto, which can be exciting and fun initially. In this game a male and a female enjoy an evening flirting with each other until one turns the other down and both leave feeling slightly uncomfortable.

A *second-degree game* occurs when the players go after bigger stakes, usually in more intimate circles, and end up with bad feelings. An example of a second-degree game is Uproar, in which two persons get angrier and angrier until one or both get very upset about being called a name or put down.

A *third-degree game* usually involves injury; the players end up in jail, the hospital, or the morgue. An example of this game is Cops and Robbers, in which people dare those in authority to catch them and yet leave clues about where they can be cornered. With each increasing degree there is greater danger of permanent damage. Very few games have a positive or neutral outcome (Berne, 1964).

Individuals who play games operate from one of three positions: victim, persecutor, or rescuer (Karpman, 1968). To keep games going, people often assume new roles. For example, in the game Why Don't You/Yes, But, one person plays the rescuer, responding to a complaint from the victim by saying, "Why don't you . . . ?" The victim answers, "Yes, but . . . ." When this game becomes tiresome, the rescuer may switch off to a persecuting role and respond sarcastically to the victim's complaint: "Ain't it awful!" Figure 11.2 represents the three positions that people assume during game interactions. The list of possible games is almost endless, and it is easy for individuals to get hooked into playing them. In the long run, however, game players avoid meaningful and healthy human interactions.

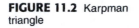

FIGURE 11.2 Karpman triangle

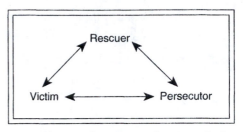

Note: From *Counseling: A Comprehensive Profession* (4th ed., p. 250) by Samuel T. Gladding. Copyright 2000. Reprinted by permission of Pearson Education, Inc., Upper Saddle River, NJ.

SCRIPT ANALYSIS

Berne contends that everyone makes a *life script*, or life plan, by the age of 5. These scripts, which determine how individuals interact with others, are based on interpretations of external events. Positive messages given to children function as permissions and do not limit them in any way. Negative messages, or *injunctions,* are more powerful and may become the basis for destructive scripts. Many parental injunctions begin with *don't*: "Don't question," "Don't contradict," "Don't play with them." Unless people make conscious attempts to overcome such injunctions, they may experience negative consequences.

Most life scripts revolve around giving and receiving *strokes* (i.e., verbal or physical recognition). Berne points out that negative strokes, or punishments, are better than no strokes at all, that is, being ignored. Strokes result in the accumulation of either good or bad feelings, known as *stamps.* When individuals collect enough stamps, they cash them in on certain behaviors. For example, a teenager may collect enough bad feelings from frequent failing grades to justify quitting school or enough good feelings from studying hard to justify attending a party. Healthy people give and receive positive strokes most often.

The following negative scripts are common:

- **Never scripts:** Individuals never get to do what they want (e.g., "Marriage is bad; never get married").
- **Until scripts:** Individuals must wait until a certain time to do something they want to do (e.g., "You cannot play until you have all your work done").
- **Always scripts:** Individuals tell themselves that they must continue doing what they have been doing (e.g., "You should always continue a job once you've started it").
- **After scripts:** Individuals expect difficulty after a certain event (e.g., "After age 40 life goes downhill").
- **Open-ended scripts:** Individuals do not know what they are supposed to do after a given time (e.g., "Be active while you're young").

There are also *miniscripts* that focus on minute-by-minute occurrences. Some of the most common miniscripts are "Be perfect," "Be strong," "Hurry up," "Try harder,"

"Please someone." These five messages, called *drivers*, allow people to escape their life scripts, but the escape is only temporary.

The ideal life script in TA terms is informed by the position *I'm OK; you're OK* (i.e., a get-on-with position) (Harris, 1967). But people may operate from three other positions: *I'm OK; you're not OK* (i.e., a get-away-from position); *I'm not OK; you're OK* (i.e., a get-nowhere-with position); and *I'm not OK; you're not OK* (i.e., a get-rid-of position). Figure 11.3 shows these positions.

Everyone operates from each of these four positions at various times, but well-functioning individuals learn to recognize unhealthy positions and modify their thoughts and behaviors accordingly. Berne holds that life scripts can be rewritten if people become more conscious of what they are thinking and make concerted efforts to change.

FIGURE 11.3 OK positions

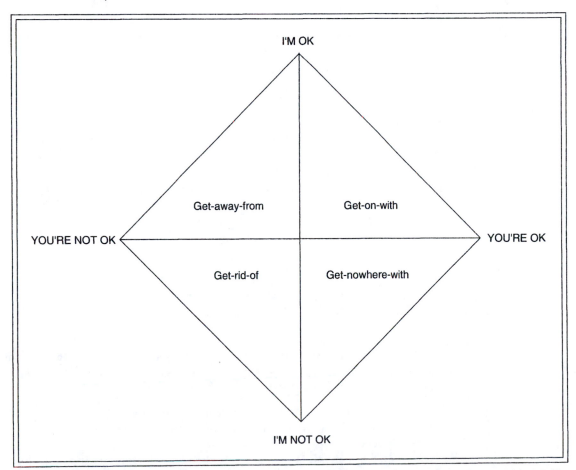

Note: From *Counseling: A Comprehensive Profession* (4th ed., p. 252) by Samuel T. Gladding. Copyright 2000. Reprinted by permission of Pearson Education, Inc., Upper Saddle River, NJ.

ROLE OF THE COUNSELOR/THERAPIST

TA treatment assigns counselors the initial role of teacher. They must explain to their clients the language and the concepts of TA, a new way of thinking about self. Thereafter, counselors contract with clients for specific changes and help them achieve them. Counselors also help their clients obtain the tools, or skills, necessary for change and empower them through various techniques (Corey, 2004).

TA counselors do not rely heavily on formal psychological tests, although counselors do assess client functioning. However, assessment is usually done through an egogram or another less formal method. The purpose is to determine how clients are spending time and from which ego states they are operating. Diagnosis based on *DSM* categories is not stressed.

GOALS

The primary goals of TA focus on transforming clients from frogs into princes and princesses. It is not enough that clients learn to adjust, as in psychoanalysis. Instead, the emphasis is on attaining health and autonomy. Counselors help their clients identify and restore distorted or damaged ego states, develop the capacity to use all ego states, use the adult ego state with its reasoning powers, alter inappropriate life scripts, and adopt a position of "I'm OK; you're OK" (Berne, 1966).

In becoming autonomous, clients exhibit more awareness, intimacy, and spontaneity; become free of games; and eliminate self-defeating scripts. They become more in touch with their past but, at the same time, are freed from previous negative influences. A major emphasis of TA is on learning about the self in order to decide whom one wishes to become (Goulding & Goulding, 1997).

PROCESS AND TECHNIQUES

TA has initiated a number of techniques for helping clients reach their goals. Most TA counselors begin with analysis—structural, transactional, game, and/or script—as described earlier. Other techniques include the following:

- *Treatment contract*—emphasizes agreed-upon responsibilities for both counselors and clients (Dusay & Dusay, 1989); reveals when counseling goals have been reached
- *Interrogation*—involves speaking to a client's adult ego state until an adult response is given; can be confrontational; can be ineffective, supplying only historical material

- *Specification*—identifies the ego state that initiated a transaction; takes place on an adult-to-adult level
- *Confrontation*—involves pointing out inconsistencies in client behavior or speech
- *Explanation*—teaches the client about some aspect of TA; occurs on an adult-to-adult ego state level
- *Illustration*—enlightens the client or elaborates on a point; may speak to both the child and the adult ego states
- *Confirmation*—points out recurrence of previously modified behavior; can be effective only when the client has a firmly established adult ego state
- *Interpretation*—explains to the child ego state of the client the reasons for the client's behavior; can be effective only when the client has a functioning adult ego state
- *Crystallization*—involves an adult-to-adult transaction in which the client becomes aware that game playing may be given up; frees the client; completes the TA process

Almost all of the techniques in TA involve some combination of questioning, confrontation, and dialogue. The following questions are among those most frequently asked by TA counselors:

What are the nicest and worst things your parents ever said to you?
What is your earliest memory?
What is the family story about your birth? What is your favorite fairy tale, story, or song?
How would you describe your mother and father?
How long do you expect to live?

To be most effective, TA counselors must always carefully assess the ego strengths of individual clients. Clients are usually capable of making new decisions about life once they discover different aspects of themselves.

TA is presently divided into three main schools of treatment: the classical school, the cathexis school, and the redecision school (Barnes, 1977). All of these schools use contracts as their primary method of intervention and have autonomy as the final goal of treatment.

MULTICULTURAL AND GENDER-SENSITIVE ISSUES

Transactional analysis appeals to many cultures. Indeed, there are TA associations in 65 countries, from Argentina to the Ukraine. TA also has an appeal within countries with diverse populations, largely because the contract basis acts "as a safeguard against therapists' imposing their cultural values" on clients (Corey, 2004, p. 351). In addition, the cognitive nature of TA and the instructive methods it uses are appealing to some cultural groups within the United States, such as African Americans, Latinos, and Asian Americans (Thompson, Rudolph, & Henderson, 2004).

Likewise, TA seems to be an appropriate theory for work on gender-sensitive issues. The emphasis on empowerment and contracts strengthens the position of women in TA therapy. Furthermore, the exploration of life scripts and family messages may help both men and women explore their roles and decide whether they wish to make any changes in what they do and how they do it.

EVALUATION OF THE THEORY

STRENGTHS AND CONTRIBUTIONS

Transactional analysis uses terms that are easily understood and clearly defined. Consequently, it can be used in varied settings with varied populations—for example, with students who want to overcome math anxiety (Eisenberg, 1992). Another strength of TA is that it is easily and effectively combined with other more action-oriented counseling theories. The use of TA and Gestalt therapy together has been especially powerful (James & Jongeward, 1971).

One other positive aspect of TA is that it puts the responsibility for change on clients. Individuals can choose to change or remain the same, but it is their decision, not their therapists'. In addition, TA is goal directed. The contractual nature of the counseling process makes it possible for both counselors and clients to know when treatment should be terminated (James & Gilliland, 2003).

Another benefit of TA is a worldwide association that sponsors certification, conferences, and publications related to the theory. The International Transactional Analysis Association (ITAA) is active in training and certifying its members and in publishing a scholarly journal, the *Transactional Analysis Journal*.

LIMITATIONS AND CRITICISM

TA has been criticized for its cognitive orientation; to understand is only the beginning of change. Although TA promotes understanding, it is limited in its effectiveness unless it is used with another more action-oriented theory.

The TA approach is also criticized for its simplicity, structure, and popularity. TA is so widely known that some people use the terminology but do not practice the theory. These individuals intellectualize their problems but take few actions to modify them. Moreover, TA terms such as "I'm OK; You're OK" have become so popular that they sometimes lose their punch.

A further criticism is that TA does not emphasize the authenticity of the counselor (Corey, 2001). Counselors and clients are seen as equals, and little attention is paid to the person of the counselor in the process.

A more serious criticism of TA is that the research behind it is relatively weak. Methodological improvements are needed to study populations receiving TA treatment (Miller & Capuzzi, 1984). In addition, some clinicians charge that the approach has not developed much since Berne's death in 1970. Although distinct emphases and schools of TA have emerged, few new ideas have been conceptualized. And there are no prominent new theorists or disciples of TA on the national or international scene. Unless there is renewal within the theory and those who practice it, TA will lose prominence as a counseling modality.

TREATING LINDA WITH TRANSACTIONAL ANALYSIS

CONCEPTUALIZATION

From a transactional analysis (TA) perspective, Linda has made some decisions that have not been very productive. Many of these decisions have been made out of her adaptive child ego state, the compliant part of the personality that conforms to the wishes and demands of parental figures. She has conformed to the wishes and demands of her father, her former husband, and her bosses at work. She has not found any of this acquiescent behavior satisfactory; in fact, it has been just the opposite, and hence her involvement with escape literature and movies. Basically, Linda has an overdeveloped child ego state and an underdeveloped adult ego state.

In addition, Linda does not operate on a complementary level in her interpersonal relationships. Instead, her responses are crossed, as when unequals speak. Most of the time these transactions leave Linda dissatisfied and discouraged. She feels that others talk down to her, and she is frustrated. Consequently, Linda plays games, most of which have left her with bad feelings, except for her most recent third-degree game involving suicide, which could have left her in the morgue. Linda feels like a victim in the games she plays and in life.

You also note that Linda has injunctions in her life, such as "Don't be too competent." Therefore, Linda's life is limited in how much she can achieve. Because Linda has received mainly negative strokes in her life, she has followed negative scripts that have allowed her to distance herself from her family, divorce her husband, and find fault with her work. Her miniscript has been to please others. She is definitely in the I'm-not-OK position, as are most of those with whom she associates.

TREATMENT PROCESS

As the TA therapist you are first of all a teacher. You explain to Linda the language and concepts of TA and the ways in which she can use these tools to think about herself. You want Linda to achieve a healthy lifestyle, to develop a strong adult ego state, and to adopt a position of I'm OK; you're OK. You want Linda to become autonomous and exhibit more awareness, intimacy, and spontaneity; become free of games; and eliminate self-defeating scripts. Therefore, you draw up a treatment contract with Linda with mutually agreed-upon goals and responsibilities.

When necessary, you confront Linda about inconsistencies in her behavior, explaining, illustrating, confirming, and interpreting as appropriate. Almost all of the TA techniques you use involve some combination of questions, confrontation, and dialogue. The techniques are aimed at helping Linda gain insight into not only what she is doing now but also how she can transform herself in time. To help in this pursuit, you use some Gestalt techniques that add action and emotion to the thought process. In the end, Linda is able to experience what it is like to be talking to others from an adult ego state and to be successful instead of frustrated and angry.

SUMMARY AND CONCLUSION

Transactional analysis was formulated in the 1960s by Eric Berne. It parallels psychoanalysis with its emphasis on ego states, yet it has a number of other assumptions and practices that differ from those of psychoanalytic theory. For instance, TA holds that people can change if they gain insight into their thinking process; thinking influences feeling and behavior. The unconscious is not important. The TA approach also stresses that therapy is a learning process and that counselors operate in the role of instructors. TA theory emphasizes the importance of clients' homework outside formal therapeutic sessions and requires clients to learn new vocabularies. TA can be used in a number of settings and with a variety of client problems.

Although TA has many strengths, it likewise has limitations. TA is so cognitively based and has so few techniques that TA counselors often must combine their theory with other approaches, such as Gestalt, to make it more active and strong. In addition, the TA research database is not strong. Many clinicians think that TA has stagnated in its development and that its popular appeal weakens its impact on clients and its status in the world of therapy.

SUMMARY TABLE: TRANSACTIONAL ANALYSIS

Major Theorist

Eric Berne

View of Human Nature/Personality

Optimistic view of change
Three interacting ego states—child, parent, adult
Importance of intrapersonal integration
Analysis of transactions, games, and scripts

Role of the Counselor/Therapist

Teaches
Contracts with clients for change
Instructs in the language of TA

Goals

Transformation of clients
Client health and autonomy
Increased awareness, freedom from games, being OK

Process and Techniques

Emphasis on teaching and learning
Treatment contract
Interrogation, specification, confrontation
Explanation, illustration
Confirmation, interpretation
Crystallization

Multicultural and Gender-Sensitive Issues

Is international
Appeals to diverse populations because of contract basis
Strengthens women through empowerment and contracts
Helps men and women explore life scripts and family messages

Strength and Contributions

Uses easily understood and clearly defined terms
Can be easily and effectively combined with other theories
Makes clients responsible for change
Is goal directed
Has a worldwide association

Limitations and Criticisms

Cognitive orientation
Simplicity, structure, and popularity
Lack of emphasis on authenticity of the counselor
Relatively weak research base
Little development since 1970s

LEARNING MORE

A number of periodicals include articles on the theory, research, and practice of transactional analysis. However, one is devoted exclusively to TA—the *Transactional Analysis Journal*.

For more information on transactional analysis organizations and institutes, contact

International Transactional Analysis Association
436 14th Street, Suite 1301
Oakland, CA 94612-2710
http://www.itaa-net.org/

Institute of Transactional Analysis
www.ita.org.uk

CLASSROOM ACTIVITIES

1. In groups of three, role-play how you think a TA counselor would act in helping an individual with the following concerns: procrastination, interpersonal conflict, stress, adjustment to a new living situation, and grief. Each student should take one role: client, counselor, or observer. After the role-playing, the observer should give feedback to the counselor; the counselor and the client should explain how they experienced the process. Then switch roles until everyone has had a chance to play each role.

2. Keep a list of the number and types of games you find yourself playing in a week. Try to notice any patterns that emerge. Share your findings with fellow classmates in an open class discussion.

3. What support does recent professional literature offer on the effectiveness of transactional analysis? Conduct a search of the literature for articles written in the last 3 years.

REFERENCES

Barnes, G. (1977). Introduction. In G. Barnes (Ed.), *Transactional analysis after Eric Berne: Teachings and practices of three TA schools* (pp. 3–31). New York: Harper & Row.

Berne, E. (1947). *The mind in action.* New York: Simon & Schuster.

Berne, E. (1964). *Games people play.* New York: Grove.

Berne, E. (1966). *Principles of group treatment.* New York: Oxford University Press.

Corey, G. (2001). *Theory and practice of counseling and psychotherapy* (6th ed.). Pacific Grove, CA: Brooks/Cole.

Corey, G. (2004). *Theory & practice of group counseling* (6th ed.). Pacific Grove, CA: Brooks/Cole.

Dusay, J. M. (1977). The evolution of transactional analysis. In G. Barnes (Ed.), *Transactional analysis after Eric Berne: Teachings and practices of three TA schools* (pp. 32–52). New York: Harper & Row.

Dusay, J. M., & Dusay, K. M. (1989). Transactional analysis. In R. J. Corsini & D. Wedding (Eds.), *Current psychotherapies* (4th ed., pp. 405–453). Itasca, IL: Peacock.

Eisenberg, M. (1992). Compassionate math. *Journal of Humanistic Education and Development, 30,* 157–166.

Goulding, M., & Goulding, R. (1997). *Changing lives through redecision therapy* (Rev. ed.). New York: Grove/Atlantic.

Harris, T. (1967). *I'm OK; You're OK.* New York: Harper & Row.

James, M., & Jongeward, D. (1971). *Born to win: Transactional analysis with Gestalt experiments.* Reading, MA: Addison-Wesley.

James, R. K., & Gilliland, B. E. (2003). *Theories and strategies in counseling and psychotherapy* (5th ed.). Boston: Allyn & Bacon.

Karpman, S. (1968). Script drama analysis. *Transactional Analysis Bulletin, 26,* 16–22.

Miller, C., & Capuzzi, D. (1984). A review of transactional analysis outcome studies. *AMHCA Journal, 6,* 30–41.

Penfield, W. (1952). Memory mechanisms. *Archives of Neurology and Psychiatry, 67,* 178–198.

Penfield, W., & Jasper, H. (1954). *Epilepsy and the functional anatomy of the human brain.* Boston: Little, Brown.

Powell, J. (1976). *Fully human, fully alive.* Niles, IL: Argos.

Thompson, C., Rudolph, L., & Henderson, D. A. (2004). *Counseling children* (6th ed.). Pacific Grove, CA: Brooks/Cole.

CHAPTER 12

Feminist Therapy

Her eyes are trained
  (for they must be)
    on the people that she meets
      in the offices and streets
        that she negotiates,
For it is how they see
  and interact with her
    that matters as much
      as who she really is
        or how she views herself.

Note: "Glances" by S. T. Gladding. Copyright 2003 by Samuel T. Gladding.

Feminist therapy is a growing approach in counseling. Feminist views of counseling sprang from the emergence of the women's movement in the late 1960s and 1970s and the development of feminist theory, which begins "with the experience of women and uses women's values and beliefs as the assumptive framework" (Nwachuku & Ivey, 1991, p. 106).

Initially, the feminist movement was seen as a challenge to patriarchal power. However, as feminism has grown, its focus has centered more on the development of females as individuals, with common and unique qualities. In a society in which women face discrimination and subordination because of their gender, feminist therapy offers women a nonsexist, active way of addressing social ills and creating a positive sense of self (Miller, 1986; Okun, 1990).

The infusion of feminist theory into counseling was gradual at first. It started to escalate after the publication of Carol Gilligan's *In a Different Voice* (1982) as the distinctions between and commonalities of women and men were more clearly defined. This approach encourages women and men to become aware of socialization patterns and personal options in altering traditional gender roles. Furthermore, it encourages clients to become involved not only in personal but in social change activities that stress equality as a way of life (Enns & Hackett, 1993).

MAJOR THEORIST: CAROL GILLIGAN

Feminist therapy can claim a number of individuals as its founders; the translation of feminist theories into therapy has seen a number of proponents. Carol Gilligan, Rachel Hare-Mustin, Paula Caplan, Laura S. Brown, Annette Brodsky, Lenore Walker, Carol Travis, Phyliss Chesler, Pam Remer, Mary Gergen, and Carol Enns all stand out as persons who have helped in this process. However, Gilligan is briefly highlighted here.

Carol Gilligan was born on November 28, 1936, in New York City. She majored in literature at Swarthmore College, from which she graduated summa cum laude in 1958. From there she went on to receive a master's degree in clinical psychology from Radcliffe in 1960 and a doctorate in social psychology from Harvard in 1964.

Gilligan began teaching at Harvard in 1967 and in 1970 became a research assistant for Lawrence Kohlberg. She disagreed with Kohlberg's focus on males and issues pertinent to them in his moral development research. Consequently,

Gilligan's primary focus came to be the moral development in girls, especially the impact of caring and relationships. In 1982 she published *In a Different Voice: Psychological Theory and Women's Development* and came to be known as the founder of "difference feminism."

Gilligan is considered to be a pioneer of gender studies, particularly the psychological and moral development of girls. In 1997 she was appointed to Harvard's first position in gender studies and coordinated the formation of the Harvard Center on Gender and Education. In 2002 Gilligan left Harvard to join the faculty of New York University in an interdisciplinary position with the Graduate School of Education and the School of Law.

The recipient of numerous awards, Gilligan was named one of *Time's* 25 most influential people in 1996. She has authored and coauthored numerous books and publications and has been instrumental in her research on adolescence, moral development, women's development, and conflict resolution. As a feminist, scholar, professor, and author, she has helped to form a new direction for women.

VIEW OF HUMAN NATURE/PERSONALITY

Feminist theory and the therapy that has sprung from it are not monolithic; diverse views about human nature exist among feminist counselors. Various feminist theories have been described as liberal, cultural, radical, or socialist with each having its unique emphasis. Yet the different points of view share some beliefs in common about people and the nature of problems within society.

Feminist counselors believe that women have been constrained and oppressed in society. Their strengths have been devalued, and they have been socialized to take care of others and deny their own needs. Thus, many problems that women experience are the result of sociopolitical and cultural forces. In addition, feminist counselors believe that clients know what is best for their lives; for example, women should determine their sexual and procreative lives.

Another assumption underlying the feminist approach is that societal relationships and institutions, as well as gender relationships, are primarily based on noncooperative values. If society and its individuals are to be more mentally healthy, values must change and society must become more nurturing, cooperative, and relational. Individual change will best occur through social change (Okun, 1997).

ROLE OF THE COUNSELOR/THERAPIST

Counselors who work from a feminist perspective play a number of roles in the treatment of their clients. As an educator the counselor demystifies what counseling is and informs clients about how the therapeutic process works. Further, a feminist therapist assumes an egalitarian and collaborative role and often uses self-disclosure to reduce the power differentiation between client and counselor.

The counselor also attempts to make the client active in the therapeutic process, focusing on the inner power a client has that may have been previously unrecognized or discounted. Through open dialogue a feminist counselor helps the client make goals and follow through on them, often using contracts to make therapy more overt and concrete.

In addition, feminist counselors challenge the traditional ways of assessing psychological health. They do not usually make diagnoses using the latest *DSM* but rather include clients in the assessment and treatment process. Somewhat like Adlerian therapists, feminist counselors have their own descriptive terms to define the concerns and problems that clients bring. They tend to reframe and relabel disorders that are especially prevalent in women—for example, depression, eating disorders, and post-traumatic stress—as ways of coping or responding to unfair societal norms and standards.

GOALS

Feminist counseling has a number of goals and objectives.

- To develop client awareness of the gender-role socialization process and internalized gender-role messages and replace them with functional beliefs
- To foster personal empowerment and the development of a wide range of freely chosen behaviors
- To help clients acquire skills to bring about change in the environment
- To promote and foster equality in society and in male/female relationships
- To enable clients to balance independence and interdependence
- To assist clients in becoming more self-nurturing
- To value diversity in all of its forms, especially in regard to gender, culture, and lifestyle (Enns, 1997)

PROCESS AND TECHNIQUES

Because many women who seek help do not recognize that the origin of their problems lies in the inferior status of women in society, part of the counseling process begins with education. Counselors emphasize the value of social, political, and economic action as a major part of treatment. Feminist counselors adapt interventions from a wide range of theoretical orientations, usually explaining the possible effects of and the rationale for their use.

- **Gender-role analysis.** Gender-role expectations begin early in life and impact the way individuals behave. In gender-role analysis counselors help clients ferret out messages they have been given by significant others about how they should behave or appear. For example, clients may have internalized messages such as "Be passive" or "Be pretty." These messages are assessed for their positive and negative impacts, and statements or self-statements are identified that clients may want to change. A plan is then developed to implement the desired changes.

- **Gender-role intervention.** In gender-role intervention, counselors conduct a social analysis of the implications of gender roles and other social expectations for clients. This process provides a broader framework within which clients can assess individual psychological problems; it gives clients insight into ways that social issues may be impacting them. For example, social expectations that women should be thin may be linked to difficulties clients are having regarding body image, weight, and self-esteem.

- **Power analysis.** In power analysis, counselors help clients recognize the difference in power between men and women in society. Power refers to the ability to access resources in order to effect change on a personal and/or external level (Worrell & Remer, 2003). As clients analyze power differences, therapists help them identify alternate kinds of power they may possess and ways to make appropriate changes. For instance, clients may not be able to individually control a chaotic situation, such as verbal or physical abuse. However, they may be able to call in allies to help rectify the situation, or they may leave the environment, and under no circumstances must they internalize the abusive messages.

- **Power intervention.** Power intervention is more spontaneous than other techniques. It involves strengthening or empowering clients by reinforcing their statements or giving them information (Sharf, 2004). Through power intervention clients become more self-sufficient, confident, courageous, and competent. For example, if clients are reinforced for being forthright in giving feedback to people who have acted inappropriately, they will most likely continue that behavior and gain enhanced status in their environments.

- **Assertiveness training.** One of the ways that clients may be empowered is by being taught how to be assertive, that is, stating what one wants in a clear and direct way. Assertiveness is different from aggression or passivity. For instance, the assertive statement "I want to go home now" differs significantly from the aggressive statement "I'm leaving you dull, boring losers" or the passive statement "I can't make up my mind whether to go or stay. What do you think I should do?" Like many other forms of behavior, assertiveness can be taught through role-playing and modeling. It is a skill that must be evaluated culturally and exercised in sensitive, sensible, and appropriate ways.

- **Reframing and relabeling.** The techniques of reframing and relabeling are used in a number of therapeutic approaches to help clients see situations from another perspective and thereby attribute a different meaning to certain behaviors. For example, behaviors that might be seen as pathological, such as depression, can be relabeled as coping mechanisms or as reactions to an oppressive policy or practice within society. In feminist therapy societal expectations are frequently explored, leading clients to understand themselves better. The result is often "a shift from blaming oneself to looking at society for an explanation" (Sharf, 2004, p. 455).

• **Bibliotherapy and scriptotherapy.** Reading and writing can help reinforce therapeutic explorations. Therefore, feminist therapists often encourage their clients to read books or magazines or view appropriate media material, such as films, to assist them in understanding themselves and society better. Journaling or keeping a log of what is being learned or thought or felt can be therapeutic, too. Materials either read or written can be the grist for much discussion in counseling sessions.

• **Demystifying therapy/self-disclosure.** When clients do not understand how counseling works, a power differentiation is created, with the professionals in charge of the therapeutic process being most powerful. To break down this barrier, feminist therapists are clear, open, and direct in explaining what therapy is and how it works. They inform clients about the parameters of the counseling process and work with them in an egalitarian way. One helpful strategy is self-disclosure, in which the counselor shares with the client personal thoughts and feelings that are educative and yet revealing of the counselor as an individual.

• **Group work/social action.** Although therapeutic groups—such as support, self-help, and advocacy groups—are not always a part of feminist therapy, they can be useful adjuncts to this approach (Corey, 2001). Such groups help connect clients with one another and promote unity among the women involved. These groups may benefit clients who are in therapy or may be a powerful follow-up after counseling ends. Similarly, joining a social action organization may help clients help themselves and others by working to change society's stereotypes of women.

MULTICULTURAL AND GENDER-SENSITIVE ISSUES

Feminist counseling is seen as both a multicultural and a gender-sensitive form of therapy. Its concepts and strategies apply equally to individuals and groups regardless of age, race, culture, gender, or sexual orientation. Issues related to various forms of discrimination are important topics of discussion within this approach. Initially, feminist therapy focused mainly on middle-class white women; however, since the 1990s it has become much more encompassing.

Gender issues are highlighted in feminist therapy, and nonsexist development is stressed. For example, in the area of career development feminist thought focuses on requirements for work instead of stressing traditional work roles by gender. Men as well as women may profit from feminist therapy by becoming more attuned to themselves and to gender-prescribed roles that inhibit their growth and restrict their relationships.

EVALUATION OF THE THEORY

STRENGTHS AND CONTRIBUTIONS

Feminist therapy has paved the way for gender-sensitive counseling practices (Corey, 2001). It has helped therapists from many other theoretical persuasions consider potential bias, especially toward women, in many traditional therapeutic practices. This awareness has made it possible for clinicians to be more fair in their work with individuals, groups, couples, and families.

A second contribution of the feminist approach is its effectiveness "with women who are motivated for change and empowerment" (Austin, 1999, p. 69). Feminist therapy gives women a way of moving past passivity and traditionally ascribed roles. It opens up women to explore the inequality of power differentials in gender interactions. Furthermore, it explores the potency of power in relationships and society and the ways in which women can become more powerful through assertive means. It also advocates self-acceptance, including one's body, and teaches clients not to devalue or discount themselves because they are female or imperfect.

Another contribution of feminist counseling is its stress on the varied roles men and women may have and the limited flexibility society promotes because of gender-ascribed behaviors. Through its emphasis on social and political realities that create problems for women and men, feminist therapy addresses oppressive factors in the fabric of society and takes the blame off women for many of their difficulties.

In addition, feminist counseling highlights the importance of interpersonal relationships and behaviors such as cooperation and self-disclosure. Feminist therapists demystify the counseling relationship and stress the egalitarian nature of counseling. This approach allows greater focus on the change process itself.

Men may benefit from feminist counseling practices, too, when they are sensitized to the plight of women and to the limitations that men face when they are forced to maintain a masculine role (Levant, 2001). These insights help men realize how gender-role stereotypes negatively impact society as a whole.

Finally, feminist therapy is extremely flexible and inclusive and can be combined with many other ways of working with clients. Few, if any, counseling theories cannot incorporate feminist principles, ideas, and techniques and thereby broaden their work with diverse client groups in various stages of life and perhaps stimulate positive social change.

LIMITATIONS AND CRITICISMS

The major drawback to feminist therapy is that there is little controlled outcome research on it. "The effectiveness of feminist therapy, both in relative and absolute terms, has not been rigorously evaluated" (Prochaska & Norcross, 2003, p. 435). Therefore, it is impossible to state whether feminist therapy is appropriate for certain clients with specific conditions and concerns.

Another limitation of feminist therapy is the difficulty of finding adequate training. The Stone Center at Wellesley College is conducting some work on what it is like to be female in society and what difficulties women in the United States face in therapeutic situations. However, the Stone Center is not a training center for feminist therapy (Sharf, 2004).

Yet another criticism of feminist therapy is that it does not take a neutral stand on issues. Instead, it actively advocates for "definite change in the social structure, especially in the area of equality, power in relationships, the right to self-determination, freedom to pursue a career outside the home, and the right to an education." Although nothing is inherently wrong with any of these goals, feminist therapists "need to be cautious to avoid pushing their own agenda on their clients" (Corey, 2001, p. 372). Some clients who come for counseling are not interested in changing social structures.

A final criticism of feminist therapy is its lack of agreement on whether the approach is a theory or a philosophical orientation. In recent years advocates of this approach have asserted that it is a theory (e.g., Crawford & Unger, 2000; Enns, 1997). However, as such, it differs significantly from other mainstream theories except for existentialism, which also is criticized for its emphasis on philosophy and its lack of concrete approaches originating from the theory itself.

TREATING LINDA WITH FEMINIST THERAPY

CONCEPTUALIZATION

From a feminist perspective Linda has failed to grow and develop as a person. Instead, she is stuck in a limiting, gender-stereotyped role in which she is stymied in her attempts to achieve and is devalued as a woman. Sociopolitical and cultural forces have conspired to keep her pigeonholed in taking care of others' needs but not her own. Linda knows in some ways that life is not working for her, but she needs to clarify exactly what she wants.

TREATMENT PROCESS

As a feminist therapist you work as an educator, a collaborator, and a partner with Linda. You explore with her the ways in which her strengths and abilities have been discounted or devalued, such as her father's negative stereotyping because of her gender. You work with Linda to define her concerns and goals as concretely as possible. Some of your goals for her include becoming aware of society's and her own internalized messages regarding women and men, becoming more empowered and developing skills that will help her grow, balancing independence with dependence, becoming self-nurturing, promoting and fostering equality in society, and valuing diversity.

To help Linda reach these goals, you conduct a gender-role analysis in which Linda focuses on identifying limiting or enabling messages in her life that were given by significant others. Thereafter, you perform a gender-role intervention, which gives Linda insight into ways that social issues may be impacting her. Next, you repeat the analysis and the intervention focusing on the topic of power. In this process you help Linda identify the power she has and reinforce herself for becoming more self-sufficient, confident, courageous, and competent.

You also teach Linda assertiveness through role-playing and modeling. In this way she is freed to ask for what she wants without being aggressive or passive. Furthermore, she learns how to reframe and relabel situations so that she does not pathologize herself. In addition, you encourage Linda to read books and magazines or view films that can assist her in understanding herself and the role of women in society. And you suggest that she keep a log of what she is learning, thinking, and feeling. Finally, you advise her to join a support group with other women to advocate for and promote equality within society. Linda finds that idea intriguing and begins to explore what it means to be a woman in the 21st century and what possibilities are available to her. A bonus from her support group is that she forms new friendships with others with whom she has much in common and learns helpful information about jobs and education, too.

SUMMARY AND CONCLUSION

A recent phenomenon growing out of the women's movement of the late 1960s and 1970s, feminist therapy is a multifaceted approach to counseling rather than a well-formulated set of constructs (Enns, 1997). It questions and challenges the attitudes of traditional counseling theories, which often advocate maintaining the status quo of a male-dominated, hierarchical society.

According to feminist therapy, gender-role expectations have a profound impact on human development. Because women and men are socialized differently, models of psychological development based on male development fail to recognize that women's identity develops in a context of connectedness and relationship with others (Jordan, 2000; Miller, 1991). Feminist counselors seek to empower women to change the social contexts that suppress them (Austin, 1999), working through gender and power analysis and intervention as well as universal interventions such as bibliotherapy and reframing/relabeling. The result is greater personal and social sensitivity and often social activism.

In feminist therapy external forces are recognized as the root of women's problems. Clients learn self-appreciation and self-value, and they learn to change their environments rather than adjust to them. They also learn to advocate for social change and to develop egalitarian rather than hierarchical relationships.

SUMMARY TABLE: FEMINIST THERAPY

Major Theorists:

Carol Gilligan	Rachel Hare-Mustin	Paula Caplan
	Carol Enns	

View of Human Nature/Personality

Some diversity of views
Social constraint and oppression
Superiority of self-knowledge
Importance of social change

Role of the Counselor/Therapist

Educator, collaborator, active participant
Diagnosis according to feminist terminology

Goals

Awareness of gender-role socialization and internalized messages, replacement with
    functional messages
Personal empowerment
Skills to bring about change in the environment
Equality in society and in male/female relationships
Balance of independence and interdependence
Self-nurturance
Appreciation of all diversity

Process and Techniques

Inferior status of women as basis
Interventions adapted from many orientations
Use of gender-role analysis and intervention
Use of power analysis and intervention
Assertiveness training, relabeling/reframing, bibliotherapy/scriptotherapy
Demystification of therapy, group work

Multicultural and Gender-Sensitive Issues

Equal application to all people
Focus on issues of discrimination
Emphasis on nonsexist development
Increased awareness of men

Strengths and Contributions

Paved the way for gender-sensitive counseling
Empowers women
Stresses varied gender roles and related inhibitions
Emphasizes interpersonal relationships
Stresses self-acceptance
Is flexible and inclusive

Limitations and Criticisms

Little controlled outcome research
Limited training available
Subjective position on social issues
Lack of agreement on orientation (theory or philosophy)

LEARNING MORE

A number of periodicals devoted to feminist therapy and theory may prove helpful in exploring this approach to counseling.

Psychology of Women Quarterly
Women and Therapy
Sex Roles

In addition to journals, several training institutes and professional associations offer clinicians an opportunity to learn more about the lives of women and the best ways to work with them in therapeutic settings.

Stone Center, Wellesley College
106 Central Street
Wellesley, MA 02481
www.wellesley.edu

Psychology of Women (Division 35)
American Psychological Association
http://www.apa.org/divisions/div35

Association for Women in Psychology
www.theworks.baka.com/awp

National Organization for Women
1000 16th Street NW, Suite 700
Washington, DC 20036
www.now.org

Newcomb College Center for Research on Women
Tulane University
20 Caroline Richardson Building
New Orleans, LA 70118-5683
http://www.tulane.edu/we

CLASSROOM ACTIVITIES

1. Stage a debate, with one group of classmates arguing that feminist therapy is a mainstream approach to working with men and women and the other group arguing that it is an adjunct to more established forms of counseling and therapy. List the pros and cons for each side, and have the class vote after listening to each side.
2. Visit the Web site of the National Organization of Women (NOW) or invite a local member of NOW to your class. Discuss current issues impacting women and the strategies being employed to address these situations.

3. Divide into groups of men and women. Have members of each gender discuss how they learned their gender roles and what their thoughts and feelings are about the opposite gender's roles. What changes would each group suggest? Which traditions or practices would each group keep?

REFERENCES

Austin, L. (1999). *The counseling primer*. Philadelphia: Accelerated Development.

Corey, G. (2001). *Theory and practice of counseling and psychotherapy*. Pacific Grove, CA: Brooks/Cole.

Crawford, M., & Unger, R. (2000). *Women and gender: A feminist psychology* (3rd ed.). New York: McGraw-Hill.

Enns, C. Z. (1993). Twenty years of feminist counseling and therapy. *Counseling Psychologist, 21*, 3–87.

Enns, C. Z. (1997). *Feminist theories and feminist psychotherapies: Origins, themes, and variations*. New York: Haworth.

Enns, C. Z., & Hackett, G. (1993). A comparison of feminist and nonfeminist women's and men's reactions to nonsexist and feminist counseling: A replication and extension. *Journal of Counseling and Development, 71*, 499–509.

Gilligan, C. (1982). *In a different voice: Psychological theory and women's development*. Cambridge, MA: Harvard University Press.

Jordan, J. V. (1997). *Women's growth in diversity: More writings from the Stone Center*. New York: Guilford.

Jordan, J. V. (2000). A relational-cultural model: Healing through mutual empathy. *Bulletin of the Menninger Clinic, 65*, 92–103.

Levant, R. E. (2001). Men and masculinity. In J. Worell (Ed.), *Encyclopedia of women and gender* (Vol. 2, pp. 717–728). San Diego: Academic Press.

Miller, J. B. (1986). *Toward a new psychology of women*. Boston: Beacon.

Miller, J. B. (1991). The development of women's sense of self. In J. V. Jordan, A. G. Kaplan, J. B. Miller, I. P. Stiver, & J L. Surrey (Eds.), *Women's growth in connection* (pp. 11–26). New York: Guilford.

Nwachuka, U., & Ivey, A. (1991). Culture-specific counseling: An alternative model. *Journal of Counseling & Development, 70*, 106–111.

Okun, B. F. (1990). *Seeking connections in psychotherapy*. San Francisco: Jossey-Bass.

Okun, B. F. (1997). *Effective helping* (5th ed.). Pacific Grove, CA: Brooks/Cole.

Prochaska, J. O., & Norcross, J. C. (2003). *Systems of psychotherapy* (5th ed.). Pacific Grove, CA: Brooks/Cole.

Sharf, R. S. (2004). *Theories of psychotherapy and counseling* (3rd ed.). Pacific Grove, CA: Brooks/Cole.

Worrell, J., & Remer, P. (2003). *Feminist perspectives in therapy* (2nd ed.). New York: Wiley.

CHAPTER 13

Bowen Family Systems Therapy

Estranged, he travels home
trying to connect
to his family and its history.
In concert, he emerges
thoughts and feelings play in harmony
life is less a mystery.

Note: "Return and Reemergence" by S. T. Gladding. Copyright 2003 by Samuel T. Gladding.

$\mathbf{F}$amily counseling is a relatively recent approach to working with clients. It grew out of the need to help families readjust to life after the upheaval of World War II. At its inception family therapy was considered radical. Most early theories dealt with how an entire family operates and interacts, both internally and externally. Such approaches differed significantly from other commonly accepted theories of the time, which were more individually oriented.

One of the oldest and most distinguished theories of working with families is Bowen family therapy. Murray Bowen and Michael Kerr have been its chief architects and advocates, with Bowen himself the major originator of this philosophy. Nonetheless, many of its concepts have been popularized by other authors, such as McGoldrick, Gerson, and Shellenberger (1999) and Friedman (1985).

This chapter covers Bowen family therapy, which can be used with individuals, couples, and families. The next chapter addresses strategic family therapy, an equally established approach and one that has some of the versatility of the Bowen approach but a different philosophy and methodology. These two family therapies, along with solution-focused therapy, represent the innovation and creativity connected with counseling families and the individuals in them.

MAJOR THEORIST: MURRAY BOWEN

Murray Bowen (1913–1990) was the oldest of five children in a tightly knit family that resided for several generations in a small town in Pennsylvania. After growing up, Bowen moved away and kept a formal distance from his parents, maintaining family relations on a comfortable but superficial level. Bowen was a psychiatrist who became interested in working with families while he was employed at the Menninger Clinic. As early as 1951, he began to require that mothers of disturbed children live in the same hospital setting as their offspring during treatment (Guerin, 1976). From this experience he became interested in studying mother-patient symbiosis, that is, the intense bond that develops between a parent and a child that does not allow either to differentiate from the other (Bowen, 1960, 1961).

In 1954 Bowen joined Lyman Wynne at the National Institute of Mental Health (NIMH), where he continued to study the dynamics of families with schizophrenic children. Bowen worked with the research team at NIMH on a pilot project to hospitalize and treat all members of such families as part of treatment. He recognized during this time that the characteristics exhibited by a schizophrenic family were similar to symptoms in many dysfunctional families. A few years later Bowen moved to Georgetown University, where he researched family dynamics and developed his therapeutic approach.

For Bowen, therapy and theory cannot be separated without doing a disservice to each. He preferred to think of himself as a theorist, one who stood alone in conceptualizing "the family as a natural system . . . which could only be fully understood in terms of the fluid but predictable processes between members" (Wylie, 1991, p. 26). Thus, Bowen viewed himself as a scientist in search of universal truths, and his theory "constantly strives to make continuous what other theories dichotomize"—for example, nature/nurture, male/female, physical illness/emotional illness (Friedman, 1991, p. 136).

During his years at Georgetown, especially in the 1970s, Bowen completed his most productive personal and professional work. Personally, he removed himself from the triangulation with his parents by returning home and reacting cognitively and neutrally to a number of emotional issues that family members presented to him (Anonymous, 1972). Professionally, he clarified his theory (Bowen, 1978); began the Georgetown Family Center Symposium; expanded the Georgetown Family Center to new, off-campus quarters; and initiated the American Family Therapy Association (AFTA) "in order to restore a serious research effort in family therapy" (Wylie, 1991, p. 77).

VIEW OF HUMAN NATURE/PERSONALITY

Murray Bowen was influenced by events in his own life, especially his difficulties with his family of origin. Thus, his personal situation had a major impact on what he proposed in regard to the development of others (Anonymous, 1972; Papero, 1991). Basically, Bowen states that individuals who do not examine and rectify patterns passed down from previous generations are likely to repeat these behaviors in their own families (Kerr, 1988). That possibility is particularly likely if family members, especially those of different generations, are either emotionally overinvolved with each other or emotionally cut off from each other. Bowen concerns himself with the family's emotional system and its impact on family members' personalities.

A key element of Bowen family therapy is that "there is a chronic anxiety in all of life that comes with the territory of living" (Friedman, 1991, p. 139). This anxiety is both emotional and physical and is shared by all protoplasm. Some individuals are more affected than others "because of the way previous generations in their families have channeled the transmission" of this anxiety to them (Friedman, 1991, p. 140).

If anxiety remains low, few problems exist for individuals or families; the family emotional system is undisturbed. However, when anxiety rises, some predictable patterns occur.

Lower scale [undifferentiated] people are vulnerable to stress and are much more prone to illness, including physical and social illness, and their dysfunction is more likely to become chronic when it does occur. Higher scale people can recover emotional equilibrium quickly after the stress passes. (Greene, Hamilton, & Rolling, 1986, p. 189)

To address chronic anxiety and emotional processes in families and society, Bowen emphasizes a number of basic concepts through which therapists can understand the dynamics within a family: differentiation, multigenerational transmission process, nuclear family emotional system, family projection process, triangles, sibling position, and societal regression (Bowen, 1978; Kerr, 1981).

Differentiation refers to the ability of persons to distinguish themselves from their family of origin on an emotional and an intellectual level, to balance the intrapsychic and interpersonal dimensions of the self (Bowen, 1978; Kerr, 2003). There are two counterbalancing life forces—togetherness and individuality. People vary in the level of self-differentiation they can achieve at any one time; the concept itself denotes a process (Bowen, 1965). On a continuum of differentiation, *autonomous*, which is at one end, signals an ability to think through a situation clearly, and *undifferentiated* at the other end implies an emotional dependence on family members, even if living away from them. Such a relationship is described as being *fused* or as an *undifferentiated family ego mass* (Bowen, 1965; Kerr, 2003). In a fused situation family members may exhibit dysfunctional behaviors such as bulimia. "Theoretically, at least four factors influence a person's level of differentiation: emotional reactivity, emotional cutoff, fusion with others, and the ability to take an 'I-position'" (Tuason & Friedlander, 2000, p. 27). It is through the process of differentiation that families and the individuals in them are able to change (see Figure 13.1).

Another of Bowen's basic concepts deals with the coping strategies and patterns that tend to be passed on from generation to generation, an important phenomenon

FIGURE 13.1 Bowen's continuum of self-differentiation

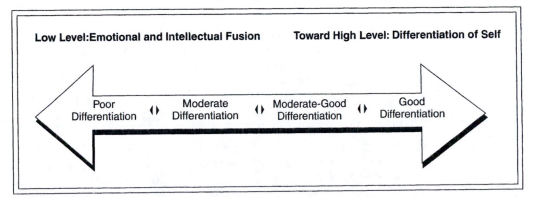

Note: From *Working with Families: An Introduction to Family Therapy* by B. Okun and L. Rappaport. Copyright 1980. Reprinted with permission of Wadsworth, a division of Thompson Learning: www.thompsonrights.com. Fax 800 730-2215.

known as the *multigenerational transmission process*. Families that present a problem have had the forces of several generations shaping and carrying it along. In marriage, people tend to select partners at their own level of differentiation (Bowen, 1976), from which union *a nuclear family emotional system* evolves.

Spouses with equally high levels of identity are able to establish and maintain clear individuality "and at the same time to have an intense, mature, nonthreatening, emotional closeness" (Bowen, 1965, p. 220). Indeed, research shows that couples that are less reactive, cutoff, or fused and that are able to relate from an I-position "experience the greatest levels of marital satisfaction" (Skowron, 2000, p. 233). This result is particularly true if the male partner remains emotionally present and available.

On the other hand, spouses with equally low levels of differentiation have difficulty establishing intimacy because they have developed only *pseudoselves*, that is, pretend selves (Kerr, 1988, p. 43). The pseudoselves fluctuate according to situations and usually result in the fusion of these selves into a "common self with obliteration of ego boundaries between them and loss of individuality to the common self" (Bowen, 1965, p. 221). Couples tend to produce offspring with the same level of differentiation that the parents have, a process Bowen describes as *family projection* (Kilpatrick, 1980).

To rid themselves of anxiety, spouses with low self-differentiation keep an emotional distance from each other. When anxiety becomes too great, it is frequently manifested in one of four ways: (1) marital conflict, (2) physical or emotional illness in one spouse, (3) projection of the problem to the children, or (4) a combination of these (David, 1979).

When working with couples, Bowen family therapists look for *triangles* (Kerr, 2003), which can occur between people or between people and things. A triangle consists of a state of calm between a comfortable twosome and an outsider (Anonymous, 1972); it is "the basic building block of any emotional system and the smallest stable relationship system" (Kilpatrick, 1980, p. 168). The original triangle is between a child and parents. Some triangles are healthy; others are not. In the latter case triangles are a frequent way of dealing with anxiety, allowing tension between two persons to be projected onto another person or object. In stressful situations anxiety can spread from one central triangle within the family to interlocking triangles outside the family, especially in work and social systems (Kerr, 1988, 2003).

Bowen therapists also examine *sibling positions* because people can develop fixed personality characteristics based on their functional birth order in the family (Toman, 1961). The more closely a marriage replicates a couple's sibling positions in their families of origin, the better the chance for success. For example, if a youngest son marries an oldest daughter, both have much to gain from the arrangement because the youngest son most likely enjoys being taken care of, and the oldest daughter probably enjoys taking care of someone.

By examining these processes, family members gain insight and understanding into the past and are freed to choose how they will behave in the present and future. Similarly, they gain a perspective on how well society as a whole is doing. In a society under too much stress (e.g., from population growth or economic decline), *societal regression* occurs because too many toxic forces counter the tendency to achieve differentiation.

ROLE OF THE COUNSELOR/THERAPIST

In the Bowen model the differentiation of the therapist is crucial. Bowen family therapists must maintain a calm presence and be differentiated from their families of origin (Friedman, 1991); objectivity and neutrality are important characteristics of Bowen therapists. To be able to work with families, therapists must first undergo emotional change (Kerr, 1981), or those they work with will not be able to experience healthy shifts.

Having personally resolved family-of-origin concerns, the Bowen therapist is usually involved in coaching on more cognitive levels. Initially, family members—primarily individuals or couples—talk to the therapist or to one another through the therapist so that emotional issues do not cloud communication (Kerr, 2003). According to Bowen, therapists should not encourage people to wallow in emotionalism but should teach them by example to transcend it, behaving with reason and self-control. Therapy should be just like a Socratic dialogue, with the teacher, or coach, calmly asking questions until the student learns to think independently (Wylie, 1991, p. 27).

Bowen family therapy looks at boundary and differentiation issues from a historical perspective. Therapists instruct individuals to search for clues as to where various family pressures have been expressed and how effectively the family has adapted to stress since its inception, through three previous generations if possible. Individuals might draw a genogram or visit their family of origin to obtain this information. By examining family dynamics, therapists become interpreters with their clients in working through multigenerational patterns of fusion and cutoffs and then resolving areas of difficulty.

GOALS

Bowen family therapy promotes differentiation in regard to self/family and also intellect/emotion. Therapists help their clients, especially couples, separate their feelings from their intellect and in the process *detriangulate*.

Another primary goal is that family members come to understand intergenerational patterns and gain insight into historical circumstances that have influenced the ways they currently interact (Learner, 1983). Then it is hoped that clients can focus on changing the "intergenerational inferences operating with the current family" (Smith, 1991, p. 25). Therapists can help family members differentiate from each other and become more diverse and fluid in their interactions (Bowen, 1978). At the end of treatment individuals should be able to relate on an autonomous, cognitive level, and projective patterns of blame should be changed (Kerr & Bowen, 1988). Nuclear family members should experience greater self-differentiation.

PROCESS AND TECHNIQUES

In Bowen family therapy the chief focus is an individual or couple; the whole family is usually not seen, even though the emphasis is systemic (Kerr, 2003). "A theoretical system that thinks in terms of family, with a therapeutic method that works toward improvement of the family system, is 'family' regardless of the number of people in the sessions" (Kerr, 1981, p. 232). By changing just one person, therapy may directly influence an entire family. Thus, the therapist may work "with all involved family members present, with any combination of family members present, or with only one family member present." However, "since the two spouses are the two family members most involved in the family ego mass, the most rapid family change occurs when the spouses are able to work as a team in family psychotherapy" (Bowen, 1965, p. 220).

Bowen family therapy is not technique oriented; rather it is process oriented, with techniques used to help clients when needed. Bowen therapists ask questions about their clients' thoughts and give homework assignments. Among the techniques most often employed are genograms, going home again, detriangulation, person-to-person relationships, differentiation of self, and asking questions.

A *genogram* is a visual representation of a family tree, depicted in geometric figures, lines, and words (McGoldrick, Gerson, & Shellenberger, 1999; Sherman, 1993) (see Figure 13.2). Genograms include information about family relationships over at least three generations. They help people gather information, hypothesize, and track relationship changes in the context of historic and contemporary events (Dunn & Levitt, 2000). "From this simple diagram, counselors and clients alike are able to view simultaneously family composition, gender, age, ethnicity, dates of birth, marriages, divorces, deaths, and other important family events" (Frame, 2000, p. 69).

The tangibility and nonthreatening nature of a genogram help family clinicians gather a large amount of information in a relatively short period of time. Furthermore, genograms can increase "mutual trust and tolerance" among all involved in their construction (Sherman, 1993, p. 91). Bowen family therapy "advises people to go 'back, back, back; and up, up, up' their family tree to look for patterns, 'recycling,' getting not just information but a feel for the context and milieu that existed during each person's formative years" (White, 1978, pp. 25–26). This process promotes the shift from emotional reactivity to clear cognitions.

Genograms can be color coded to indicate everything from substance abuse to forms of spirituality (Frame, 2000). Data in genograms are scanned for (1) repetitive patterns, such as triangles, cutoffs, and coalitions; (2) coincidences, such as the deaths of members or the ages of symptom onset; and (3) the impact of change and untimely life cycle transitions, such as off-schedule events (e.g., marriage, death, and the birth of children) (McGoldrick et al., 1999).

In *going home again*, the family therapist instructs the individual client or family members to return home in order to get to know better their family of origin (Bowen, 1976). With this type of information, individuals can differentiate themselves more

FIGURE 13.2 Family genogram

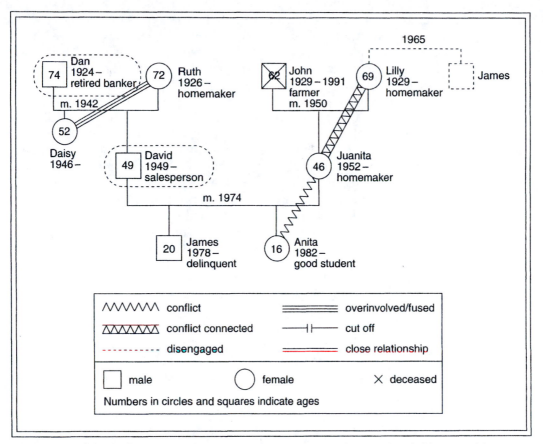

Note: From *Family Therapy: History, Theory, and Practice* (3rd ed., p. 137) by Samuel T. Gladding. Copyright 2002. Reprinted by permission of Pearson Education, Inc., Upper Saddle River, NJ.

clearly and thus can operate more fully within all family contexts of which they are a part. However, before returning home, clients may need to learn and practice how to remain calm (Bowen, 1976).

The concept of *detriangulation* involves "the process of being in contact and emotionally separate" (Kerr, 1988, p. 55). It operates on at least two levels. On one level individuals resolve their anxiety over family situations and do not project feelings onto anyone else. On a second level Bowen therapists help those individuals separate themselves from the tension that arises in the family, refusing to allow themselves to become targets or scapegoats for others who may be overcome with anxiety. For example, if a usually triangulated person stays rational during times of emotional stress, he or she will seldom become the focus of attention for the others in the triangle (Bowen, 1972). On both levels individuals will be free to voice their concerns and try out new ways of acting.

In *person-to-person relationships* two family members "relate personally to each other about each other; that is, they do not talk about others (triangling) and do not talk about impersonal issues" (Piercy & Sprenkle, 1986, p. 11). For instance, a father may say to his son, "Your actions remind me of myself when I was your age." In return the son may say, "I really don't know much about you when you were a boy. Please tell me about what you did and how you felt when you were my age." Such a process helps promote individuation, or autonomy, and intimacy.

"*Differentiation of self* has to do with the degree to which a person is able to distinguish between the subjective feeling process and the more objective intellectual (thinking) process" (Gibson & Donigian, 1993, p. 28). This procedure may involve all of the preceding techniques plus some confrontation between family members and the therapist. As was mentioned earlier, a failure to differentiate results in fusion, in which "people are dominated by their automatic emotional system"; they have "less flexibility, less adaptability, and are more emotionally dependent on those around them" (Sauber, L'Abate, & Weeks, 1985, p. 43). Over generations, children most involved in family fusion move toward a lower level of differentiation of self (Bowen, 1972). For example, they may develop eating disorders. In such cases Bowen therapists try to help these individuals (usually young women) increase their degree of self-differentiation through assertiveness training, healthier family boundaries, enhanced cognitive communication skills, and new coping behaviors for stress (Levy & Hadley, 1998).

In each of the techniques in Bowen family theory, a consistent strategy is to ask questions. In fact, *asking questions* is deemed the magic bullet of Bowen therapists. For instance, when major events such as deaths, births, and marriages disturb the equilibrium of a family, emotional shock waves may result (Bowen, 1976). Questions can help individuals involved in Bowen family therapy learn to better understand the reactions of those in their families.

MULTICULTURAL AND GENDER-SENSITIVE ISSUES

Bowen family therapy is flexible in its applications, but some of its concepts are limited in their applicability to different cultures. On the positive side genograms can be multicultural in nature and can include worldview and cultural factors that influence the behavior of family members (Thomas, 1998). In addition, there is evidence that differentiation is applicable multiculturally. However, for some groups such as Filipinos and North Americans, "psychological well-being in adulthood may well be affected by factors outside of the family, such as peer relationships, employment, or societal influences" (Tuason & Friedlander, 2000, p. 33).

The Bowen approach is somewhat controversial in regard to gender-specific issues. Bowen theory proposes that the genogram is gender neutral in its display of facts and patterns. However, Knudson-Martin (2002) suggests that many women, as well as persons from less individualistic cultures and very spiritual persons, develop a connected self that is significantly different from Bowen's image of separate selves engaged with each other. Basically, Knudson-Martin contends that Bowen theory ignores many of the positive aspects of togetherness.

EVALUATION OF THE THEORY

STRENGTHS AND CONTRIBUTIONS

A strength of Bowen theory is that it calls attention to family history, emphasizing the importance of noticing and dealing with past patterns to enable individuals and families to avoid repeating these behaviors in the future. The genogram is a specific tool developed to plot historical linkages and as such is increasingly used by theorists of all persuasions in assessing client families.

Another strength of Bowen family therapy is that it is a well-established and heuristically appealing approach. Its emphasis on theory as well as its practical nature makes it attractive. In addition, the theory and the therapy are extensive and intertwined. The theory is a blueprint for the therapy; the therapy is consistent with and inseparable from the theory. Family therapists are indebted to Bowen for intertwining these two aspects.

Another strength is that Bowen was insightful and detailed in suggesting the course of working with families. And he established a center for educating practitioners, ensuring that the Bowen approach will continue to be learned and used.

One final contribution is that Bowen family therapy is systemic in nature, controlled in focus, and cognitive in practice, thereby giving clinicians and their clients a concrete way of evaluating progress (Bowen, 1975). Furthermore, unlike many other systemic family approaches, Bowen family therapy can be used extensively with individuals or couples.

LIMITATIONS AND CRITICISMS

The Bowen approach is vulnerable to criticism for its failure to fully validate its intergenerational hypothesis (Tuason & Friedlander, 2000). In other words, the ideas behind this approach are intriguing but are not always verified. A related concern is that the theory underlying the approach is its own paradigm (Friedman, 1991). Thus, setting up research questions to refute or verify this approach is a challenge of the highest order.

Another drawback is that Bowen's stress on the importance of the past encourages some families or family members to examine their history rather than deal immediately with present circumstances. Such a process may promote insight but not action.

One other limitation is the time and, consequently, the financial resources that Bowen family therapy requires of its clients. Most people cannot afford to invest as heavily in this process as is necessary. Thus, as with psychodynamically oriented therapy, the number of people who can benefit from this approach is limited.

A final criticism of the Bowen approach is the complex and convoluted nature of Bowen's writings about the continuity of and connection between theory and therapy (Kaplan, 2000). Reading Bowen is not easy.

TREATING LINDA WITH BOWEN FAMILY SYSTEMS THERAPY

CONCEPTUALIZATION

From a Bowen family systems perspective Linda is most likely undifferentiated from her family of origin. Therefore, she suffers from chronic anxiety and has difficulty relating to others from an I-position. This inability to relate on a deep level has resulted in Linda's developing a pseudoself that fluctuates with situations. She becomes angry when threatened and either lashes out, as in her past jobs, or withdraws, as with her family and her fascination with adventure books and films. Linda's state of functioning is a result of multigenerational transmissions; she reflects the low level of differentiation in her family. If this condition is not rectified, Linda will most likely start forming triangles to scapegoat people and activities about which she becomes anxious.

TREATMENT PROCESS

As a Bowen family therapist you maintain a calm presence in the midst of Linda's anxiety because you have dealt with your own family-of-origin issues. You work cognitively with Linda as a coach, a teacher, and a catalyst, being as objective and neutral as possible. It is not necessary for Linda to bring her family to therapy because you can help her make changes and gain insight that will alter the system dynamics in her family.

Initially, you press Linda to search for clues on how her family has dealt with stress. You ask her questions. You also have her draw a genogram, a multigenerational family diagram that reveals how past generations in the family have acted and reacted in times of significant turmoil and transition. Your goal in each of these activities is to have Linda draw on historical information to influence the present. If Linda can separate her thoughts from her feelings and herself from her family, she may become more autonomous, differentiated, and healthy.

You also assign Linda homework: She is to go home again and have person-to-person relationships with as many family members as possible. In addition, she is to ask questions of her parents and siblings about relationships in the family. The hope is that she will learn information that will help her detect family patterns and then change her ways of relating. If successful, she will be able to differentiate herself from her family and form deep and lasting bonds with others. The process of therapy takes several months, but in the end Linda is calmer and has begun to think about what her next steps will be vocationally, as well as in the community and in her family.

SUMMARY AND CONCLUSION

Bowen family therapy is one of the most established approaches to working with families. A psychoanalytically trained psychiatrist, Murray Bowen devised his own approach to working with families, especially couples, based in part on his life experiences and in part on psychoanalytic theory.

Bowen theory emphasizes the importance of unconscious forces in family life. The therapy is systemic, although its primary clients are individuals and couples. It emphasizes the importance of historical intergenerational patterns and uses a cognitive strategy to help couples and family members differentiate and change their ways of thinking. In the process the therapist acts as a coach, a teacher, and a catalyst.

Overall, this approach emphasizes in-depth exploration of clients' families and concentrates on long-term results. It requires a considerable investment of time and resources. Yet Bowen theory is concrete in outcome and gives its clients a way to recognize dysfunctional patterns transmitted across generations.

SUMMARY TABLE: BOWEN FAMILY SYSTEMS THERAPY

Major Theorists

Murray Bowen   Michael Kerr

View of Human Nature/Personality

Impact of a family's emotional system on personalities
Focus on previous generations' transmission of anxiety
Basic concepts: differentiation, multigenerational transmission process, nuclear family emotional system, family projection process, triangles, sibling position, societal regression

Role of the Counselor/Therapist

Is objective and neutral
Has resolved family-of-origin concerns
Teaches, coaches, displays self-control
Instructs individuals to search for clues through construction of genograms

Goals

Promote differentiation
Understand intergenerational patterns
Change troublesome patterns

Process and Techniques

Focus on process
Questions and homework assignments
Use of genograms, going home again, detriangulation, person-to-person relationships, differentiation of self, and asking questions

Multicultural and Gender-Sensitive Issues

Multicultural genograms
Differentiation applicable multiculturally
Little consideration of factors outside the family
Focus on individuality, not togetherness

Strengths and Contributions

Calls attention to family history, deals with past patterns
Is well-established and heuristic
Has a blueprint for therapy
Has a center for educating practitioners
Is systemic, controlled, and cognitive

Limitations and Criticisms

Has failed to validate intergenerational hypothesis
Stresses the past, sometimes at the expense of the present
Is difficult to refute or verify
Requires substantial time and money
Can be complex and convoluted

LEARNING MORE

A number of periodicals carry articles on the theory, research, and practice of Bowen family therapy. One journal devoted exclusively to this theory/therapy is *Family Systems*, an interdisciplinary journal published by the Georgetown Family Center.

Bowen family therapy is a popular approach to use with a variety of clients. Further information about the therapy. conferences, and publications is available:

Bowen Center for the Study of the Family
Georgetown Family Center
4400 MacArthur Blvd NW, Suite 103
Washington, DC 20007-2521
800-GFC-6882 or 202-965-4400
http://www.thebowencenter.org/index.html

CLASSROOM ACTIVITIES

1. With the permission of your instructor and the cooperation of your family-of-origin, make a genogram of your family for the past three generations. Afterwards, discuss with a classmate what you learned either about your family or about the process of making genograms. (If this activity is not suitable for you, make a genogram of a well-known historical family and note the patterns you observe.)

2. Evaluate your emotional and cognitive reactions to the following events: a wedding, a funeral, the birth of a baby, the completion of a mundane task like vacuuming, studying for a test, and reading a story about your hometown in a national newspaper. Did you find yourself reacting more affectively, thoughtfully, or with balance in regard to these events? What do you believe Bowen's ideal response to each would be?

3. What family or work-based triangles are active in your community, for example, mother/child/school, boss/subordinate/product? With a classmate make a list. After you have completed the list discuss what factors would make people more susceptible to forming triangles and how individuals could detriangulate in the situations you have listed.

REFERENCES

Anonymous. (1972). Differentiation of self in one's family. In J. L. Framo (Ed.), *Family interaction*. New York: Springer.

Bowen, M. (1960). A family concept of schizophrenia. In D. Jackson (Ed.), *The etiology of schizophrenia*. New York: Basic Books.

Bowen, M. (1961). Family psychotherapy. *American Journal of Orthopsychiatry, 31*, 40–60.

Bowen, M. (1965). Family psychotherapy with schizophrenia in the hospital and in private practice. In I. Boszormenyi-Nagy & J. T. Framo (Eds.), *Intensive family therapy* (pp. 213–243). Hagerstown, MD: Harper & Row.

Bowen, M. (1972). Toward the differentiation of self in one's family of origin. In F. D. Andres & J. P. Lorio (Eds.), *Georgetown Family Symposia* (pp. 70–86). Washington, DC: Georgetown University.

Bowen, M. (1975). Family therapy after twenty years. In S. Arieti, D. X. Freedman, & J. E. Dyrud (Eds.), *American handbook of psychiatry, V. Treatment* (2nd ed.). New York: Basic Books.

Bowen, M. (1976). Theory in the practice of psychotherapy. In P. J. Guerin (Ed.), *Family therapy: Theory and practice* (pp. 42–90). New York: Gardner Press.

Bowen, M. (1978). *Family therapy in clinical practice*. New York: Jason Aronson.

David, J. R. (1979). The theology of Murray Bowen or the marital triangle. *Journal of Psychology and Theology, 7*, 259–262.

Dunn, A. B., & Levitt, M. M. (2000). The genogram: From diagnostics to mutual collaboration. *The Family Journal: Counseling and Therapy for Couples and Families, 8*, 236–244.

Frame, M. W. (2000). Constructing religious/spiritual genograms. In R. E. Watts (Ed.), *Techniques in marriage and family counseling* (pp. 69–74). Alexandria, VA: American Counseling Association.

Friedman, E. H. (1985). *Generation to generation: Family process in church and synagogue*. New York: Guilford.

Friedman, E. H. (1991). Bowen theory and therapy. In A. S. Gurman & D. P. Kniskern (Eds.), *Handbook of family therapy* (Vol. II, pp. 134–170). New York: Brunner/Mazel.

Gibson, J. M., & Donigian, J. (1993). Use of Bowen theory. *Journal of Addictions and Offender Counseling, 14*, 25–35.

Greene, G. J., Hamilton, N., & Rolling, M. (1986). Differentiation of self and psychiatric diagnosis: An empirical study. *Family Therapy, 8*, 187–194.

Guerin, P. J. (1976). Family therapy: The first twenty-five years. In P. J. Guerin (Ed.), *Family therapy: Theory and practice* (pp. 2–22). New York: Gardner.

Kaplan, D. M. (2000). Who are our giants? *The Family Digest, 12*(4), 1, 6.

Kerr, M. (1981). Family systems theory and therapy. In A. S. Gurman & D. P. Kniskern (Eds.), *Handbook of family therapy*. New York: Brunner/Mazel.

Kerr, M. E. (1988). Chronic anxiety and defining a self. *The Atlantic Monthly, 262*, 35–37, 40–44, 46–58.

Kerr, M. E. (2003, August 9). *Process of differentiation*. Paper presented at the 111th Annual Convention of the American Psychological Association, Toronto, Canada.

Kerr, M. E., & Bowen, M. (1988). *Family evaluation: An approach based on Bowen theory*. New York: Norton.

Kilpatrick, A. C. (1980). The Bowen family intervention theory: An analysis for social workers. *Family Therapy, 7*, 167–178.

Knudson-Martin, C. (2002). Expanding Bowen's legacy to family therapy: A response to Horne and Hicks. *Journal of Marital and Family Therapy, 28*, 115–118.

Learner, S. (1983). *Constructing the multigenerational family genogram: Exploring a problem in context* [Videotape]. Topeka, KS: Menninger Video Productions.

Levy, P. A., & Hadley, B. J. (1998). Family-of-origin relationships and self-differentiation among university students with bulimic-type behavior. *The Family Journal: Counseling and Therapy for Couples and Families, 6,* 19–23.

McGoldrick, M., Gerson, R., & Shellenberger, S. (1999). *Genograms: Assessment and intervention.* New York: Norton.

Papero, D. V. (1990). *Bowen family systems theory.* Boston: Allyn & Bacon.

Papero, D. V. (1991). The Bowen theory. In A. M. Horne & J. L. Passmore (Eds.), *Family counseling and theory* (2nd ed., pp. 47–76). Itasca, IL: Peacock.

Piercy, F. P., & Sprenkle, D. H. (1986). *Family therapy sourcebook.* New York: Guilford.

Sauber, S. R., L'Abate, L., & Weeks, G. R. (1985). *Family therapy: Basic concepts and terms.* Rockville, MD: Aspen.

Sherman, R. (1993). The intimacy genogram. *The Family Journal: Counseling and Therapy for Couples and Families, 1,* 91–93.

Skowron, E. A. (2000). The role of differentiation of self in marital adjustment. *Journal of Counseling Psychology, 47,* 229–237.

Smith, R. L. (1991). Marriage and family therapy: Direction, theory, and practice. In J. Carlson & J. Lewis (Eds.), *Family counseling* (pp. 13–34). Denver, CO: Love.

Thomas, A. J. (1998). Understanding culture and worldview in family systems: Use of the multicultural genogram. *The Family Journal: Counseling and Therapy for Couples and Families, 6,* 24–32.

Toman, W. (1961). *Family constellation: Its effects on personality and social behavior.* New York: Springer.

Tuason, M. T., & Friedlander, M. L. (2000). Do parents' differentiation levels predict those of their adult children? and other tests of Bowen theory in a Philippine sample. *Journal of Counseling Psychology, 47,* 27–35.

White, H. (1978). Exercises in understanding your family. In *Your family is good for you.* New York: Random House.

Wylie, M. S. (1991, March/April). Family therapy's neglected prophet. *Family Therapy Networker, 15,* 24–37, 77.

CHAPTER 14

Strategic Family Therapy

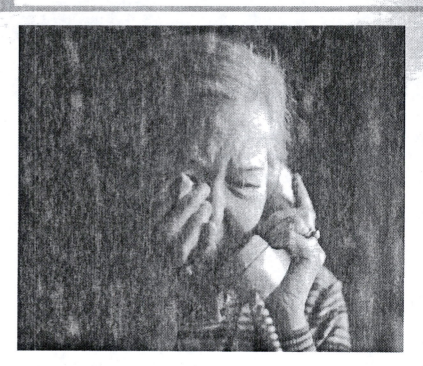

Widow Wood did all she could
    to keep her lover amused
She cleaned and cooked and even lied
    but still she was abused.

Note: "Abused" by S. T. Gladding. Copyright 2003 by Samuel T. Gladding.

Strategic family therapy is method oriented and brief in duration. Varied strategic therapies are indebted to the genius of Milton Erickson, whose work influenced their founders. Erickson's goal in treatment was change; he believed in utilizing the resources of his clients and designing a "strategy for each specific problem" (Madanes, 1991, p. 396). Erickson then gave directives and indirect suggestions to help his clients assist themselves. He did not care whether people gained insight as long as their actions produced beneficial results. "If Freud was a philosopher-priest from Vienna, Erickson was a samurai warrior from Wisconsin" (Wylie, 1990, p. 28).

Although inspired by Erickson, the ideas and techniques of strategic family therapy have been generated and refined primarily in two different centers: the Mental Research Institute (MRI) in Palo Alto, California, and the Washington School of Jay Haley and Cloe Madanes. The MRI form of strategic family therapy is the older of these therapeutic approaches. It is a descendent of the Bateson communications studies group, which was conducted in Palo Alto from 1952 to 1962. Among the most active modern proponents of this approach are Paul Watzlawick and John Weakland; other related professionals are Lynn Hoffman, Peggy Penn, and Richard Rabkin. The Washington School, organized in the mid-1970s, is most associated with Jay Haley and Cloe Madanes (Keim, 2000).

The strategic family therapy approaches have a history that is both long and distinguished. Jay Haley (1963, 1973) coined the term *strategic therapy* to describe the work of Milton Erickson, who paid extreme attention to the details of the symptoms his clients presented. His focus, like that of most present-day strategic therapists, was to change behavior by manipulating it, not to instill insight. Erickson achieved his objectives in therapy by accepting and emphasizing the positive, framing all symptoms and maladaptive behaviors as helpful; using indirect and ambiguous directives; and encouraging or directing routine behaviors so that resistance is shown through change and not through normal and continuous actions (Haley, 1963).

MAJOR THEORIST: JAY HALEY

Jay Haley is one of the most distinguished and controversial pioneers in the field of family therapy. He influenced the Bateson group and the MRI group as a founding member of each and set up the Family Therapy Institute of Washington, DC, with

Cloe Madanes in 1974. In addition, he has served as an effective communicator between people and groups and has been a strong advocate of family therapy in public and professional settings.

Haley's development is unique among family therapists; he learned from and with the three people who had the most influence on the evolution of family therapy—Milton Erickson, Gregory Bateson, and Salvador Minuchin. Haley began his career with Gregory Bateson in 1952. Because Haley had a master's degree in communications, his chief responsibility on Bateson's research team was to take the lead in diagnosing communication patterns in schizophrenic families. As a result of that work, Haley became interested in the hypnotherapy communication process of Milton Erickson. Haley learned hypnosis from Erickson in 1953 and later taught and practiced it (Simon, 1982). He also incorporated many of Erickson's ideas into his own concepts about therapy and learned to become a therapist under Erickson's supervision. Basically, Haley adopted and modified Erickson's individual emphasis so that it would work with families.

In 1962, after the Bateson team dissolved, Haley joined the Mental Research Institute staff and worked there until 1967. At this time he stopped doing therapy and became primarily involved in "family research and the observation of therapy" (Simon, 1982, p. 20). He also became the first editor of the initial journal in the field of family therapy, *Family Process*, and held that position from 1962 to 1969. Haley became even more involved in supervision when he moved east to join Salvador Minuchin at the Philadelphia Child Guidance Center in 1967. With Minuchin he organized "the Institute for Family Counseling (IFC), a project training people from the Philadelphia ghetto, who had no formal education beyond high school, to be family therapists" (Simon, 1982, p. 20). This effort further established his prominence.

In 1976 he moved to the Washington, DC, area to establish the Family Therapy Institute with Cloe Madanes. Thereafter he published two of his most influential books, *Problem-Solving Therapy* (1976) and *Leaving Home* (1980). These books spell out the essence of strategic family therapy as he views it, with an emphasis on power and hierarchy. Haley is described as having the skills of a power broker and a military strategist and making these skills "respectable therapeutic techniques" (Wylie, 1990, p. 28). Haley retired in 1995 and currently lives in La Jolla, California.

VIEW OF HUMAN NATURE/PERSONALITY

In general, strategic family therapists concentrate on the following dimensions of family life:

- *Family rules*—the overt and covert rules that families use to govern themselves
- *Family homeostasis*—the tendency of the family to remain in the same pattern of functioning unless challenged to do otherwise,
- *Quid pro quo*—the tendency of family members to treat others in the way they are being treated

- *Redundancy principle*—a family's repetition of limited behavioral sequences
- *Punctuation*—the belief that what individuals say in a transaction is caused by what others say
- *Symmetrical relationships and complementary relationships*—relationships that are both among equals (symmetrical) and among unequals (complementary)
- *Circular causality*—the idea that events are interconnected and that behaviors are caused by multiple factors

ROLE OF THE COUNSELOR/THERAPIST

As a group, strategic family therapies follow Ericksonian principles, emphasizing short-term treatment of about 10 sessions. Often strategic therapies are characterized as *brief* therapy, referring to the clarity about what needs to be changed rather than to the time required. "A central principle of brief therapy is that one evaluates which solutions have so far been attempted for the patient's problem" (Priebe & Pommerien, 1992, p. 433). Then, different solutions are tried that are often the opposite of what has already been attempted (Watzlawick, 1978). "Brief therapists hold in common the belief that therapy must be specifically goal-directed, problem-focused, well-defined, and, first and foremost, aimed at relieving the client's presenting complaint" (Wylie, 1990, p. 29).

The roles of strategic therapists differ among the subschools. However, those who work within this methodology believe in being active and flexible with their clients. It is the therapist's responsibility to plan strategies to resolve family problems. Therefore, therapists often proceed quickly and specifically to resolve presenting problems and virtually ignore family histories and personal diagnoses (Wylie, 1990). "They are symptom focused and behaviorally oriented" (Snider, 1992, p. 20).

"The first task of the therapist is to define a presenting problem in such a way that it can be solved" (Madanes, 1991, p. 396). Thus, the therapist usually tries to define it as something that the family has voluntary control over and that involves a power struggle. The therapist tries to help family members make changes that alter family dynamics from a competitive stance, in which there are winners and losers, to a cooperative position, in which everyone wins (Watzlawick, 1983).

Most strategic therapists are overtly active. For instance, Haley (1990) believes that it is essential to make changes in individuals and families within the first three sessions. Thus, he works hard at reframing a client's perceptions and the presenting complaints. Haley also strives for a unique and innovative approach in each case, tailored to the family as Erickson would have done, much as a surgeon would plan an operation. "Therapists also use structural interventions such as attempting to unbalance family systems by joining with one or more members on a conflictual point, fortifying generational boundaries, and supporting members at particular times to accomplish a specific objective" (Snider, 1992, p. 20). Families usually have homework assignments between sessions.

GOALS

The goal of strategic family therapy is to resolve, remove, or ameliorate the problem that the family has agreed to work on (Snider, 1992). In addition, the family must learn, at least indirectly, how to address other problems in a constructive manner. Often, resolving family difficulties involves a multitude of interventions, or steps. Four common procedures help to ensure a successful outcome:

1. Defining a problem clearly and concisely
2. Investigating all solutions that have previously been tried
3. Defining a clear and concrete change to be achieved
4. Formulating and implementing a strategy for change (Watzlawick, 1978)

Overall, the emphasis in strategic therapy is on process rather than content. The methods used focus on breaking up vicious cycles of interaction and replacing them with virtuous cycles that highlight alternative ways of acting (Friesen, 1985).

PROCESS AND TECHNIQUES

Strategic family therapists are innovative. They believe that it is not helpful to tell people what they are doing wrong or to encourage catharsis (Haley, 1976). If families are going to change, alterations in behaviors must precede new perceptions and feelings. This goal can be accomplished in an almost endless number of ways.

Each intervention in strategic therapy is tailored to the idiosyncrasies of individuals and problems. This customization makes strategic therapies some of the most technique driven of all family therapies. In general, strategic family therapists emphasize reframing, directives, paradoxes, ordeals, pretending, and positioning.

Reframing involves the use of language to induce a cognitive shift within family members and alter the perception of a situation. In reframing, a different interpretation is given to a family's situation or behavior, a circumstance is given new meaning, and as a consequence, other ways of behaving are explored. Reframing does not change a situation, but "the alteration of meaning invites the possibility of change" (Piercy & Sprenkle, 1986, p. 35). For instance, depression may be conceptualized as irresponsibility or stubbornness. Overall, reframing helps establish rapport between the therapist and the family and breaks down resistance. What was once seen as out-of-control behavior may become voluntary and open to change.

A *directive* is an instruction from a family therapist to a family to behave differently. "The directive is to strategic therapy what the interpretation is to psychoanalysis. It is the basic tool of the approach" (Madanes, 1991, p. 397). Many types of directives can be given, including nonverbal messages (e.g., silence, voice tone, and posture), direct and indirect suggestions (e.g., "Go fast" or "You may not want to change too quickly"), and assigned behaviors (e.g., when you think you won't sleep, force yourself to stay up all night). The purpose of outside assignments is to help individuals behave differently so that they can have different subjective experiences. Directives also increase the influence of the therapist in the change process and give the therapist information about how family members react to suggested changes. One example of a directive is to tell a family to go slowly in working to bring about change. If they disobey the directive, their resistance to change may dissolve. If they follow the directive, the therapist may gain more influence in their lives.

One of the most controversial and powerful techniques in strategic family therapy is *paradox* (Sexton & Montgomery, 1994). Although fine distinctions can be made between them, this process is very similar to prescribing the symptom. It gives families permission to do something they are already doing and is intended to lower or eliminate resistance. Jay Haley (1976) is one of the best-known proponents of this technique, which can take many forms.

1. In *restraining*, the therapist tells the client family that they are incapable of doing anything other than what they are doing. For example, a therapist might say, "In considering change, I am not sure you can do anything other than what you are presently doing."
2. In *prescribing*, family members are instructed to enact a troublesome dysfunctional behavior in front of the therapist. For instance, parents may be asked to show how they argue with their 16-year-old about getting a driver's license. They are told to continue the argument as long as it usually lasts and to come up with the same impasses.
3. *Redefining* is attributing positive connotations to symptomatic or troublesome actions. The underlying idea is that symptoms have meaning for those who display them, whether such meaning is logical or not. In the case of a school-phobic daughter, the therapist might redefine her behavior as an attempt to keep her parents together by focusing their attention on her.

The ordeals technique involves helping clients give up symptoms that are troublesome to maintain (Haley, 1984). In this method the therapist assigns an *ordeal*, which is a constructive or neutral behavior that must be performed before one can engage in the undesirable behavior. For example, an ordeal might be to exercise before the onset of depression. The ordeal is always healthy but is not an activity that the client wants to engage in. The hope is that the client will give up the symptom in order to avoid performing the constructive behavior.

The *pretend technique* is a more gentle and less confrontational technique than most of the other procedures used in strategic family therapy. Cloe Madanes (1981, 1984) is identified as the creator of this concept. Basically, the therapist asks family members to pretend to engage in a troublesome behavior, such as having a fight. The act of pretending helps individuals change by experiencing control of a previously involuntary action.

The act of *positioning* by the therapist involves acceptance and exaggeration of what family members are saying (Piercy & Sprenkle, 1986). If conducted properly, it helps the family see the absurdity of what they are doing, thereby freeing them to do something else. For example, if a son states that his relationship with his father is difficult, the therapist might respond, "No, it is absolutely hopeless" (Watzlawick, 1983).

MULTICULTURAL AND GENDER-SENSITIVE ISSUES

Strategic family counseling has been used effectively in many cultures and subcultures. For example, Santisteban et al. (2003) found brief strategic family therapy to be effective in working with Hispanic youth exhibiting behavioral problems and drug use. Likewise, Soo-Hoo (1999) found brief strategic family therapy effective in working with Chinese American families and consistent with their family values. The concept of reframing was an especially effective principle in this work.

In short, strategic family therapists seem to be sensitive to different cultures and are able to work within them. Richeport-Haley (1998) describes a brief strategic family therapy approach that can be an alternative to a culture-focused therapy. A culture-oriented counselor focuses on understanding cultural premises and then attempts to do therapy within the worldview of the clients. In contrast, the strategic approach emphasizes the structure of the family and offers techniques that can be used whatever the culture.

Strategic family therapy is also noted for its gender sensitivity as addressed by Cloe Madanes (1990). Many of today's strategic family therapy practitioners use pretend techniques, which are much gentler and more gender friendly than paradox or ordeals. Counselors also pay attention to gender-related issues. For example, Madanes has devised a 16-step procedure for working with sex offenders and their victims. This approach is notable for obtaining clear facts, connecting sexuality with spirituality, and persuading the offender to seek forgiveness while kneeling before the victim.

EVALUATION OF THE THEORY

STRENGTHS AND CONTRIBUTIONS

A major strength of strategic family therapy is its flexibility with a variety of client families. This approach has been successfully used with family members who display such dysfunctional behaviors as enmeshment, eating disorders, and substance abuse (Haley, 1980; Stanton, Todd, & Associates, 1982).

Another positive characteristic of the strategic approach is that most therapists who use it "now concede that real change is possible at the individual and dyadic level—that the entire system need not always be involved in lower-order change" (Fish, 1988, p. 15). Because significant change can be brought about without having the entire family involved in treatment sessions, the chances of a desirable outcome are increased.

A third contribution of strategic family therapy is its focus on innovation and creativity. Strategic therapists trace their lineage to Milton Erickson, who was especially skilled in devising novel ways to help his clients. Strategic family clinicians have continued that effort, and through their "introduction of the novel or unexpected, a frame of reference is broken and the structure of reality is rearranged" (Papp, 1984, p. 22).

An additional strength of strategic family therapy is its ability to be employed with a number of other therapies (Alexander & Parsons, 1982; Fish, 1988; Haley, 1976; Steinberg, Sayger, & Szykula, 1997). Because many influential therapists have a historical or personal connection with strategic therapy, they continue to be influenced in their thoughts and actions by dialogue and debate with and among strategic family therapists.

LIMITATIONS AND CRITICISMS

One aspect of strategic family therapy that may be considered a limitation is its concentration on one problem. Even though the one problem approach may help families marshal their resources to deal with an identified difficulty quickly and efficiently (Snider, 1992), many families have more than one presenting problem that needs attention.

A second criticism of strategic therapy is that the approach is too cookbookish and mechanical (Simon, 1984). This charge results from the prescribed methods of treatment by the MRI and Jay Haley, although therapists who embrace this theory do experience considerable flexibility. Another criticism of strategic family therapy linked to Jay Haley is his denial of the existence of schizophrenia.

An additional limitation of this approach is the skill necessary to implement some of its methods. For instance, the use of paradox can be powerful in the hands of a skilled clinician, but it can be a catastrophe if employed in a naive way (Friesen, 1985). Some strategic approaches demand considerable training before practitioners can implement them properly.

Another drawback of strategic family therapy concerns time and emphasis. All subschools within this orientation restrict the number of therapeutic sessions, hoping to motivate families to work. However, the seriousness or extent of problems may not be dealt with adequately (Wylie, 1992). It is also hoped that families will learn problem-solving skills by resolving one specific situation, although some families may not achieve this goal.

A final downside of strategic family therapy is its lack of collaborative input from client families. Some models, such as those devised by Haley, emphasize power techniques and the expertise of the therapist. All stress the creativity of the therapist to find a solution for the family. Thus, the strategic therapist who does not produce the desired results in clients usually takes the blame. This approach is the antithesis of most other forms of family therapy.

TREATING LINDA WITH STRATEGIC FAMILY THERAPY

CONCEPTUALIZATION

From the perspective of strategic family therapy, Linda is stuck in a homeostatic pattern of difficult interaction with older authority figures, especially demanding and demeaning men. Linda's husband was apparently much like her father, and she obeyed him even when it meant having an abortion that she did not want. Linda's bosses have not been any better in their treatment of Linda, displaying sexist behavior. In many ways Linda has acted with her husband and her bosses as she did with her father.

Linda began this behavior when she followed the rule in her family that women are inferior. This pattern has led her to function below her abilities and act out in ways that are potentially harmful to her. For example, she pursued a 2-year business degree instead of a 4-year college degree, then started working as a secretary instead of seeking a more challenging career, and recently gave notice on one job before she found another. Linda has consistently set up complementary relationships in which she is unequal. These relationships and her associated actions have left her depressed, discouraged, and trapped in situations that are unfulfilling and disheartening. She has also followed the redundancy principle of repeating a limited number of behaviors again and again. Because she blames others, especially her family, for where she is today, she avoids them but has not broken out of her self-defeating behavior to create new friends and opportunities.

TREATMENT PROCESS

As a strategic family therapist you are quite active as you begin your work with Linda. First, you evaluate the effectiveness of solutions Linda has tried so far, for example, obedience, passive-aggressive behavior, depression. You then help Linda define her problem in such a way that it becomes solvable: "The problem is being passive and not utilizing my abilities."

After the problem is defined, you give Linda a homework assignment. Because she came alone initially, you give her the task of bringing her family into therapy with her the next time. You want her family to collaborate with her to find better ways to experience life, thereby setting up a cooperative and potentially exciting relationship. Your goal is to help Linda formulate and implement a strategy for change in which she can be successful, breaking out of the vicious cycle she has been in and into a virtuous cycle.

When Linda comes in with her family, you are creative in finding a strategy that will work for everyone. You reframe the family's difficulties as members having forgotten to give positive and helpful messages to each other. As with anything forgotten, learning to remember is quite possible. This reframing of the problem from a negative to a positive and from a basis of blame to one of remembering is appealing to all family members. Therefore, you give them the following directive: During their Sunday lunch time each person is to give to every other family member a sincere and helpful message framed in a positive manner. No one resists the assignment, and you remind them that they can pretend to be sincere if they find that aspect difficult.

The next week the family reports that it carried out the directive. Thus, you see no need to use paradox or ordeals. You exaggerate and accept all that the family members say and compliment them on helping one another. You learn that Linda has received feedback that she is capable, smart, and able to do anything she sets her mind to. You notice that family members are sitting closer to one another and are more jovial. As the strategic family therapist you are functioning as the expert, using your power as a physician does to bring about healing and growth through powerful interventions. After several more sessions Linda and her family terminate their treatment with you. They are interacting positively and often with each other.

SUMMARY AND CONCLUSION

Strategic family therapy is among the most popular approaches to working with families. It was formulated in the 1960s by the Mental Research Institute (MRI) and Jay Haley, following the creative genius of Milton Erickson. It is short-term, specific, positive, and designed to change behaviors and thoughts often overlooked by other therapeutic approaches. As they did originally, strategic family therapists continue to limit to 10 the number of sessions in which they see a family. They work actively on clearly defined problems.

Strategic family therapists are innovative and creative. They use a variety of techniques including reframing, directives, prescribing the symptom, ordeals, pretending, and positioning. This approach is used in multicultural contexts and, thanks to the work of Cloe Madanes, is gender sensitive. Strategic family therapy emphasizes the power and expertise of the therapist.

SUMMARY TABLE: STRATEGIC FAMILY THERAPY

Major Theorists

Milton Erickson   John Weakland
Jay Haley   Paul Watzlawick
Cloe Madanes

View of Human Nature/Personality

View of dysfunction as attempt to adapt
Developmental framework of the family life cycle
Personalities of individuals and families shaped by various factors: for example,
    family rules and family homeostasis, quid pro quo, circular causality

Role of the Counselor/Therapist

Systemic view of problem behaviors, focus on process rather than content
Resolution of presenting problems, little attention to insight
Action and goal orientation
Brief, limited therapy—10 sessions or fewer

Goals

Resolve problematic behaviors
Generate new functional behaviors

Motivate by limiting number of sessions
Instill skills for resolving future conflicts

Process and Techniques

Innovative intervention tailored to specific situation
Acceptance of presenting problem(s)
Technique-driven approach
Use of reframing, directives, and paradoxes
Use of ordeals and pretending
Frequent homework assignments

Multicultural and Gender-Sensitive Issues

Used effectively in many cultures and subcultures
Employed with gender-related concerns

Strengths and Contributions

Pragmatic and flexible
Innovative and creative
Intent on changing perceptions to foster new behaviors
Focused on one problem and limited sessions to enhance motivation

Limitations and Criticisms

May short change clients who have multiple problems or who need more time
May appear too cookbookish or mechanical
Denies biological basis for schizophrenia
Demands considerable training for certain techniques
May not empower families

LEARNING MORE

A number of periodicals feature articles on the theory, research, and practice of strategic family therapy. Most are mainstream family therapy journals.

Family Process
American Journal of Family Therapy
Journal of Family Psychotherapy
Contemporary Family Therapy: An International Journal

Strategic therapy is practiced in multiple settings; its innovative techniques and strategies make it a popular approach in counseling and therapy, especially with families. For more information contact the oldest strategic training institute:

Mental Research Institute (MRI)
555 Middlefield Road
Palo Alto, CA 94301
650-321-3055
http://www.mri.org/

CLASSROOM ACTIVITIES

1. With another classmate role-play a situation in which one of you presents a problem that is vague. The other person, as the strategic therapist, should then attempt to clarify the problem and put it into a form in which it can be solved.
2. Take four common concerns that you have heard before and try to reframe them. Talk with the class as a whole about your perceptions of the concerns before and after your reframing.
3. Make up an ordeal that you must perform before you can do something that you want to do—for example, count to 150 before you get mad or take a shower before you eat an extra dessert. After you have completed the ordeal several times, talk to classmates about how it helped or hindered you.

REFERENCES

Alexander, J., & Parsons, B. (1982). *Functional family therapy*. Pacific Grove, CA: Brooks/Cole.

Fish, J. M. (1988, July/August). Reconciling the irreconcilable. *Family Therapy Networker, 12*, 15.

Friesen, J. D. (1985). *Structural-strategic marriage and family therapy*. New York: Gardner.

Haley, J. (1963). *Strategies of psychotherapy*. New York: Grune & Stratton.

Haley, J. (1973). *Uncommon therapy*. New York: Norton.

Haley, J. (1976). *Problem-solving therapy*. San Francisco: Jossey-Bass.

Haley, J. (1980). *Leaving home: The therapy of disturbed young people*. New York: McGraw-Hill.

Haley, J. (1984). *Ordeal therapy*. San Francisco: Jossey-Bass.

Haley, J. (1990). Interminable therapy. In J. Zeig & S. Gilligan (Eds.), *Brief therapy: Myths, methods, and metaphors*. New York: Brunner/Mazel.

Keim, J. (2000). Strategic family therapy. In A. Horne (Ed.), *Family counseling and therapy* (3rd ed., pp. 170–207). Itasca, IL: Peacock.

Madanes, C. (1981). *Strategic family therapy*. San Francisco: Jossey-Bass.

Madanes, C. (1984). *Behind the one-way mirror: Advances in the practice of strategic therapy*. San Francisco: Jossey-Bass.

Madanes, C. (1990). *Sex, love, and violence*. New York: Norton.

Madanes, C. (1991). Strategic family therapy. In A. S. Gurman & D. P. Kniskern (Eds.), *Handbook of family therapy* (Vol. 2, pp. 396–416). New York: Brunner/Mazel.

Papp, P. (1984, September/October). The creative leap. *Family Therapy Networker, 8*, 20–29.

Piercy, F. P., & Sprenkle, D. H. (1986). *Family therapy sourcebook*. New York: Guilford.

Priebe, S., & Pommerien, W. (1992). The therapeutic system as viewed by depressive inpatients and outcome: An expanded study. *Family Process, 31*, 433–439.

Richeport-Haley, M. (1998). Ethnicity in family therapy: A comparison of brief strategic therapy and culture-focused therapy. *American Journal of Family Therapy, 26*, 77–90.

Santisteban, D. A., Coatsworth, J. D., Perez-Vidal, A., Kurtines, W. M., Schwartz, S. J., LaPerriere, A., & Szapocznik, J. (2003). Efficacy of brief strategic family therapy in modifying Hispanic adolescent behavior problems and substance use. *Journal of Family Psychology, 17*, 121–133.

Sexton, T. L., & Montgomery, D. (1994). Ethical and therapeutic acceptability: A study of paradoxical techniques. *The Family Journal: Counseling and Therapy for Couples and Families, 2*, 215–228.

Simon, R. (1982, September/October). Behind the one-way mirror: An interview with Jay Haley. *Family Therapy Networker, 6*, 18–25, 28–29, 58–59.

Simon, R. (1984, November/December). Stranger in a strange land: An interview with Salvador Minuchin. *Family Therapy Networker, 8*, 20–31.

Simon, R. (1986, September/October). Behind the one-way kaleidoscope: An interview with Cloe Madanes. *Family Therapy Networker, 10*, 19–29, 64–67.

Simon, R. (1987, September/October). Good-bye paradox, hello invariant prescription: An interview with Mara Selvini Palazzoli. *Family Therapy Networker, 11*, 16–33.

Snider, M. (1992). *Process family therapy*. Boston: Allyn & Bacon.

Soo-Hoo, T. (1999). Brief strategic family therapy with Chinese Americans. *American Journal of Family Therapy, 27,* 163–179.

Stanton, D., Todd, T., & Associates. (1982). *The family therapy of drug abuse and addiction.* New York: Guilford.

Steinberg, E. B., Sayger, T. V., & Szykula, S. A. (1997). The effects of strategic and behavioral family therapies on child behavior and depression. *Contemporary Family Therapy, 19,* 537–551.

Watzlawick, P. (1978). *The language of change.* New York: Basic Books.

Watzlawick, P. (1983). *The situation is hopeless but not serious.* New York: Norton.

Wylie, M. S. (1990, March/April). Brief therapy on the couch. *Family Therapy Networker, 14,* 26–35, 66.

Wylie, M. S. (1992, January/February). The evolution of a revolution. *Family Therapy Networker, 16,* 17–29, 98–99.

CHAPTER 15

Solution-Focused Therapy

She tells her story
   of pain and sorrow
      it is heavy like a day
         without a tomorrow;
She speaks again
   and highlights new facts
      her face is calm
         her manner relaxed;
Time has been extended
   hope has been awakened.

Note: "Hope and Change" by S. T. Gladding. Copyright 2003 by Samuel T. Gladding.

One of the most recent theoretical developments in the field of counseling is the creation of solution-focused therapy. This approach grew out of strategic family therapy, particularly the MRI model, but departs from that tradition by concentrating on finding solutions instead of dealing with problems.

One of the most experienced and articulate spokespersons for solution-focused therapy is Steve deShazer, who studied with Milton Erickson. This model appeared first in deShazer's writings and those of his associates at the Brief Family Therapy Center in Milwaukee, Wisconsin (deShazer, 1982, 1985, 1988, 1991). Current advocates of the solution-focused position include Bill O'Hanlon and his associates (O'Hanlon & Weiner-Davis, 1989; O'Hanlon & Wilk, 1987), Patricia O'Hanlon Hudson (Hudson & O'Hanlon, 1991), Michele Weiner-Davis, Alan Gurman, Eve Lipchik, and Scott Miller. Solution-focused therapy has a midwest origin with a worldwide application.

MAJOR THEORISTS: STEVE DESHAZER AND BILL O'HANLON

Although Steve deShazer and William O'Hanlon developed their ideas separately, the various forms of this theory spring from the work of Milton Erickson. Steve deShazer began his career at the Mental Research Institute in the mid-1970s. In the late 1970s he and other individuals in Milwaukee established the Brief Family Therapy Center (Kaplan, 2000). There deShazer first gained attention as a therapist and began to emerge as a major theorist through his writings in the 1980s. Initially, deShazer was considered a strategic family therapist influenced by the work of not only Milton Erickson but also Gregory Bateson and the staff of the MRI. However, beginning in the 1980s and continuing into the present, deShazer's writings and presentations have become distinct from the mainstream of the strategic family therapy approach.

DeShazer (1982) identifies his theory as *brief family therapy*, sometimes called just *brief therapy*, and describes it as an ecosystemic approach. Whenever possible, he employs a team, collectively known as consultants, which observes a session from behind a one-way mirror and transmits messages to the therapist at a designated break time. Thus, a client can benefit from multiple inputs.

Bill O'Hanlon entered the therapeutic world because of his own life experiences. As an adolescent he was unhappy and shy; as a college student he was isolated and uncomfortable in the world. He reports that he felt like "all exposed nerve—no skin—everything hurt" (Krauth, 1995, p. 24). He experimented with drugs and noticed that "the reality we all take for granted could be changed by a couple of micrograms of something introduced into one's body" (Bubenzer & West, 1993, p. 366). He also contemplated suicide but changed his mind when a friend offered him a lifetime of free rent on a Nebraska farm if he would stay alive. That possibility changed his outlook on life and led to his interest in therapeutic work that went beyond repairing damage or dealing with pathology.

After earning a tailor-made master's degree from Arizona State University in family therapy, O'Hanlon went on to receive special tutelage under Milton Erickson in exchange for tending Erickson's garden. Erickson's influence on O'Hanlon was profound and shifted his attention to a focus on solutions. He was also influenced by MRI work. In 1980 O'Hanlon became a major proponent of solution-focused therapy, which he now prefers to call *possibility therapy* (Bubenzer & West, 1993; Krauth, 1995). He characterizes his approach as one that is pragmatic and full of midwest values.

VIEW OF HUMAN NATURE/PERSONALITY

The view of human nature characteristic of solution-focused therapy is built on the philosophy of *social constructionism*, that is, including the social or cultural context of people or families. Because culture influences the way individuals view the world, therapy must incorporate the philosophy of *constructivism*, which states that reality is not an objective entity, but a reflection of observation and experience (Maturana & Varela, 1987; Simon, Stierlin, & Wynne, 1985).

At the foundation of this approach is the belief that dysfunctional people get stuck in dealing with their problems (deShazer, 1985). They use unsatisfactory methods to solve their difficulties, relying on patterns that do not work (Bubenzer & West, 1993). Solution-focused therapy is aimed at breaking such repetitive, nonproductive behavioral patterns by enabling individuals and families to take a more positive view of troublesome situations and actively participate in doing something different. "It is not necessary to know the cause of the complaint or even very much about the complaint itself in order to resolve it" (Cleveland & Lindsey, 1995, p. 145). The presenting problem is simply the problem for which a solution needs to be worked out (Kaplan, 2000). No extensive analysis is needed.

Another premise of solution-focused therapy is that individuals really want to change. To underscore this idea, deShazer (1984, 1989) considers resistance no longer a valid concept. When clients do not follow therapists' directions, they are actually cooperating by teaching therapists the best way to help them.

A related concept is that only a small amount of change is necessary. An analogy used to illustrate this point notes that a 1° error in a plane's path across the United States results in a destination that is considerably off course (deShazer, 1985). Small amounts of change can also encourage people to realize that they can make progress. Even minute change boosts confidence and optimism and creates a ripple effect (Spiegel & Linn, 1969).

ROLE OF THE COUNSELOR/THERAPIST

Solution-focused therapists construct solutions in collaboration with clients (Kiser, Piercy, & Lipchik, 1993). However, one of the therapists' first roles is to determine how active clients will be in the process of change. Clients usually fall into one of three categories: visitors, complainants, or customers. *Visitors* are not involved in the problem and are not part of the solution. *Complainants* complain about situations but can be observant and describe problems even if they are not invested in solving them. *Customers* are not only able to describe a problem and their involvement in it, but are also willing to work to solve it. If therapists are working with customers or can help visitors and complainants evolve into customers, appropriate intervention strategies can be developed (Fleming & Rickord, 1997).

A solution-focused therapist becomes a "facilitator of change, one who helps clients access the resources and strengths they already have but are not aware of or are not utilizing" (Cleveland & Lindsey, 1995, p. 145). In this process practitioners work with clients to change their perspective on a problem, paying special attention to language (West, Bubenzer, Smith, & Hamm, 1997). Positive assumptions about change are constantly conveyed. For example, therapists might ask a *presuppositional question*, such as, "What good thing happened since our last session?" In addition, "by selecting a specific verb tense, or implying the occurrence of a particular event, . . . individuals are . . . led to believe that a solution will be achieved" (Gale, 1991, p. 43). Likewise, when an improvement occurs, therapists use *positive blame* and recognition of competence through such questions as, "How did you make that happen?" (Fleming & Rickord, 1997).

Solution-focused therapists believe that it is important to fit therapeutic interventions into the context of individual or family behavior. This fit has been articulated by deShazer (1985), who contends that a solution does not have to be as complex as the presenting problem. The example of locks and keys illustrates what he means. Locks may be complex, but opening them does not require a similar complexity of keys. In fact, skeleton keys (i.e., standardized therapeutic techniques) can be helpful in dealing with most locks, regardless of complexity.

To obtain a good solution fit, deShazer (1985) uses a team whenever possible to begin mapping, or sketching out, a course of successful intervention. However, it is up to clients to define what they wish to achieve; therapists then help them define clear, specific goals that can be conceptualized concretely (deShazer, 1985; O'Hanlon & Weiner-Davis, 1989). In this process clients and therapists begin to identify solutions, that is, desired behaviors. "Therapy is over when the agreed upon outcome has been reached" (O'Hanlon & Wilk, 1987, p. 109).

Solution-focused therapists encourage individuals and families to make small changes—in both perception and behavior—and to do so rapidly (deShazer, 1985; O'Hanlon & Weiner-Davis, 1989). Once that small change is achieved, regardless of the method used, therapists get out of the way and let the "beneficial difference amplify itself naturally" (Fleming & Rickord, 1997, p. 289). Solution-focused therapists do not distinguish between short-term and long-term problems; some problematic behaviors endure longer than others because the right solutions have not been tried. Instead, solution-focused therapists are always challenging their clients to envision a "future that has possibilities of change" (Bubenzer & West, 1993, p. 372), a practice that "provides hope and expands the options for solutions" (Erdman, 2000, p. 100).

GOALS

Solution-focused therapy encourages clients to seek solutions and tap internal resources. The belief is that all individuals and families have resources and strengths with which to resolve complaints (Cleveland & Lindsey, 1995); the task is simply to get them to use the abilities they already have. Thus, solution-focused therapy encourages, challenges, and sets up expectations for change. Therapists try to help clients unlock their set views, be creative, and generate novel approaches with broad applicability. The concept of pathology, as defined in the *DSM*, does not play a part in the treatment process.

Identifying what is a problem and what is not a problem is a key component in the solution-focused process (deShazer, 1988). It emphasizes exceptions to generally accepted ways of behaving and viewing situations (O'Hanlon & Wilk, 1987). Solution-focused therapy takes the Ericksonian position that change is inevitable and helps clients reframe their situations positively.

PROCESS AND TECHNIQUES

The processes and techniques in solution-focused therapy are also geared to solutions, not problems. Focus on a detailed personal or family history of problems is believed to be unhelpful (deShazer, 1985; O'Hanlon & Weiner-Davis, 1989). To stress the idea that causal understanding is unnecessary, O'Hanlon and Wilk (1987) state that every psychotherapy office should have a couch for therapists instead of clients, because "every now and then, in the course of a session, a hypothesis might accidentally enter the therapist's head, and the best remedy for it is to lie down until it goes away" (p. 98). To increase motivation and expectation, solution-focused therapy, like strategic therapy, emphasizes short-term treatment, between 5 and 10 sessions.

One subtle but primary technique used in this therapy is to *cocreate a problem*. Initially, an agreement is made as to which problem is to be solved. For example, both therapist and family must agree that a family's failure to discipline a child properly is the difficulty that needs to be addressed.

A second technique is to ask clients for a hypothetical solution to their situation, often using the *miracle question*. For example, "If a miracle happened tonight and you woke up tomorrow and the problem was solved, what would you do differently?" (Walter & Peller, 1993, p. 80). Such a question invites clients to suspend their present frame of reference and enter a reality that they wish to achieve.

Another novel technique in solution-focused therapy is to *focus on exceptions*, that is, to look for times when clients' goals may be happening (Krauth, 1995). "In a practical sense, exceptions do not exist in the real world of clients; they must be cooperatively invented or constructed by both the client and the therapist while exploring what happens when the problem does not occur" (Fleming & Rickord, 1997, p. 289). For example, a couple that is quarreling a lot might find that they are peaceful whenever they sit down to eat. By examining the dynamics of particular situations or at various times, clients may learn something about who they are and how they interact. And in the process they may become different. "Inventing exceptions to problems deconstructs the client's frame: I am this way, or it always happens that way" (Fleming & Rickord, 1997, p. 289).

Solution-focused therapists may also use the technique of *scaling*, in which questions are asked using a scale of 1 (low) to 10 (high) to help clients move toward their goal. For example, a therapist might say, "On a scale of 1 to 10, how far do you think you have come in solving your problem?" If the client chooses 6, the therapist might ask what it would take to reach 7. By answering the question, the client may reach a new understanding about what immediate, realistic, and measurable steps should be taken (Fleming & Rickord, 1997).

Another technique in this approach involves *second-order*, or *qualitative change*. The goal is to change client patterns by intervening in the order of events in clients' lives or altering the frequency and duration of a dysfunction (O'Hanlon, 1987). For example, a couple that has been having long fights at dinner might agree to finish their meal before arguing and then limit their time of disagreement to 15 minutes. This type of change in the structure and duration of events is likely to alter family dynamics.

Another intervention is to give clients *compliments*. For solution-focused therapists, especially deShazer (1982), a compliment is a written message designed to praise a client strength and build a *yes-set*, that is, a tendency to respond affirmatively. A compliment consists of a positive statement with which the client(s) can agree. For example, a therapist might say, "I am impressed with your hard work to bring about change and the way all of you are discussing what needs to happen next." A compliment is always planned as a lead-in to giving clients a task or assignment.

An additional technique is to provide clients with a *clue*, or an intervention that mirrors the clients' usual behavior. It is intended to alert clients to the idea that some behavior is likely to continue (deShazer, 1982). For example, a therapist's intervention might be, "Don't work too hard trying to spend time talking, because conversation is something that regularly occurs in your environment and you can do it naturally." The idea behind a clue is "to build mutual support and momentum for carrying out later interventions" (Sauber, L'Abate, & Weeks, 1985, p. 23).

One final strategy, mentioned earlier, is to use procedures that have worked before and that have a universal application. These *skeleton keys* help clients unlock a variety of problems (deShazer, 1985). DeShazer has refined five interventions that have been useful to him in a number of situations (deShazer, 1985; deShazer & Molnar, 1984):

1. "Between now and next time we meet, we (I) want you to observe, so that you can tell us (me) next time, what happens in your (life, marriage, family, or relationship) that you want to continue to happen" (p. 298). Such an assignment encourages clients to look at the stability, or steadiness, of the problems on which they wish to work.

2. "Do something different" (p. 300). This type of request encourages individuals to explore their range of possibilities, rather than to continue to do what they believe is correct. DeShazer gives an example of a woman who complained that her husband, a police detective, was staying out late every night with his friends. The deShazer team suggested that her husband might want more mysterious behavior from her. Therefore, one night she hired a babysitter, rented a motel room, and stayed out until 5:00 A.M. Her husband had come in at 2:00 A.M. Nothing was said, but her husband began staying home at night.

3. "Pay attention to what you do when you overcome the temptation or urge to . . . perform the symptom or some behavior associated with the complaint" (p. 302). This instruction helps clients to realize that symptom behaviors are under their control.

4. "A lot of people in your situation would have . . . " (p. 302). This type of statement again helps clients realize that they may have options other than those they are exercising. With such awareness they can begin to make needed changes.

5. "Write, read, and burn your thoughts" (p. 302). This experience consists of writing about past times and then reading and burning the writings the next day, in an attempt to move on. (deShazer, 1985)

Overall, solution-focused interventions help clients view their situations differently. They can also give them hope, thereby assisting them in powerful ways (Bubenzer & West, 1993). In the words of deShazer and Molnar (1984), "It now appears to us that the therapists' ability to see change and to help the clients to do so as well, constitutes a most potent clinical skill" (p. 304).

MULTICULTURAL AND GENDER-SENSITIVE ISSUES

Solution-focused therapy has made strides in recent years to become more sensitive to and appropriate for different cultural groups—for example, Chinese (Cheung, 2001; Yeung, 1999) and African-American and Mexican-American families (Corcoran, 2000). Practitioners of the approach have also sought to integrate it with other cultural views of helping. For instance, Hung-Hsiu-Chang and Ng (2000) compare the phenomenon of change in two different world views—I Ching and solution-focused therapy—and attempt to integrate these views for therapeutic usefulness.

Solution-focused therapy is also sensitive to gender issues. O'Hanlon & Bertolino (2002), for example, address the matter of sexual abuse and the ways in which solution-focused therapy can help victims work through their trauma. Another gender-sensitive approach to change is a "gender solution-focused genogram to help clients identify the beliefs and behaviors related to their presenting problems" (Softas-Nall, Baldo, & Tiedemann, 1999, p. 179). This special type of genogram may be particularly useful in identifying past gender-role messages that have negatively influenced present behaviors.

EVALUATION OF THE THEORY

STRENGTHS AND CONTRIBUTIONS

One strength of solution-focused therapy is that it concentrates on and is directed by a client's theory, or story. Before any attempt is made to create change, clients' experiences are accepted. Whatever clients bring to therapy is examined from a broad context, but the past is emphasized only when it calls attention to the present. O'Hanlon compares this type of approach with the Rogerian concept of first listening attentively to how people are feeling before trying to implement change (Bubenzer & West, 1993).

A second contribution of solution-focused therapy is that therapists assist clients in defining their situations with clarity, precision, and possibilities. These therapists emphasize that "the defined problem should be achievable" (Todd, 1992, p. 174). Sometimes success is measured in the elimination of a problem; at other times clients may change their perception of a situation or discover exceptions to troublesome times. Small changes in behavior are seen as the basis for larger systemic changes, and therapists encourage and reinforce any type of change. Their belief is that once change starts, it will continue. "Solution-focused brief therapy . . . asserts that change is inevitable" (Kok & Leskela, 1996, p. 398).

Another positive aspect of solution-focused therapy is that it does not focus on a clinical understanding of a client's situation; instead, the focus is on change. The therapist's job is to produce change by helping clients focus on their solutions to the problems they have reported. Therapists may prompt change by challenging their clients' worldviews, asking appropriate questions, and assigning tasks that help clients unlock their own potential.

A related strength of solution-focused therapy is that it is empowering as it assists clients in assessing and utilizing their resources. Formula tasks and awareness exercises help people help themselves. Clients "are encouraged to imagine a future without the problem(s) so that they can identify what they will be doing (solutions)" (Kok & Leskela, 1996, p. 398).

Furthermore, the flexibility of solution-focused therapy is exceptional. It can be employed in working with a variety of disoders and situations, such as children and adolescents in a family context (Berg & Steiner, 2003), problem drinkers (Berg & Miller, 1992), and eating disorders (McFarland, 1995).

LIMITATIONS AND CRITICISMS

One drawback to solution-focused therapy is that little attention is paid to client history. Sometimes individuals need to resolve issues from their past before they can move into the present or future. However, solution-focused therapy makes no provision for such a need.

A second criticism of solution-focused therapy is that it ends when a behavioral goal is reached (O'Hanlon & Wilk, 1987). If there is no further complaint or objective, there is no further treatment. In this respect solution-focused therapy is similar to many forms of behavioral therapy; it concentrates on resolving a concrete objective. Although behavioral accomplishments are important, some clients need additional help changing accompanying thoughts and/or feelings. And again, solution-focused therapy does not provide for such needs.

Another limitation of solution-focused therapy is that some proponents, mainly deShazer and Berg, use a team approach in helping clients. Even though there are generally fewer sessions in such an approach, the expense of this treatment may be great.

TREATING LINDA WITH SOLUTION-FOCUSED THERAPY

CONCEPTUALIZATION

From a solution-focused perspective Linda is temporarily stuck in a pattern of dysfunctional behavior. She really wants to change but does not know how and, as a consequence, has suicidal thoughts. She has found some solace from the pain of her divorce in romance novels, television shows, and action movies. When she is engaged in any of these activities, she does not feel depressed. You see that these activities are exceptions. And although you do not dwell on history, you notice that Linda could have gone to a 4-year college and wonder if her intelligence is one of her assets.

TREATMENT PROCESS

As a solution-focused therapist you want to set up a collaborative working relationship with Linda and challenge her to envision a new future. Linda is a customer who wants to get better and is willing to work. Consequently, you convey to her that change is inevitable and set up expectations for such change, even if it is small. You also remind Linda that you have only 5 to 10 sessions in which to treat her, so it is important to get right to work.

Initially, you work with Linda to cocreate a problem, which turns out to be that she is lonely and cut off from people. When you ask Linda the miracle question, you find out that if the problem were resolved, she would have a new lover in her life and would be closer to her family and premarital friends. When you ask her to scale her handling of her problem, she puts it at a 3. For that rating to be higher, that is, more positive, Linda says she would be reading fewer books, watching less television, and seeing fewer movies.

You compliment Linda on her strength and suggest that a lesser person would have caved in to the circumstances. At the same time, you work with her to find all the exceptions to her feeling depressed, such as when she is reading. You work with her as well to find skeleton keys that she can use to overcome her situation. One such key is a telephone call to family and friends to set up times to do things together, such as share a meal. Another skeleton key is to ask friends and relatives to help her locate activities that she would enjoy and that would introduce her to new people. In both of these situations Linda is less apt to be depressed.

After Linda completes her initial homework, you ask her to scale her feelings about her life again. Her score increases to a 6. You then challenge her to envision a future that is even brighter and let her convey to you the ways that future might come about, such as her becoming more active in social outlet groups and reconnecting with her family. After this session and one more, you terminate therapy although Linda can refer herself back if necessary. You do ask her to report back to you about her progress in a couple of months, reemphasizing the fact that change is inevitable and need not be large to make a big difference in her life.

SUMMARY AND CONCLUSION

In the 1980s and especially in the 1990s, the work of deShazer and O'Hanlon brought national attention to solution-focused therapy. This approach concentrates on bringing change to a wider range of client problems. It is short-term, specific, and positive and concentrates on effecting small changes in the process of facilitating larger ones. Both deShazer and O'Hanlon have been greatly influenced by Milton Erickson.

Solution-focused therapy is concerned with changing present behaviors rather than examining past histories. It stresses that individuals and families have untapped resources that can and should be marshaled in helping them help themselves. This approach is creative in innovative ways that go beyond traditional forms of therapy; for example, it emphasizes that change is inevitable. Overall, solution-focused therapy represents the best of the developing therapeutic approaches.

SUMMARY TABLE: SOLUTION-FOCUSED THERAPY

Major Theorists

Steve deShazer   William O'Hanlon
Insoo Kim Berg   Michele Weiner-Davis

View of Human Nature/Personality

Importance of social constructionism
Dysfunctional use of unsatisfactory methods to solve difficulties
Availability of personal resources/strengths

Innate desire to change
Value of small change

Role of the Counselor/Therapist

Collaborates with client
Assesses client involvement as visitor, complainant, or customer
Fosters a new perspective
Fits intervention to client
Lets small change grow
Does not distinguish between short- and long-term problems
May use team approach

Goals

Tap internal client resources and seek solutions
Change client focus, reframe situations positively

Process and Techniques

Use of short-term framework
Focus on single problem
Use of miracle question and scaling
Focus on exceptions, change in organization and structure
Use of compliments, clues, skeleton keys

Multicultural and Gender-Sensitive Issues

Applicable to different cultural groups
Sensitive to victims of sexual abuse
Appropriate for gender solution-focused genograms

Strengths and Contributions

First accepts clients' stories/experiences
Defines situations carefully
Focuses on change
Helps clients utilize resources
Emphasizes small change, inevitability of change
Is flexible

Limitations and Criticisms

Pays little attention to client history
Ends when behavioral goal is reached
May increase expense with team approach

LEARNING MORE

A number of periodicals carry articles on the theory, research, and practice of solution-focused therapy.

Journal of Family Therapy
American Journal of Family Therapy
Journal of Systemic Therapies

Solution-focused therapy is a popular approach to use with a variety of clients. More information is available from the following related organizations and institutes:

Brief Family Therapy Center
P.O. Box 13736
Milwaukee, WI 53213
414-302-0650
http://www.brief-therapy.org/

European Brief Therapy Association
http://www.ebta.nu/index.html/

Creating Solutions, Inc.
2061 First Street
Brookings, SD 57006
605-692-8113
www.creatingsolutions.org/

CLASSROOM ACTIVITIES

1. Think of a small change that you made in the past that made an important difference in your life. Talk with another classmate about that change and other small changes you have seen others make that were beneficial.
2. Look at a behavior that is troublesome to you or somebody else. Then focus on exceptions, that is, times when the behavior is not happening. What do exceptions tell you about the dynamics of the behavior and the person displaying it?
3. Practice asking the miracle question to friends or relatives who complain that they are having a problem. What do you notice about their reactions?

REFERENCES

Berg, I. K., & Miller, S. (1992). *Working with the problem drinker: A solution-focused approach*. New York: Norton.

Berg, I. K., & Steiner, T. (2003). *Children's solution work*. New York: Norton.

Bubenzer, D. L., & West, J. D. (1993). William Hudson O'Hanlon: On seeking possibilities and solutions in therapy. *The Family Journal, 1*, 365–379.

Cheung, S. (2001). Problem-solving and solution-focused therapy for Chinese: Recent developments. *Asian Journal of Counselling, 8*, 111–128.

Cleveland, P. H., & Lindsey, E. W. (1995). Solution-focused family interventions. In A. C. Kilpatrick & T. P. Holland (Eds.), *Working with families* (pp. 145–160). Boston: Allyn & Bacon.

Corcoran, J. (2000). Solution-focused family therapy with ethnic minority clients. *Crisis Intervention and Time Limited Treatment, 6*, 5–12.

deShazer, S. (1982). *Patterns of brief family therapy*. New York: Guilford.

deShazer, S. (1984). The death of resistance. *Family Process, 23*, 11–21.

deShazer, S. (1985). *Keys to solution in brief therapy*. New York: Norton.

deShazer, S. (1988). *Clues: Investigating solutions in brief therapy*. New York: Norton.

deShazer, S. (1989). Resistance revisited. *Contemporary Family Therapy, 11*, 227–233.

deShazer, S. (1991). *Putting differences to work*. New York: Norton.

deShazer, S., & Molnar, A. (1984). Four useful interventions in brief family therapy. *Journal of Marital and Family Therapy, 10*, 297–304.

Erdman, P. (2000). Bringing a symbol: An experiential exercise for systematic change. In R. E. Watts (Ed.), *Techniques in marriage and family counseling* (pp. 99–102). Alexandria, VA: American Counseling Association.

Fleming, J. S., & Rickord, B. (1997). Solution-focused brief therapy: One answer to managed mental health care. *The Family Journal, 5*, 286–294.

Gale, J. E. (1991). *Conversion analysis of therapeutic discourse: The pursuit of a therapeutic agenda*. Norwood, NJ: Ablex.

Hudson, P. O., & O'Hanlon, W. H. (1991). *Rewriting love stories: Brief marital therapy*. New York: Norton.

Hung-Hsiu-Chang, T., & Ng, K. S. (2000). I Ching, solution-focused therapy and change: A clinical integrative framework. *Family Therapy, 27*, 47–57.

Kaplan, D. M. (2000). Who are our giants? *The Family Digest, 12*(4), 1, 6.

Kiser, D. J., Piercy, F. P., & Lipchik, E. (1993). The integration of emotion in solution-focused therapy. *Journal of Marital and Family Therapy, 19*, 233–242.

Kok, C. J., & Leskela, J. (1996). Solution-focused therapy in a psychiatric hospital. *Journal of Marital and Family Therapy, 22*, 397–406.

Krauth, L. D. (1995, December). Strength-based therapies. *Family Therapy News, 26*, 24.

Maturana, H., & Varela, F. (1987). *The tree of knowledge*. Boston: New Science Library.

McFarland, B. (1995). *Brief therapy and eating disorders : A practical guide to solution-focused work with clients*. San Francisco: Jossey-Bass.

O'Hanlon, B., & Bertolino, B. (2002). *Even from a broken web: Brief, respectful solution-oriented therapy for sexual abuse and trauma*. New York: Norton.

O'Hanlon, W. H. (1987). *Taproots: Underlying principles of Milton Erickson's therapy and hypnosis*. New York: Norton.

O'Hanlon, W. H., & Weiner-Davis, M. (1989). *In search of solutions: A new direction in psychotherapy*. New York: Norton.

O'Hanlon, W. H., & Wilk, J. (1987). *Shifting contexts: The generation of effective psychotherapy*. New York: Guilford Press.

Sauber, S. R., L'Abate, L., & Weeks, G. R. (1985). *Family therapy: Basic concepts and terms*. Rockville, MD: Aspen.

Simon, F., Stierlin, H., & Wynne, L. (1985). *The language of family therapy*. New York: Family Process Press.

Softas-Nall, B. C., Baldo, T. D., & Tiedemann, T. R. (1999). A gender-based, solution-focused genogram case: He and she across the generations. *The Family Journal, 7*, 177–180.

Spiegel, H., & Linn, L. (1969). The "ripple effect" following adjunct hypnosis in analytic psychotherapy. *American Journal of Psychiatry, 126*, 53–58.

Todd, T. (1992). Brief family therapy. In R. L. Smith & P. Stevens-Smith (Eds.), *Family counseling and therapy* (pp. 162–175). Ann Arbor, MI: ERIC/CAPS.

Walter, J., & Peller, J. (1993). Solution-focused brief therapy. *The Family Journal, 1*, 80–81.

West, J. D., Bubenzer, D. L., Smith, J. M., & Hamm, T. L. (1997). Insoo Kim Berg and solution-focused therapy. *The Family Journal, 5*, 346–354.

Yeung, F. K. C. (1999). The adaptation of solution-focused therapy in Chinese culture: A linguistic perspective. *Transcultural-Psychiatry, 36*, 477–489.

CHAPTER 16

Ethical and Legal Aspects of Counseling

Her last words in leaving were:
  "I'll see you in court!
Your practice of counseling
  is cause for a tort!"
Stunned, he consulted a worn textbook
  and with studious scrutiny
    he sought and looked
To see if he had followed a proper course
  where professional ethics were the source
    of what he did in the session
      and why.

Note: "The Source" by S. T. Gladding. Copyright 2003 by Samuel T. Gladding.

Regardless of the theory or theories a therapist chooses to use, counseling is not a value-free or neutral activity (Cottone & Tarvydas, 2003; Schulte, 1990). Instead, it is an active profession based on values that are "orienting beliefs about what is good . . . and how that good should be achieved" (Bergin, 1985, p. 99). Values are at the core of counseling relationships, for all goals in counseling, "whether they are goals for symptom relief or goals to modify a lifestyle, are subtended by value systems" (Bergin, 1992, p. 9).

Because counseling and its theories are so complex and multifaceted, counselors must be dependent on codes of ethics as well as external codes of law (DePauw, 1986; McGovern, 1994). Counselors who are not clear about their values, ethics, and legal responsibilities, as well as those of their clients, can cause harm despite their best intentions (Gladding, Remley, & Huber, 2001; Remley, 1991). Therefore, it is vital for counselors to be knowledgeable first about themselves and then about the ethics of and laws pertaining to the profession of counseling and the use of its theories.

This chapter explores ethical standards and legal constraints under which counselors operate. Both are crucial, for they promote the professionalism of counseling, directly and indirectly. In some cases ethical and legal considerations overlap (Wilcoxon, 1993). However, at other times, just like distinct theories, ethics and the law may be poles apart and may operate according to different premises (Rowley & MacDonald, 2001).

DEFINITIONS: ETHICS, MORALITY, AND LAW

Ethics involves "making decisions of a moral nature about people and their interaction in society" (Kitchener, 1986, p. 306). The term is often used synonymously with *morality*, and in some cases the two terms overlap. Both deal with "what is good and bad or the study of human conduct and values" (Van Hoose & Kottler, 1985, p. 2), yet each has a different meaning.

"Ethics is generally defined as a philosophical discipline that is concerned with human conduct and moral decision making" (Van Hoose & Kottler, 1985, p. 3). Ethics focuses on principles and standards that govern relationships between individuals, such as those between counselors and clients. Morality, on the other hand, involves judgment or evaluation of action. It is associated with such words as *good*, *bad*, *right*, *wrong*, *ought*, and *should* (Brandt, 1959; Grant, 1992). Counselors have morals, and the theories that counselors employ have embedded within them moral presuppositions about human nature that explicitly and implicitly question first, "What is a person and second, what should a person be or become?" (Christopher, 1996, p. 18).

Law is the precise codification of governing standards that are established to ensure legal and moral justice (Hummell, Talbutt, & Alexander, 1985). Law is created by legislation, court decision, and tradition, as in English common law (Anderson, 1996). Law does not dictate what is ethical in a given situation but what is legal. Sometimes what is legal at a given time (e.g., matters pertaining to race, age, or sex) is considered unethical or immoral by significant segments of society.

ETHICS AND COUNSELING

As a group, professional counselors are concerned with ethics and values. Indeed, many counselors treat ethical complaints with the same seriousness with which they treat lawsuits (Chauvin & Remley, 1996). Patterson (1971) has observed that counselors' professional identity is related to their knowledge and practice of ethics. Welfel (1998) adds that the effectiveness of counselors is connected to their ethical knowledge and behavior as well. Just knowing counseling theories is not sufficient.

Unethical behavior in counseling can take many forms; the temptations common to people everywhere exist also for counselors. These include "physical intimacy, the titillation of gossip, or the opportunity (if the gamble pays off) to advance one's career" (Welfel & Lipsitz, 1983b, p. 328). Some forms of unethical behavior are obvious and willful, whereas others are more subtle and unintentional. Regardless, the harmful outcome is the same. Following are some of the most prevalent forms of unethical behaviors in counseling (Levenson, 1986; Pope & Vetter, 1992; Swanson 1983):

* violation of confidentiality
* exceeding one's level of professional competence
* negligent practice
* claiming expertise one does not possess
* imposing one's values on a client
* creating dependency in a client
* sexual activity with a client
* certain conflicts of interest, such as dual relationships
* questionable financial arrangements, such as charging excessive fees
* improper advertising

PROFESSIONAL CODES OF ETHICS AND STANDARDS

To address ethical situations, counselors have developed professional codes of ethics and standards of conduct "based upon an agreed-on set of values" (Hansen, Rossberg, & Cramer, 1994, p. 362). Professionals in counseling voluntarily abide by such codes for many reasons. "Among its many purposes, a code of ethical conduct is designed to offer formal statements for ensuring protection of clients' rights while identifying expectations of practitioners" (Wilcoxon, 1987, p. 510). Furthermore, "without a code of established ethics, a group of people with similar interests cannot be considered a professional organization" (Allen, 1986, p. 293). A code of ethics not only helps professionalize an association on a general level but also is "designed to provide some guidelines for the professional behavior of members" on a personal level (Swanson, 1983, p. 53). In addition, according to Van Hoose and Kottler (1985),

- Ethical codes protect the profession from government. They allow the profession to regulate itself and function autonomously instead of being controlled by legislation.
- Ethical codes help control internal disagreements and bickering, thus promoting stability within the profession.
- Ethical codes protect practitioners from the public, especially in regard to malpractice suits. If counseling professionals behave according to ethical guidelines, their behavior is judged to be in compliance with accepted standards.

Ethical codes also help increase public trust in the integrity of the profession and provide clients with some protection from charlatans and incompetent counselors (Swanson, 1983; Vacc, Juhnke, & Nilsen, 2001). Like counselors, clients can use codes of ethics and standards as a guide in evaluating questionable treatment.

A number of professional codes of ethics exist. Among the most useful for counselors is the American Counseling Association (ACA) ethics code, which is entitled *Code of Ethics and Standards of Practice*. Its eight sections contain material similar to that found in many other ethical codes (Allen, Sampson, & Herlihy, 1988) but unique to the profession of counseling. Section 1 deals with the nature of the counseling relationship, including counselors' professional responsibilities to clients and their welfare (e.g., respect for diversity and client rights). This section also discusses counselors' personal needs and ways to handle troublesome subjects, such as dual relationships, fees, and termination. It clearly states that sexual intimacy between counselors and clients is unethical. In addition, it addresses related skills that may be associated with the treatment of clients, such as computer use.

Section 2 covers confidentiality in counseling, including the right to privacy, records, minor or incompetent clients, consultation, and research and training. Section 3 focuses on issues related to professional responsibility, such as professional competence, advertising and solicitation, credentials, and public responsibility. Section 4 covers relationships with other professionals, including employers and employees, referral fees (which are unethical), and subcontractor arrangements.

Section 5 deals with evaluation, assessment, and interpretation. In addition to general information, it includes material on using and interpreting tests, informed consent, release of information to competent professionals, proper diagnosis of mental disorders, testing conditions, and test security. Section 6 focuses on issues related to teaching, training, and supervision, including expectations of counselor educators and trainers, counselor education programs, and students and supervisees. Section 7 deals with research and publications and delineates research responsibilities, informed consent practices, and reporting of research results. Section 8 addresses ways to resolve ethical issues, including the handling of suspected violations and cooperation with ethics committees.

LIMITATIONS OF ETHICAL CODES

Remley (1985) notes that ethical codes are general and idealistic; they seldom answer specific questions. Furthermore, he points out that ethics documents do not address "foreseeable professional dilemmas" (p. 181). Rather, they provide guidelines, based on experiences and values, of how counselors should behave. In many ways ethical standards represent the collected wisdom of a profession at a particular time.

Specific limitations exist in any code of ethics; some of those most frequently mentioned are listed here (Beymer, 1971; Corey, Corey, & Callanan, 2003; Mabe & Rollin, 1986; Talbutt, 1981):

- Some issues cannot be resolved by a code of ethics.
- Enforcing ethical codes is difficult.
- Conflicts may exist within the standards delineated by the code.
- Some legal and ethical issues are not covered in codes.
- Because ethical codes are historical documents, what may be acceptable practice at one time may later be considered unethical.
- Sometimes conflicts arise between ethical and legal codes.
- Ethical codes do not address cross-cultural issues.
- Ethical codes do not address every possible situation.
- Bringing together systematically the interests of all parties involved in an ethical dispute is often difficult.
- Ethical codes are not proactive documents that help counselors decide what to do in new situations.

Thus, ethical codes are useful in many ways, but they do have their limitations. Counselors need to be aware that they will not always find all of the guidance they want in these documents. Nevertheless, whenever an ethical issue arises, a counselor should first consult ethical standards to see whether the situation is addressed.

CONFLICTS WITHIN AND AMONG ETHICAL CODES

The adoption of ethical codes and the emphasis placed on them have paralleled the increased professionalism of counseling (Stude & McKelvey, 1979). Nonetheless, the presence of such standards poses a potential dilemma for many counselors. First, as

Stadler (1986) points out, to act ethically, counselors must be aware of ethical codes and be able to differentiate an ethical dilemma from another type of dilemma, a differentiation that is not always easy to make. For example, counselors may take a stand on a controversial issue that they seem to support with ethical principles when, in reality, that support comes only from personal beliefs or biases.

Second, different ethical principles in one code may sometimes offer conflicting guidelines about what to do in a given situation (Stadler, 1986). One example is the potential conflict between respecting confidentiality and acting in clients' best interests when clients reveal that they are going to harass someone or harm themselves. Counselors who keep such information confidential may actually be acting against the best interests of their clients and their communities.

A third conflict may occur when counselors belong to two or more professional organizations whose codes of ethics differ, as do the codes of the American Psychological Association and the ACA. These therapists may face situations in which ethical action is unclear.

MAKING ETHICAL DECISIONS

Ethical decision making is often difficult yet is a part of being a counselor and using theories properly. It requires "virtues such as character, integrity, and moral courage" as well as knowledge (Welfel, 1998, p. 9). Some counselors operate according to personal ethical standards without regard to the guidelines developed by professional counseling and therapy associations. Such therapists usually function well until faced with a dilemma "for which there is no apparent good or best solution" (Swanson, 1983, p. 57). At such times these counselors experience anxiety, hesitation, and confusion; and their behavior may turn out to be unethical because it is not grounded in any ethical code.

This situation is illustrated by a study conducted in New York (Hayman & Covert, 1986). Researchers there found five types of ethical dilemmas most prevalent among the university counselors they surveyed; confidentiality, role conflict, counselor competence, conflicts with employer or institution, and degree of dangerousness. The situational dilemmas that involved danger were the least difficult to resolve; those that dealt with counselor competence and confidentiality were the most difficult. Fewer than one third of the respondents indicated that they relied on published professional codes of ethics in resolving dilemmas. Instead, most used common sense, a strategy that may be most unwise.

In difficult situations counselors need to be aware of their resources for ethical decision making, especially when questions arise over controversial behaviors, such as setting fees or maintaining dual relationships (Gibson & Pope, 1993). *Ethical reasoning* is crucial—"the process of determining which ethical principles are involved and then prioritizing them based on the professional requirements and beliefs" (Lanning, 1992, p. 21). Counselors should take actions "based on careful, reflective thought" about which responses are professionally appropriate in particular situations (Tennyson & Strom, 1986, p. 298).

Several ethical principles can guide counselors' decision making:

- *beneficence*—doing good
- *nonmaleficence*—not inflicting harm
- *autonomy*—respecting freedom of choice and self-determination
- *justice*—acting fairly
- *fidelity*—being faithful and honoring commitments (Herlihy, 1996; Stadler, 1986)

Some experts identify nonmaleficence as the primary ethical responsibility of counselors. It involves not only the "removal of present harm" but the "prevention of future harm, and passive avoidance of harm" (Thompson, 1990, p. 105). From this basis counselors respond to clients who may endanger themselves or others and to colleagues who behave unethically (Daniluk & Haverkamp, 1993).

Swanson (1983) lists other guidelines for ethical behavior. The first is personal and professional honesty. Counselors need to operate openly with themselves and those with whom they work. Hidden agendas or unacknowledged feelings hinder relationships and place counselors on shaky ethical ground. Another guideline is to act in the best interests of clients, an ideal that is easier to discuss than to achieve. Counselors must guard against imposing personal values on their clients (Gladding & Hood, 1974) and must always be alert to client emergencies.

A third guideline is that counselors should act without malice or personal gain. Counselors must be especially careful with difficult clients and with likable clients. Errors in judgment are most likely to occur when counselors' emotions or self-interest becomes a part of the client relationship (St. Germaine, 1993). And finally, counselors should be able to justify an action "as the best judgment of what should be done based upon the current state of the profession" (Swanson, 1983, p. 59). To make such a decision, counselors must keep up with current trends and theories—reading professional literature, attending in-service workshops and conventions, and becoming actively involved in local, state, and national counseling activities.

The *ACA Ethical Standards Casebook* (Herlihy & Corey, 1996) contains examples of difficult ethical situations, each of which involves a standard of the ethical code. The book gives helpful guidelines and questions to consider. However, in many counseling situations the proper behavior is far from obvious (Gladding et al., 2001). For example, counselors struggle with the question of confidentiality in balancing the individual rights of a person with AIDS and society's right to be protected from the spread of disease (Harding, Gray, & Neal, 1993). There are also multiple ethical dilemmas in counseling adult survivors of incest—questions of confidentiality and the consequences of reporting abuse (Daniluk & Haverkamp, 1993). When counselors are in doubt, it is crucial for them to use all available resources: consulting with colleagues as well as using principles, guidelines, casebooks, and professional codes of ethics.

When counselors face new circumstances that are not addressed by professional ethical standards, they can attempt to make ethical decisions by applying *principle ethics*, which is based on a set of obligations that focus on finding socially and historically appropriate answers to the question, "What shall I do?" (Corey et al., 2003). In other words, "Is this action ethical?" Counselors can also employ *virtue ethics*, which focuses on the "character traits of the counselor and nonobligatory ideals to which professionals aspire" (p. 13). Rather than solving a specific ethical question, virtue ethics looks at the question: "Am I doing what is best for my client?" Counselors would be wise to integrate both of these forms of ethical reasoning into their deliberations whenever clear standards are unavailable. Unfortunately, there are no absolute guidelines for most situations, making it critical for counselors to stay abreast of current issues, trends, and legislation related to the situations they face.

EDUCATING COUNSELORS IN ETHICAL DECISION MAKING

One of the best ways to promote ethical decision making in counseling is through course offerings that are now required in most counseling programs and are available for continuing education credit. Such courses can bring about significant attitudinal changes in students and practicing professionals, as well as increased knowledge about various ethical areas such as self-awareness, dual relationships, impairment, and multiculturalism (Coll, 1993). Van Hoose and Paradise (1979) conceptualize the ethical behavior of counselors in a five-stage developmental continuum.

1. *Punishment orientation.* At this stage counselors are motivated by the thought of punishment. If clients or counselors violate any external societal rule, they should be punished.
2. *Institutional orientation.* Counselors who operate at this stage believe in and abide by the rules of the institutions for which they work. They do not question the rules and base their decisions on them.
3. *Societal orientation.* Counselors at this stage base decisions on societal standards. If a question arises about the needs of society versus those of an individual, the needs of society are always given priority.
4. *Individual orientation.* The individual's needs receive top priority at this stage. Counselors are aware of societal needs and are concerned about the law, but they focus on what is best for the individual.
5. *Principle, or conscience, orientation.* At this stage concern for the individual remains primary, but ethical decisions are based on internalized ethical standards, not external considerations.

As Welfel and Lipsitz (1983a) point out, the work of Van Hoose and Paradise is especially important because it "is the first conceptual model in the literature that attempts to explain how counselors reason about ethical issues" (p. 36). It is *heuristic* (i.e., able to be researched) and thus can form the basis for empirical studies of the promotion of ethical behavior.

Several other models have been proposed for educating counselors and therapists in ethical decision making. Pelsma and Borgers (1986) suggest a process-oriented model based on the assumption that counselors do not learn to make ethical decisions on their own. Pelsma and Borgers emphasize the *how* as opposed to the *what* of ethics—that is, how to reason ethically in a constantly changing field. Other guides include a seven-step decision-making model based on a synthesis of the professional literature (Forester-Miller & Davis, 1996) and a nine-step model based on critical-evaluative judgments (Welfel, 1998). These models follow explicit steps or stages and are often used for specific areas of counseling practice.

In addition, the ACA Ethics Committee offers a variety of educational experiences. For example, members of the committee offer learning institutes at national and regional ACA conferences. They also publish articles in the ACA newsletter, *Counseling Today*, and they produce a consumer's guide entitled *The Layperson's Guide to Counselor Ethics: What You Should Know about the Ethical Practice of Professional Counselors*, available in print as well as on the ACA Web site (Williams & Freeman, 2002).

SPECIFIC ETHICAL CONCERNS

WORKPLACE PRESSURE

The difficulty in making ethical decisions can sometimes be attributed to the environments in which counselors work. "Most organizations that employ counselors are organized not collegially or professionally, as is in part the case with universities and hospitals, but hierarchically. In a hierarchical organization, the administrator or executive decides which prerogatives are administrative and which are professional" (Ladd, 1971, p. 262). Thus, implementing ethical decisions can sometimes involve "substantial personal and professional risk or discomfort" (Faiver, Eisengart, & Colonna, 1995, p. 121).

Counselors should thoroughly check the policies and principles of an institution before accepting employment, which implies agreement. When counselors find themselves in institutions that misuse their services and do not act in the best interests of clients, the counselors must act either to change the institution or to find other employment.

DUAL RELATIONSHIPS

The issue of dual relationships as an ethical consideration emerged from debates in the 1970s on the ethical nature of counselor-client sexual relations. When professional groups concluded that such relationships were unethical, questions were raised about other types of relationships between counselors and clients, such as business interactions or friendships. Because of the counseling connection, these relationships are not entirely mutual, leaving clients more vulnerable than counselors.

Professional groups concluded that nonsexual dual relationships should be avoided because "no matter how harmless a dual relationship seems, a conflict of interest almost always exists, and any professional counselor's judgment is likely to be affected" (St. Germaine, 1993, p. 27). Counselors lose their objectivity, and clients may be unable to be assertive. For example, if a business transaction takes place between a counselor and a client and is not successful, there is apt to be a negative impact on the therapeutic relationship, no matter what theory or theories are being employed. Even with former clients objectivity is lost. Therefore, as a matter of ethics, counselors should avoid socializing or doing business with present or former clients; accepting gifts from them; or entering into a counseling relationship with a friend, family member, student, lover, or employee.

Although these principles may seem clear, implementing them is sometimes difficult. For instance, many substance abuse counselors are in recovery. "For these individuals, existing ethical codes do not specifically or adequately address the unique circumstances in which they periodically find themselves" (Doyle, 1997, p. 428). They must often struggle with issues of confidentiality and anonymity, attendance at self-help groups with clients, social relationships among self-help group members, and sponsorship in self-help programs.

UNETHICAL COLLEAGUES

Although most counselors are ethical, occasionally some are not. In these circumstances other counselors must take some action or risk eroding their own sense of moral self-hood and perhaps finding it easier to condone future ethical breaches, a phenomenon known as the *slippery slope effect*.

Herlihy (1996) suggests several steps to take in working through potential ethical dilemmas, especially with impaired professionals. The first is to identify the problem as objectively as possible and the concerned counselor's relationship to it. Such a process is best done on paper to clarify thinking. The second step is to apply a code of ethics to the matter in the hope that a clear course of action might emerge. If not, the counselor should consider the moral principles of the helping profession discussed earlier, such as beneficence, justice, and autonomy. Consultation with another colleague is an option, also.

If action is warranted, the concerned counselor should approach the colleague in question informally in a caring context. If the colleague does not address the problem, the confronting counselor should consider the potential consequences of all other options and then define a course of action. One approach might be to file an ethical complaint with a professional counseling association or with a state licensure or national certification board. Such a complaint should be filed by either the concerned counselor or a client who was treated unethically (Piercy, 2000).

In examining courses of action, the concerned counselor must evaluate various criteria: the fairness of the action, any lingering feelings of doubt, the universality of the option (i.e., Would I recommend this course to others?), and the possibility of publicity. Whatever action is chosen, some will disagree, and the counselor must prepare for both criticism and credit.

THE LAW AND COUNSELING

The profession of counseling is also governed by legal standards. *Legal* refers to "law or the state of being lawful," and *law* refers to "a body of rules recognized by a state or community as binding on its members" (Shertzer & Stone, 1980, p. 386). Contrary to popular opinion, "law is not cut and dried, definite and certain, or clear and precise" (Van Hoose & Kottler, 1985, p. 44). Rather, it seeks compromise between individuals and parties. It offers few definite answers but many notable exceptions.

There is "no general body of law covering the helping professions" (Van Hoose & Kottler, 1985, p. 45), but a number of court decisions and statutes influence legal opinion on counseling. The 1993 Napa County, California, case involving Gary Ramona is one such decision. In this widely publicized trial Ramona sued his daughter's therapists, "charging that by implanting false memories of sexual abuse in her mind they had destroyed his life" (Butler, 1994, p. 10). Ramona was awarded $475,000 after the jury "found the therapists had negligently reinforced false memories" (Butler, 1994, p. 11). The legal opinion on which the case was decided was *duty to care*, a health provider's legal obligation not to act negligently.

Another important legal case was the 1996 U.S. Supreme Court decision in *Jaffee v. Redmond*, which held that communications between licensed psychotherapists and their clients are privileged and do not have to be disclosed in federal cases (Remley, Herlihy, & Herlihy, 1997). The importance of this case is that a legal precedent was set protecting confidentiality between a master's-level clinician, in this case a social worker, and her client. The case also brought positive attention to mental health services, including counseling.

A third legal case that has affected counselors is the *amicus curiae* brief argued before the United States Supreme Court in 1997. This brief dealt with mental health issues associated with physician-assisted suicide (Werth & Gordon, 2002). In this court action several mental health groups joined together to protect the rights of counselors and other helping specialties in hastening death—protecting the suffering person, the person's significant others, and society as a whole from the problems associated with aid-in-dying.

In most cases the law is "generally supportive or neutral" toward professional codes of ethics and counseling in general (Stude & McKelvey, 1979, p. 454). It supports licensure or certification of counselors and therapists as a means of ensuring that those who enter the profession attain at least minimal standards. It also supports the general "confidentiality of statements and records provided by clients during therapy" (p. 454). In addition, the law is neutral in allowing "the profession to police itself and govern counselors' relations with their clients and fellow counselors" (p. 454). The only time the law overrides a professional code of ethics is when it is necessary "to protect the public health, safety, and welfare" (p. 454), as in cases of confidentiality when disclosure of information is necessary to prevent harm. In such cases counselors and therapists have a duty to warn potential victims about the possibility of a client's violent behavior (Costa & Altekruse, 1994).

LEGAL ASPECTS OF THE COUNSELING RELATIONSHIP

Counselors must follow specific legal guidelines in working with certain populations. For example, counselors have a legal obligation under all child abuse laws to report suspected cases of abuse to proper authorities, usually specific personnel in a state social welfare office (Henderson, 2003). Such situations may be especially troubling when counselors are working directly with the families in which the abuse is suspected (Stevens-Smith & Hughes, 1993).

Counselors have considerable difficulty when the law is not clear or a conflict exists between the law and professional counseling ethics. Such situations often involve the sharing of information among clients, counselors, and the court system. *Confidentiality* is "the ethical duty to fulfill a contract or promise to clients that the information revealed during therapy will be protected from unauthorized disclosure" (Arthur & Swanson, 1993, p. 7). Confidentiality becomes a legal as well as an ethical concern if it is broken, whether intentionally or not. It prompts many inquiries every year to the ACA Ethics Committee.

"*Privacy* [italics added] is an evolving legal concept that recognizes individuals' rights to choose the time, circumstances, and extent to which they wish to share or withhold personal information" (Herlihy & Sheeley, 1987, p. 479). Clients who think they have been coerced into revealing information they would not normally disclose may seek legal recourse against counselors.

Privileged communication, a narrower concept, protects clients from having their confidential communications disclosed in court without their permission. It is defined as "a client's legal right, guaranteed by statute, that confidences originating in a thera-peutic relationship will be safeguarded" (Arthur & Swanson, 1993, p. 7). Most states recognize and protect privileged communication in counselor-client relationships, with nine categories of exceptions (Glosoff, Herlihy, & Spence, 2000):

> "(a) in cases of a dispute between counselor and client; (b) when a client raises the issue of mental condition in legal proceedings; (c) when a client's condition poses a danger to self or others; (d) in cases of child abuse or neglect (in addition to mandated reporting laws); (e) when the counselor has knowledge that the client is contemplating commis-sion of a crime; (f) during court ordered psychological evaluations; (g) for purposes of involuntary hospitalization; (h) when the counselor has knowledge that a client has been a victim of a crime; and (i) in cases of harm to vulnerable adults." (p. 455)

It is essential that counselors and therapists know and communicate to their clients potential situations in which confidentiality may be broken (Glosoff et al., 2000; Woody, 1988).

And even though "the legal concept of privileged communication generally does not apply in group and family counseling" (Anderson, 1996, p. 35), therapists should protect the confidentiality of those individuals as much as possible.

A landmark court case that reflects the importance of limiting confidentiality is *Tarasoff v. Board of Regents of the University of California* (1976). Prosenjit Poddar was a student and a voluntary outpatient at the student health services on the Berkeley campus of the University of California. He informed the psychologist who was counseling him that he intended to kill his former girlfriend, Tatiana Tarasoff, when she arrived back on campus. The psychologist notified the campus police, who detained and questioned the student about his proposed activities. The student denied any intention of killing Tarasoff, behaved rationally, and was released. Poddar refused further treatment from the psychologist, and no additional steps were taken to deter him from his intended action. Two months later he killed Tarasoff, whose parents sued the regents of the University of

California for failing to notify the intended victim of a threat against her. The California Supreme Court ruled in their favor, holding, in effect, that a therapist has a duty to protect the public that overrides any obligation to maintain client confidentiality.

Thus, there is a limit to how much confidentiality counselors can or should maintain. When it appears that a client is dangerous to him- or herself or to others, state laws specify that this information must be reported to proper authorities. Knapp and Vandecreek (1982) note, however, that state laws do vary, and reporting such information is often difficult. They suggest that counselors try to defuse the danger while also satisfying any legal duty when client violence is at risk. They recommend consulting with professional colleagues who have expertise in working with violent individuals, and all actions should be documented.

CIVIL AND CRIMINAL LIABILITY

The *Tarasoff* case raises the question of liability and malpractice in regard to counselors and therapists. Basically, *liability* relates to whether counselors have caused harm to clients (Wittmer & Loesch, 1986). It is directly connected with malpractice. *Malpractice* is defined as "harm to a client resulting from professional negligence, with *negligence* [italics added] defined as the departure from acceptable professional standards" (Hummell et al., 1985, p. 70). Until recently, there were relatively few counselor malpractice lawsuits; but with the increased number of licensed, certified, and practicing counselors, such suits have become more common.

Two ways that counselors and therapists can protect themselves from malpractice claims are to follow professional codes of ethics and to follow normal practice standards (Hopkins & Anderson, 1990). Nonetheless, because malpractice lawsuits can still occur, liability insurance is a must (Bullis, 1993). *Avoiding Counselor Malpractice* (Crawford, 1994) is an excellent book explaining the nature and scope of malpractice and reasonable precautions to avoid being implicated in lawsuits.

Liability can be classified as either civil or criminal. *Civil liability* means that "one can be sued for acting wrongly toward another or for failing to act when there [is] a recognized duty to do so" (Hopkins & Anderson, 1990, p. 21). *Criminal liability*, on the other hand, involves a counselor's interaction with a client in a way the law does not allow (Burgum & Anderson, 1975). Civil liability rests on the concept of *tort*, "a wrong that legal action is designed to set right" (Hopkins & Anderson, 1990, p. 21). That wrong can be against a person, property, or even someone's reputation and may be unintentional or direct. Counselors and therapists are most apt to face civil liability suits for malpractice in the following situations: (a) failure to present options or pressure to choose an option in particular situations (e.g., birth control, abortion, prescribing and administering drugs, treatment), (b) illegal search, (c) defamation, (d) invasion of privacy, and (e) breach of contract (Hopkins and Anderson, 1990). Counselors and therapists risk criminal liability for civil disobedience, for being an accessory to a crime, and for contributing to the delinquency of a minor (Burgum & Anderson, 1975; Hopkins & Anderson, 1990).

CLIENT RIGHTS AND RECORDS

Client rights may be implied or explicit (Hansen et al., 1994), and both relate to due process. *Implied rights* are linked to substantive due process. When a rule is made that arbitrarily limits an individual (i.e., deprives the person of constitutional rights), he or she has been denied substantive due process. *Explicit rights* focus on procedural due process (i.e., the steps necessary to initiate or complete an action when an explicit rule is broken). An individual's procedural due process is violated when an explicit rule is broken and the person is not informed about how to remedy the matter. A client has a right to know what recourse is available when either of these types of rights is violated.

All client records are legally protected except under special circumstances. The Buckley Amendment provides an individual the legal right to inspect his or her record. However, in some cases (cited by Hummell et al., 1985) third parties also have access to educational information without the consent of the student or parent. Nevertheless, in the vast majority of cases, counselors are legally required to protect clients of all ages by keeping their records under lock and key, separate from any required business records, and by refusing to disclose any information about the clients without their written permission (Mitchell, 2001). A release-of-information form, which can be drawn up by an attorney, is the best method to use in meeting a request to disclose information (Rosenthal, 1998). In no case should counselors release client information that they have not obtained firsthand.

Because record keeping is one of the most important areas of legal liability for counselors (Snider, 1987), it is important to know what should go into records. Basically, records should contain "all information about the client necessary for his or her treatment" (Piazza & Baruth, 1990, p. 313). Six categories of documents are usually included:

1. *Identifying or intake information*—name, address, telephone number(s), date of birth, gender, occupation
2. *Assessment information*—psychological evaluation(s), social/family history, health history
3. *Treatment plan*—presenting problem, plan of action, steps to be taken to reach targeted behavior
4. *Case notes*—documentation of progress in each session toward the stated goal
5. *Termination summary*—outcome of treatment, final diagnosis (if any), after-care plan
6. *Other data*—client's signed consent for treatment, copies of correspondence, notations about any unusual interventions, any administrative problems

Counselors must check their state legal codes for exact guidelines about record keeping. Counselors who receive third-party reimbursement must note progress in terms of a treatment plan and a diagnosis, if required (Hinkle, 1994).

THE COUNSELOR IN COURT

The court system in the United States is divided into federal and state courts. Each is similarly patterned with "trial courts, a middle-level appellate court, and a supreme court" (Anderson, 1996, p. 7). Most counselors who appear in court do so on the state level; federal courts deal with cases arising from federal laws or from disputes involving citizens of different states and monetary amounts exceeding $50,000.

Most counselors wind up in court in one of two ways. The first is voluntary and professional and occurs when the counselor serves as an *expert witness*. "An expert witness is an objective and unbiased person with specialized knowledge, skills, or information, who can assist a judge or jury in reaching an appropriate legal decision" (Remley, 1992, p. 33). A counselor who serves as an expert witness is compensated financially. A counselor may also appear in court through a *court order*, a *subpoena* to appear in court at a certain time in regard to a specific case. Such a summons is issued so that the counselor will testify on behalf of or against a present or former client.

Because the legal system is adversarial, counselors are wise to seek the advice of their attorneys before responding to court orders (Remley, 1991). In addition, in preparing for legal encounters, counselors should read some or all of the 12 volumes in the American Counseling Association Legal Series. Edited by Theodore P. Remley, Jr., these volumes are written by experts in the field of counseling who have either legal degrees or expert knowledge on important legal issues, such as preparing for court appearances, documenting counseling records, counseling minors, understanding confidentiality and privileged communication, receiving third-party payments, and managing a counseling agency. Role-playing possible situations before appearing in court may also help counselors function better in such situations.

SUMMARY AND CONCLUSION

Counselors and therapists, like other professionals, have established codes of ethics to guide them in the practice of helping others. The ethical standards of the ACA are a primary resource for counselors when they face ethical dilemmas. Acting ethically is not always easy, comfortable, or clear.

In making an ethical decision, counselors rely on personal values as well as ethical standards and legal precedents. They also consult professional colleagues, casebooks, and accepted principles. It is imperative that counselors become well informed in the area of ethics for the sake of their own well-being and that of their clients. It is not enough to have an academic knowledge of ethical standards; counselors must also have a working knowledge and be able to assess the developmental level at which they and their colleagues are operating.

In addition, counselors must be informed about state and national legislation and legal decisions, for these will affect the ways in which they work. Counselors are liable for civil and criminal malpractice if they violate client rights or societal rules. One way for counselors to protect themselves legally is to follow the ethical standards of the professional organizations with which they are affiliated and operate according to recognized practices. Counselors must be able to justify what they do, and they should carry malpractice insurance.

Ethical standards and legal codes reflect current conditions and are ever-evolving documents. They do not cover all situations, but they do offer guidance beyond counselors' personal beliefs and values. The ethical and legal aspects of counseling will probably become more complicated in the future, and enforcement procedures will become stricter. No practicing counselor should be ignorant of ethics or the law.

CLASSROOM ACTIVITIES

1. Obtain copies of ethical codes for counseling, social work, marriage and family therapy, and psychology. Compare their ethical standards. What differences do you notice? Discuss your observations with fellow class members.
2. In groups of four, enact before your classmates specific ethical dilemmas that you think might arise in counseling. Have the other groups write down at least two courses of action to pursue in solving each dilemma and have them explain the personal and professional reasons for their actions. Discuss each of these situations with the class as a whole and with your instructor.
3. Write down ways that you, as a professional counselor, can influence the development of counseling ethics and law. Be specific. Share your thoughts with fellow classmates.

REFERENCES

Allen, V. B. (1986). A historical perspective of the AACD ethics committee. *Journal of Counseling and Development, 64,* 293.

Allen, V. B., Sampson, J. P., Jr., & Herlihy, B. (1988). Details of the 1988 AACD ethical standards. *Journal of Counseling and Development, 67,* 157–158.

American Counseling Association. (1995). *Ethical standards of the American Counseling Association.* Alexandria, VA: Author.

Anderson, B. S. (1996). *The counselor and the law* (4th ed.). Alexandria, VA: American Counseling Association.

Anderson, D., & Swanson, C. (1994). *Legal issues in licensure.* Alexandria, VA: American Counseling Association.

Arthur, G. L., & Swanson, C. D. (1993). *Confidentiality and privileged communication.* Alexandria, VA: American Counseling Association.

Bergin, A. E. (1985). Proposed values for guiding and evaluating counseling and psychotherapy. *Counseling and Values, 29,* 99–115.

Bergin, A. E. (1992). Three contributions of a spiritual perspective to counseling, psychotherapy, and behavior change. In M. T. Burke & J. G. Miranti (Eds.), *Ethical and spiritual values in counseling* (pp. 5–15). Alexandria, VA: American Counseling Association.

Beymer, L. (1971). Who killed George Washington? *Personnel and Guidance Journal, 50,* 249–253.

Brandt, R. (1959). *Ethical theory.* Upper Saddle River, NJ: Prentice Hall.

Bullis, R. K. (1993). *Law and the management of a counseling agency or private practice.* Alexandria, VA: American Counseling Association.

Burgum, T., & Anderson, S. (1975). *The counselor and the law.* Washington, DC: APGA Press.

Butler, K. (1994, July/August). Duty of care. *Family Therapy Networker, 18,* 10–11.

Chauvin, J. C., & Remley, T. P., Jr. (1996). Responding to allegations of unethical conduct. *Journal of Counseling and Development, 74,* 563–568.

Christopher, J. C. (1996). Counseling's inescapable moral visions. *Journal of Counseling and Development, 75,* 17–25.

Clawson, T. W., & Wildermuth, V. (1992, December). The counselor and NBCC. *CAPS Digest,* EDO-CG–92–14.

Coll, K. M. (1993). Student attitudinal changes in a counseling ethics course. *Counseling and Values, 37,* 165–170.

Corbia, D. C., & Pipes, R. B. (2002). Mandated supervision: An intervention for disciplined professionals. *Journal of Counseling and Development, 80,* 140–144

Corey, G., Corey, M. S., & Callanan, P. (2003). *Issues and ethics in the helping professions* (6th ed.). Pacific Grove, CA. Brooks/Cole.

Costa, L., & Altekruse, M. (1994). Duty-to-warn guidelines for mental health counselors. *Journal of Counseling and Development, 72,* 346–350.

Cottone, R. R., & Tarvydas, V. M. (2003). *Ethical and professional issues in counseling* (2nd ed.). Upper Saddle River, NJ: Merrill/Prentice Hall.

Crawford, R. L. (1994). *Avoiding counselor malpractice.* Alexandria, VA: American Counseling Association.

Daniluk, J. C., & Haverkamp, B. E. (1993). Ethical issues in counseling adult survivors of incest. *Journal of Counseling and Development, 72,* 16–22.

DePauw, M. E. (1986). Avoiding ethical violations: A timeline perspective for individual counseling. *Journal of Counseling and Development, 64,* 303–305.

Dingman, R. L. (1990, November). *Counselor credentialing laws.* Paper presented at the Southern Association for Counselor Education and Supervision, Norfolk, VA.

Doyle, K. (1997). Substance abuse counselors in recovery: Implications for the ethical issue of dual relationships. *Journal of Counseling and Development, 75,* 428–432.

Faiver, C., Eisengart, S., & Colonna, R. (1995). *The counselor intern's handbook.* Pacific Grove, CA: Brooks/Cole.

Forester-Miller, H., & Davis, T. E. (1996). *A practitioner's guide to ethical decision making.* Alexandria, VA: American Counseling Association.

Fretz, B. R., & Mills, D. H. (1980). *Licensing and certification of psychologists and counselors.* San Francisco: Jossey-Bass.

Gibson, W. T., & Pope, K. S. (1993). The ethics of counseling: A national survey of certified counselors. *Journal of Counseling and Development, 71,* 330–336.

Gladding, S. T., & Hood, W. D. (1974). Five cents, please. *School Counselor, 21,* 40–43.

Gladding, S. T., Remley, T. P., Jr., & Huber, C. H. (2001). *Ethical, legal and professional issues in the practice of marriage and family therapy* (3rd ed.). Upper Saddle River, NJ: Merrill/Prentice Hall.

Glosoff, H. (1992). Accrediting and certifying professional counselors. *Guidepost, 34*(12), 6–8.

Glosoff, H. L., Herlihy, B., & Spence, E. B. (2000). Privileged communication in the counselor-client relationship. *Journal of Counseling and Development, 78,* 454–462.

Grant, B. (1992). The moral nature of psychotherapy. In M. T. Burke & J. G. Miranti (Eds.), *Ethical and spiritual values in counseling* (pp. 27–35). Alexandria, VA: American Counseling Association.

Hansen, J. C., Rossberg, R. H., & Cramer, S. H. (1994). *Counseling: Theory and process* (5th ed.). Boston: Allyn & Bacon.

Harding, A. K., Gray, L. A., & Neal, M. (1993). Confidentiality limits with clients who have HIV: A review of ethical and legal guidelines and professional policies. *Journal of Counseling and Development, 71,* 297–304.

Hayman, P. M., & Covert, J. A. (1986). Ethical dilemmas in college counseling centers. *Journal of Counseling and Development, 64,* 318–320.

Henderson, D. A. (2003). School counseling. In R. R. Cottone & V. M. Tarvydas, *Ethical and professional issues in counseling* (2nd ed., pp. 236–259). Upper Saddle River, NJ: Prentice Hall.

Henderson, D. A., & Fall, M. (1998). School counseling. In R. R. Cottone & V. M. Tarvydas (Eds.), *Ethical and professional issues in counseling* (pp. 263–294). Upper Saddle River, NJ: Prentice Hall.

Herlihy, B. (1996). When a colleague is impaired: The individual counselor's response. *Journal of Humanistic Education and Development, 34,* 118–127.

Herlihy, B., & Corey, C. (1996). *ACA ethical standards casebook* (5th ed.). Alexandria, VA: American Counseling Association.

Herlihy, B., & Sheeley, V. L. (1987). Privileged communication in selected helping professions: A comparison among statutes. *Journal of Counseling and Development, 64,* 479–483.

Hinkle, J. S. (1994, September). *Psychodiagnosis and treatment planning under the DSM-IV* Workshop presentation of the North Carolina Counseling Association, Greensboro.

Hopkins, B. R., & Anderson, B. S. (1990). *The counselor and the law* (3rd ed.). Alexandria, VA: American Counseling Association.

Hummell, D. L., Talbutt, L. C., & Alexander, M. D. (1985). *Law and ethics in counseling.* New York: Van Nostrand Reinhold.

Kitchener, K. S. (1986). Teaching applied ethics in counselor education: An integration of psychological processes and philosophical analysis. *Journal of Counseling and Development, 64,* 306–310.

Kitchener, K. S. (1994, May). Doing good well: The wisdom behind ethical supervision. *Counseling and Human Development,* 1–8.

Knapp, S., & Vandecreek, L. (1982). *Tarasoff:* Five years later. *Professional Psychology, 13,* 511–516.

Ladd, E. T. (1971). Counselors, confidences, and the civil liberties of clients. *Personnel and Guidance Journal, 50,* 261–268.

Lanning, W. (1992, December). Ethical codes and responsible decision-making. *ACA Guidepost, 35,* 21.

Levenson, J. L. (1986). When a colleague practices unethically: Guidelines for intervention. *Journal of Counseling and Development, 64,* 315–317.

Mabe, A. R., & Rollin, S. A. (1986). The role of a code of ethical standards in counseling. *Journal of Counseling and Development, 64,* 294–297.

McGovern, T. F. (1994, May/June). Being good and doing good: An ethical reflection around alcoholism and drug abuse counseling. *The Counselor,* 14–18.

Mitchell, R. (2001). *Documentation in counseling records* (2nd ed.). Alexandria, VA: American Counseling Association.

Patterson, C. H. (1971). Are ethics different in different settings? *Personnel and Guidance Journal, 50,* 254–259.

Pelsma, D. M., & Borgers, S. B. (1986). Experience-based ethics: A developmental model of learning ethical reasoning. *Journal of Counseling and Development, 64,* 311–314.

Piazza, N. J., & Baruth, N. E. (1990). Client record guidelines. *Journal of Counseling and Development, 68,* 313–316.

Piercy, F. P. (2000, March/April). To tell or not to tell? *Family Therapy Networker, 24,* 21.

Pope, K. S., & Vetter, V. A. (1992). Ethical dilemmas encountered by members of the American Psychological Association. *American Psychologist, 47,* 397–411.

Remley, T. P., Jr. (1985). The law and ethical practices in elementary and middle schools. *Elementary School Guidance and Counseling, 19,* 181–189.

Remley, T. P., Jr. (1991). *Preparing for court appearances.* Alexandria, VA: American Counseling Association.

Remley, T. P., Jr. (1992, Spring). You and the law. *American Counselor, 1,* 33.

Remley, T. P., Jr., Herlihy, B., & Herlihy, S. B. (1997). The U.S. Supreme Court decision in *Jaffee v. Redmond:* Implications for counselors. *Journal of Counseling and Development, 75,* 213–218.

Romano, G. (1992). The power and pain of professionalization. *American Counselor, 1,* 17–23.

Rosenthal, H. (1998). *Before you see your first client.* Holmes Beach, FL: Learning Publications.

Rowley, W. J., & MacDonald, D. (2001). Counseling and the law: A cross-cultural perspective. *Journal of Counseling and Development, 79,* 422–429.

St. Germaine, J. (1993). Dual relationships: What's wrong with them? *American Counselor, 2,* 25–30.

Schulte, J. M. (1990). The morality of influencing in counseling. *Counseling and Values, 34,* 103–118.

Shertzer, B., & Stone, S. (1980). *Fundamentals of counseling* (3rd ed.). Boston: Houghton Mifflin.

Shimberg, B. (1981). Testing for licensure and certification. *American Psychologist, 36,* 1138–1146.

Snider, P. D. (1987). Client records: Inexpensive liability protection for mental health counselors. *Journal of Mental Health Counseling, 9,* 134–141.

Stadler, H. (1986). Preface to the special issue. *Journal of Counseling and Development, 64,* 291.

Stevens-Smith, P., & Hughes, M. M. (1993). *Legal issues in marriage and family counseling.* Alexandria, VA. American Counseling Association.

Stude, E. W., & McKelvey, J. (1979). Ethics and the law: Friend or foe? *Personnel and Guidance Journal, 57,* 453–456.

Swanson, C. D. (1983). Ethics and the counselor. In J. A. Brown & R. H. Pate, Jr. (Eds.), *Being a counselor* (pp. 47–65). Pacific Grove, CA: Brooks/Cole.

Talbutt, L. C. (1981). Ethical standards: Assets and limitations. *Personnel and Guidance Journal, 60,* 110–112.

Tennyson, W. W., & Strom, S. M. (1986). Beyond professional standards: Developing responsibleness. *Journal of Counseling and Development, 64,* 298–302.

Thompson, A. (1990). *Guide to ethical practice in psychotherapy.* New York: Wiley.

Vacc, N. A., Juhnke, G. A., & Nilsen, K. A. (2001). Community mental health service providers' code of ethics and the *Standards for Educational and Psychological Testing. Journal of Counseling and Development, 79,* 217–224.

Van Hoose, W. H., & Kottler, J. (1985). *Ethical and legal issues in counseling and psychotherapy* (2nd ed.). San Francisco: Jossey-Bass.

Van Hoose, W. H., & Paradise, L. V. (1979). *Ethics in counseling and psychotherapy.* Cranston, RI: Carroll.

Welfel, E. R. (1998). *Ethics in counseling and psychotherapy.* Pacific Grove, CA: Brooks/Cole.

Welfel, E. R., & Lipsitz, N. E. (1983a). Ethical orientation of counselors: Its relationship to moral reasoning and level of training. *Counselor Education and Supervision, 23,* 35–45.

Welfel, E. R., & Lipsitz, N. E. (1983b). Wanted: A comprehensive approach to ethics research and education. *Counselor Education and Supervision, 22,* 320–332.

Werth, J. L., Jr., & Gordon, J. R. (2002). Amicus curiae brief for the United States Supreme Court on mental health issues associated with "physician-assisted suicides." *Journal of Counseling and Development, 80,* 160–172.

Wilcoxon, S. A. (1987). Ethical standards: A study of application and utility. *Journal of Counseling and Development, 65,* 510–511.

Wilcoxon, S. A. (1993, March/April). Ethical issues in marital and family counseling: A framework for examining unique ethical concerns. *Family Counseling and Therapy, 1,* 1–15.

Williams, C. B., & Freeman, L. T. (2002). Report of the ACA Ethics Committee: 2000–2001. *Journal of Counseling and Development, 80,* 251–254.

Wittmer, J. P., & Loesch, L. C. (1986). Professional orientation. In M. D. Lewis, R. L. Hays, & J. A. Lewis (Eds.), *The counseling profession* (pp. 301–330). Itasca, IL: Peacock.

Woody, R. H. (1988). *Fifty ways to avoid malpractice.* Sarasota, FL: Professional Resource Exchange.

Epilogue

Compared to others
  you're physically small
    so your heart must be big
      and your senses strong
Amid such a contrast
  people may see
    the gifts that you bring to humanity
      and know anew that quality in life
        is not one measured in inches.

Note: "A Note to Tim on Life" by S. T. Gladding. Copyright 2003 by Samuel T. Gladding.

In the preceding chapters you have read about the importance of theories and have been able to surmise how the most popular theories of today work. You have also read about the importance of ethical and legal issues in using theories. Beginning counselors and even some experienced therapists sometimes question which theory or theories work best. They may even engage in heated debates about minor issues associated with various theories. The public as well as management groups connected to mental health issues, such as HMOs, frequently have such discussions as well. The reason is that clinicians, insurance companies, and the public may become more assured and confident about outcomes and the value of treatment if a theory or theories can be proven to be effective in certain situations or with specific populations.

In recent years there has been a tendency for cognitive, behavioral, and cognitive-behavioral theories to experience a good deal of validity in regard to their helpfulness. This trend is not surprising, given that these approaches to counseling and therapy are probably the most objectively measured. Still the classic question persists when a new client is seen: "What treatment, by whom, is most effective for this individual with that specific problem (or set of problems) and under which set of circumstances?" (Paul, 1967, p.111).

It is beyond the scope of this text to give a definitive answer to Paul's pondering, which would require delving into an almost inexhaustible number of variables related to a client before counseling and therapy begins—for example, family background, physical and psychological issues, and so on. Research has verified, though, that a number of psychologically oriented treatments are valuable with some specific disorders (Murdock, 2004; Seligman, 2003). In addition, a number of emerging theories hold significant promise (Corsini, 2001).

THEORIES, CLIENTS, AND YOU

Regardless of the current state of research about theories, it is important to emphasize that having and utilizing a theory in counseling is important both singularly and in combination. Theories ground you as a professional helper by making you aware of what other practitioners and researchers have proposed and how their ideas and implementations have worked. However, it must be stressed that clients respond differently to diverse theories. As stated at the beginning of this text, counselors may even change theories during the course of counseling with the same client. As you have seen in the chapter vignettes, Linda's outcomes are related to the approaches employed with her.

Yet, as crucial as the qualities and backgrounds of theories and clients are, you as the counselor are equally important. Applying theoretical approaches to therapeutic situations is both an art and a science. It involves knowing the research behind what you do and being aware of yourself, your client, and the developmental stage of therapy in which you are engaged. There are no cookbooks for or shortcuts to think-ing, feeling, and acting within the moments that you are engaged in helping others. If you remember this fact, you will likely do well in applying the theories you have learned here and others that you may master later. Your sensitivity to the complexity of counseling will have been increased, and the helping relationships you establish will be informed by the past as well as the present.

FINAL CONSIDERATIONS

As you have seen from reading about how the different theories work, many reasons are associated with what various approaches emphasize and what techniques they use. These reasons are based on developmental and situational factors. Thus, the same client may be conceptualized in a number of ways, depending on who is providing services. However, even though theories are unique, they are paradoxically similar in using specialized vocabularies, terms, and procedures. Counseling has its own special language that must be mastered. However, therapists' backgrounds and personalities enter treatment, too, and appropriate ways of responding and interacting with clients must be learned and mastered so that the personhood of therapists does not detract from theories that they know or use.

You will do well to remember that despite some drawbacks and limitations, theories provide guidance about what is occurring in the lives of clients and how such issues might best be handled (Austin, 1999). Theories also influence the process of therapy— that is, what will be done and how, as well as outcomes, or results. In the end, all theories deal with perception and persuasion (Frank & Frank, 1991). They seek to make life better for clients. But it is how they are used that makes a difference. Like a knife, a theory may help heal or it may wound; it depends on who uses it and how.

In developing a theoretical model of your own or finding your comfort level in using already-developed models, you should remember that most theories involve a number of components, such as their view of human nature, processes, techniques, multicultural issues, strengths, and limitations. No theory is perfect. Indeed, the best theories are always evolving and growing because they are being researched and practiced. You as a professional are emerging also. When all of these factors are taken into consideration, you may find working with clients more complicated than you had initially imagined, but you may also find it more stimulating, rewarding, and fulfilling than you had expected. Theories can help lead the way—what could be more exciting and inviting!

REFERENCES

Austin, L. (1999). *The counseling primer*. Philadelphia: Accelerated Development.

Corsini, R. J. (2001). *Handbook of innovative therapy*. New York: Wiley.

Frank, J. D., & Frank, J. B. (1991). *Persuasion and healing: A comparative study of psychotherapy*. Baltimore: Johns Hopkins Press.

Murdock, N. L. (2004). *Theories of counseling and psychotherapy*. Upper Saddle River, NJ: Prentice Hall.

Paul, G. L. (1967). Strategy of outcome research in psychotherapy. *Journal of Consulting Psychology, 31*, 109–118.

Seligman, M. E. P. (2003, August 8). *Positive psychology: Applications to work, love, and sports*. Paper presented at the 111th annual convention of the American Psychological Association, Toronto, Canada.

Simon, F., 212
Simon, G. M., 8
Simon, R., 198, 203
Singer, E., 24
Skeleton keys, 213, 215–216
Skinner, B. F., 15, 105, 106, 108, 116–117
Sklare, G., 144
Skowron, E. A., 184
Slavik, S., 39
Slippery slope effect, 233
Smith, J. M., 213
Smith, R. L., 185
Snider, M., 199, 203
Snider, P. D., 237
Social action, 173
Social-cognitive theory, 105, 108–109
Social constructionism, 212
Social interest, 35, 38. *See also* Adlerian therapy
Socialization, 93
Social Modeling, 105, 108–109
Societal orientation, 231
Societal regression, 184
Society, and Adlerian therapy, 37
Society of Individual Psychology, 35
Socratic method
  Bowen family therapy, 185
  cognitive and cognitive-behavioral therapy, 126, 128, 133
  existential therapy, 52
Softas-Nall, B. C., 217
Soltz, V., 36, 37, 40
Solution-focused therapy, 210–221
  case study, 218–219
  counselor/therapist role, 213–214
  deShazer, Steve, 211–212
  goals, 214
  human nature/personality, 212–213
  multicultural and gender-sensitive issues, 216–217
  O'Hanlon, Bill, 211, 212
  process and techniques, 214–216
  strategic family therapy and, 211
  theory evaluation, 217–218
Soo-Hoo, T., 202
Spangenberg, J. J., 68
Specification, 161
Specifying automatic thoughts, 129
Spence, E. B., 235

Sperry, L., 39
Spiegel, H., 213
Spirituality, 37
Spitting in the client's soup, 40
Splitting, 20
Sprenkle, D. H., 188, 200, 201
Sprinthall, N. A., 117
Stadler, H., 229
Stamps, 158
Standards
  ethical standards, 227–229
  legal standards, 233–234
Stanton, D., 202
Stations of the Mind (Glasser), 92
Statton, J. E., 39
Steinberg, E. B., 203
Steiner, T., 217
Stevens, M. J., 53–54
Stevens-Smith, P., 235
Stevic, R. R., 4
Stierlin, H., 212
Stimulus control, 9
Stimulus-response model, 105, 107–108
Stoic philosophy, 142
Stolz, S., 116
Stone, Irving, 15
Stone, S., 233
Stone, S. C., 4
Stone Center, 174–175
Strategic family therapy, 196–206
  case study, 203–205
  counselor/therapist role, 199
  Haley, Jay, 197–198
  human nature/personality, 198–199
  multicultural and gender-sensitive issues, 202
  process and techniques, 200–201
  solution-focused therapy and, 211
  theory evaluation, 202–203
Strategic therapy, 197
Stress inoculation, 130–131
Stress Inoculation Training (Meichenbaum), 126
Strokes, 158
Strom, S. M., 230
Structural analysis, 154–155
Stuart, R. B., 116
Stude, E. W., 228, 234
Style-shift counseling, 8

Sublimation, 21
Subpoenas, 238
Substantive due process, 237
Success identity, 92–93, 94
Suicide, physician-assisted, 234
Sullivan, Harry Stack, 15
Superego, 17–18
Superiority complex, 36
Swanson, C. D., 226, 227, 229, 230, 235
Sweeney, T. J., 36, 41
Syllogisms, 144
Symmetrical relationships, 199
Symptoms, and behavioral therapy, 116
Syncretism, 8
Systematic desensitization, 113–114
Szapocznik, J., 202
Szykula, S. A., 203

TA. *See* Transactional analysis
Talbutt, L. C., 226, 228, 236, 237
Talk therapies, 6–7
Tang, T. Z., 127
Tantam, D., 83
Tarasoff, Tatiana, 235–236
Tarasoff v. Board of Regents of the University of California (1976), 235–236
"Tar baby," 40
Tarvydas, V. M., 225
Task setting, 40
Taylor, J., 144
Teaching
  rational emotive behavior therapy technique, 143
  reality therapy technique, 96
Technical eclecticism, 8–9
Techniques. *See* Processes and techniques
Tennyson, W. W., 230
Thanatos, 18
Thematic Apperception Test, 25–26
Theoretical eclecticism, 8
Theoretical integrationism, 8
Theories, 2–12. *See also* Psychoanalysis and psychoanalytic theories; *and other specific theories and therapies*
  antiquated theories, 6–7
  case study, 9–12
  characteristics of sound theories, 4